Felix Academicus
Tales of a Happy Academic

Also by Skip Eisiminger

Poetry
Nonprescription Medicine (Mardi Gras Press, 1995)

Essays
The Consequences of Error and Other Language Essays (Peter Lang, 1991)

Word Games
Wordspinner (Rowman and Littlefield, 1991)

Non-fiction
Omi and the Christmas Candles (Clemson University Digital Press, 2005)

Edited Work
Integration with Dignity (Clemson University Digital Press, 2003)

Co-edited work
Business in Literature (with Charles Burden, Elke Burden, and Lynn Ganim, David McKay, 1977)

Why Can't They Write? A Symposium on the State of Written Communication (with John Idol, University Press of America, 1979)

Felix Academicus
Tales of a Happy Academic

Skip Eisiminger

Contents

Preface

Lou Holtz, the former football coach at USC, observed that happiness is a poor memory. My recall is not particularly good: I swear I know many of the answers on *Jeopardy*; I just can't remember them. No, my academic contentment has little to do with having a bad memory; I recall the bad times all too well, and the good times I make an effort to take note of in my journal and card file. I've taken to heart the advice of Kurt Vonnegut's Uncle Alex: "Please notice when you are happy." But Alex and I both know that diamonds burn, and gold cannot stay.

My old American literature professor at Auburn, Dr. Robert Pierle, was closer to the mark than Coach Holtz when Pierle observed that he had the best job in the world: he was being "paid to read books and talk about them." When I heard him say that, I knew I was in the right major because I loved to read and write, and I could not think of another job in which I'd be paid to do those things that I would have done regardless of the profession I chose. As an academic, however, I could read those things I chose to read (for the most part), say the things I wanted to say (for the most part), write the things I wanted to write (for the most part), and be paid for doing them. Grading a stack of papers and attending a committee meeting every so often seemed well worth what I was getting in return: a tenured job (eventually), a private office, the respect of society, a secretary, the summer off if I chose to take it, free access to a copier, a computer, a telephone, a fax machine, a good library and ILL service, smart caring colleagues, a handful of good students (God bless them!), access to a fitness center and cafeterias, a concert series, a free lecture series, a four-day-a-week schedule with classes starting at 11 AM, paid travel, a year off every six years, and (finally) a decent salary. Indeed, if my calculations are correct, I should receive about as much when I retire as I am currently making teaching over two hundred students a year. The South Carolina TERI program, of course, had a lot to do with my financial security, and whoever dreamed up the academic handout has my eternal gratitude because it ranks right up there with Medicare, the G.I. Bill, and Social Security.

One of John Updike's characters says that "America is one vast conspiracy to make you happy," and, in my case, it seems to be working. All I ever expected was the opportunity to pursue Dame Felicia, and now it appears I have caught her.

The essays which follow, the product of what V. S. Pritchett called a "congenial monotony," are the evidence of my felicity; I trust they will give my readers as much pleasure as they gave the *felix academicus* who wrote them. Enjoy!

Skip Eisiminger

Foreword

The writer of personal essays, like the creator of the form, Montaigne, seeks to engage readers by sharing experiences, opinions, discoveries, observations, responses to books, speeches, works of art, and a myriad of facts and ideas gleaned from a lifetime of desultory reading. Perhaps better than in any other form of writing, including what hopes to pass as straightforward, truthful autobiography, personal essays enable authors to unveil themselves, even if, as in the case of Nathaniel Hawthorne in a personal essay introducing his *Mosses from an Old Manse*, they proclaim themselves not to be "one of those supremely hospitable people, who serve up their hearts delicately fried, with brain-sauce, as a tidbit for their beloved public."

The personal essay, by its very nature, is self-revelatory even in the act of concealing. It allows us to see what makes the author tick. Word by well-chosen word, sentence by well-wrought sentence, paragraph by richly informed or impressively opinioned paragraph, the author comes into being before our very eyes and grasps our minds, challenges our ideas and codes of behavior, tickles us, infuriates us, leads us, and touches our hearts. It does not overwhelm us with its length nor underwhelm us with its lack of solid content. It raises a point, makes it, and clears out, leaving us room to reflect before our brains turn to jelly or cement. As we reflect, we have the sense that we have shared companionable moments, as though we had sat at a table breaking bread with someone possessing a richly stored mind, someone who had lived fully, thoughtfully, conscientiously, someone whose experiences ranged from the humorous to the tragic.

In defining and describing the personal essay, I find I have given an overview of the artistry of the personal essays you now hold in your hand. Indeed, my friend and former colleague, Sterling (Skip) Eisiminger has mastered the art of the personal essay. Taking a cue from the aforementioned Hawthorne, I invite you to join me in Skip's study to observe him at work, to read over his shoulder, to ask him to keep preparing delicious and hearty dishes of "brain sauce." Come prepared to be well-fed, engaged, and even envious, for few people today write as well as does this prose-poet.

John Lane Idol, Jr.

Acknowledgments

Six of the essays in this volume were previously published. "Word Wise," "When the Teacher's Wrong," and "The Long and Short of Brevity" originally appeared on-line in *The Vocabula Review*. "A Continual Allegory," "The Language of Race," and "An Apology for Expediency" were first published in the *South Carolina Review*. The author wishes to thank the editors of both journals for their permission to reprint.

ঽ

Dedication

Felix Academicus is dedicated to all the happy academics (though some are admittedly happier than others), especially, but in no particular order:

Harold, Ray, Hallman, Fred, Dick, Mark, Bill, Roger, Claire, Albert, Malcolm, Tharon, Sylvia, Meredith, Dixie, Charlie, Ron, Roger, Lucy, Michael, Elizabeth, Teddi, Michelle, Wayne, Keith, John, Jack, Joan, Ed, Richard, Summer, Chip, Morris, Deuel, Louis, Corinne, Ben, David, Carol, Ned, Marion, Donna, Jill, Allen, Ryan, Victor, Jennie, Jason, Sean, Ardyce, Susanna, Kara, Clint, Laurie, Lynn, Jennifer, Neil, Ashley, Frank, Jonathon, Laura, Terry, Mary, Amy, Cynthia, Barbara, Susan, Jan, Justin, Martin, Allison, Stephen, Mason, Xioll, Amanda, Stephen, Kimberly, Robert, Patrick, Kira, Bart, Catherine, Philip, Donna, Art, Angie, Mark, Joseph, Elisa, Skye, Lenny, Rob Roy, Bruce, Jim, Jerry, Bob, Joel, Hal, Cecil, Debbie, Joe, Cecelia, and Dan.

EPIPHANIES OF PURPOSE

My mother, who hated an empty wall, garden row, or canvas, taught me an early lesson in purpose: "Make the desert bloom." She issued this directive a few days after my twelfth Christmas when I was whining about my "poverty." A painter by avocation, she pulled out a balsa airplane model that I'd just received from my father in Korea who probably knew I wasn't getting the chrome-plated pogo stick Santa had promised. Together she and I cut, glued, and pinned down one side of the fuselage of my Piper Cub, and before I realized it, I'd forgotten the pogo stick. Supper slowly called Mother to the kitchen, and as my plane rose from the plans, I was left with the "desert" blooming within.

My development as an individual for better or worse has been assisted by several people like my mother who consciously or unconsciously taught me lessons in purpose. These lessons often arrived like an epiphany and like bones were buried, but like the forgotten femur, the buried purpose continues to nourish even as it decomposes. My family and friends' reasons for living became my own through a nuanced process of understanding and imitation.

As a military engineer, my father was pleased with my models; he thought they showed promise. Occasionally we built airplanes together and flew them in the park. During these excursions, Dad instilled in me what he called the "paradox of the arch": counterintuitive as it sounds, the more weight a builder places on an arch, the stronger it becomes. I suppose there are limits to what one can stack upon the keystone, but I know that a well-made stone arch supporting a hundred pounds is much less stable than one supporting five times as much. My father, who had earned an Eagle Scout badge while delivering for a bakery and going to high school during the Depression, expected no less of me in better economic times. So I joined the Boy Scouts and took a job delivering a morning newspaper. I was pleased that my grades did not suffer although the time I had for playing football and baseball did. Still my arches did not flatten.

When I took a sick friend's route on top of my own and my grades did suffer, I told my father of my academic woes. Dad revealed something I'd never suspected—he too had failed. At the University of Illinois, he'd been nominated for the ROTC "Honor Graduate" award at the start of his final semester. "Unfortunately," Dad said, "a personality conflict developed between me and the instructor in my last required design course, and, to put it briefly, I flunked." Unfortunately, the class was not being offered again until the following year, so he lost his scholarship and went home in disgrace. Dad's commission was presented to his roommate, who thought himself lucky when he was sent to Bataan in the summer of 1939 to serve under Gen. MacArthur. Though this was the Depression, Dad found work cleaning large chemical drums at an East St. Louis refinery after being turned down by over ninety employers. Living at home, he saved his money, reread the textbook, went back to Champaign-Urbana in the spring of 1940, enrolled in a section of the course he needed but taught by a different instructor, made an "A," and graduated. That summer with commission in hand, instead of being shipped to the Philippines, he was sent to Ft. Benning, Georgia, where he soon met and married the woman who would become my mother. Incidentally, Dad's roommate was shot and killed on the infamous Death March while attempting to escape his Japanese captors. The tale gives me an unholy shiver every time I think about the handful of points in a grade book that meant the death of one man and my own existence. If nothing else, Dad's failure has forced me to think hard about the judgments I pass on students.

When I did poorly in chemistry and failed my English class at Georgia Tech in 1959,

I chose to take a "time out": I enlisted in the U.S. Army and asked to be sent to Germany. I had no interest in cleaning chemical drums, and the war we were currently fighting was considerably cooler than the one I was born into. Growing up, I had mistakenly assumed that I shared my father's purpose, and I needed some time to determine what I wanted to do with my life. Why had I chosen engineering as my major when I loved poetry and fiction? At Tech, we had not read a single book that miserable quarter, and four misspellings in any written assignment for English spelled "F." Though Mother and Dad were not happy with my decision to enlist, I knew it was best for me. As luck would have it, I landed in a remote corner of Germany within a stone's throw of the badly rusted Iron Curtain. Here with a mosaic of college dropouts, I had ample time to read books of my choosing. My "military operational specialty" required that I intercept and record East German and Russian radar signals, but a uniformed ape could have performed those duties. With one hand on the toggle switch scanning the radar frequencies, I did my work. My other hand held a book, which occupied my mind. As a result, Remarque, Steinbeck, Spillane, and others became my companions, so much so that by the time I re-entered college, I made an "A" in freshman English with the unconscious assistance of my "friends," who'd taught me to spell.

Though I was not the best soldier, four years of military duty did yield an enhanced sense of purpose, and I've been a proponent of national service ever since. Being married and expecting a child, however, produced an even greater change especially in my attitude toward academics. Looming responsibility like being shot at has a way of focusing one's attention. My wife, Ingrid, worked until the day before giving birth to our son and returned to her bank job just four weeks later. Her dedication to our small family led me to conclude that I had no alternative but to perform. I know many men exploit their wives' selfless commitment, but my parents had installed a Presbyterian conscience in me very early.

Besides resuming my education, I returned to the arms of the church, where I had long been my grandmother's designated "tithe," but mother church didn't embrace me for long. I'd attended various German churches, but the language barrier was too high for me to hurdle. Since the mid-1950s, I had attended the First Presbyterian Church in Columbus, Georgia where the Rev. Robert McNeill was making national waves by inviting blacks to worship beside their white brothers and sisters. Before leaving for Germany, I read an article in *Look* that he'd written about his commitment to non-violent integration. After returning from Europe where I'd tracked the nascent Civil Rights movement in *The Stars and Stripes* and *Time*, I was eager to hear Rev. McNeill preach again, but I learned that the elders had dismissed him for turning the national spotlight on their congregation and his premature righteousness.

The latest issue at this church's door was a proposal to use the Sunday-school wing as a day-care center during the week. The problem was that most of the families who might benefit from such a facility were African-American. Despite what Rev. McNeill had said about the church existing to give itself away, the proposal was dismissed, and I went with it. My sympathies were largely with the oppressed, thinking, as I did, that Martin Luther King was the apotheosis of courage and integrity. I was working with two black men at the plumbing wholesaler where I had a part-time job, and I knew how much inexpensive day care would have meant to their families. It was not to be, however, but from disappointment comes renewed purpose when one is young. I wasn't ready to give up yet.

Just as my wife's example of familial dedication turned my attention toward the books and a career, so did my Aunt Clarice re-energize my commitment to a career in education. Clarice was a first-grade teacher in Harris County, Georgia during the integration turmoil of the 1960s. School administrators in consultation with Clarice chose her to teach the first two black children admitted to a white school in that district since Reconstruction.

Court-ordered desegregation would be accomplished best, the administrators decided, if there was a minimum of fanfare, so she was ordered not to make a public issue of her black charges. All went well until one day Clarice held up the work of one of her black students as a model for the rest. When white parents learned from their children that not only were they being taught in the same classroom as black children, but that the penmanship of a black child was being used as an example of excellence, whites started withdrawing their progeny and sending them to the segregation academies that were sprouting like acorns under a mature oak. Clarice was reassigned to the county high school to teach home economics, but she always maintained that she did nothing wrong, and I concurred.

Justice, I came to understand, is a slippery concept; how it is defined and related to purpose depends on a number of greasy variables. Before their deaths, my wife's parents taught me that lesson in the stories I collected over their supper table. During the Second World War, my wife's mother, Ilse, had become a convert to civil disobedience while her husband was at the eastern front. Responsible for her two frail parents as well as two children, she asked the farmer who employed her occasionally if she could barter a few automobile parts for some potatoes since her cupboard and basement were bare. "You know the law, Ilse" said Herr Schultze. "Everything I grow must be sent to the front. God knows we don't want our boys to starve before they're shot. I can't sell you any potatoes, but you can steal some," said the farmer with a wink. And so on moonless nights during the harvest, Ilse, dressed in black, dodged the guards, and gathered all of Schultze's precious tubers that she could carry. She knew at least one soldier who wouldn't begrudge her "theft."

In December of 1947, Ilse's husband, Otto, returned to his family in Germany from a French war prison where he had learned lessons in self-reliance and expediency himself. The shortages of food and fuel that his family was suffering struck him hard, but he soon decided on a course of action: after planting some seeds in old jars in the kitchen, he sharpened his bow saw, pruned the overgrown orchard, and built a wagon of cherry, apple, and pear. As soon as the snow melted, he put out his seedlings and took his two children into the forest around the village of Wolsdorf. With his son stationed a hundred meters to his left and his daughter a hundred meters to his right, he threw a weighted string over a leafless branch. To the string, he tied a heavier rope and pulled it over the limb. When the moment was ripe, he snapped off the dead limb, hoping the forest master was far enough away not to hear the report. Although the medieval ordinance that only fallen deadwood could be gathered was still in effect, providing for his family outweighed the letter of an antiquated law. On the way home, he and the children gathered various berries, mushrooms, and beechnuts, which could be pressed for cooking oil.

As much as my family inspired my admiration, which in turn stoked the furnace of my purpose, I must credit the German governess my parents hired in 1946 for nurturing my interests in fields as diverse as bullfighting and anatomy. When I showed an interest in the Spanish national pastime, Annelore found someone in war-ravaged Rüsselsheim with a toreador costume and traded some coffee for it. My parents and I were expecting nothing more than a *papier-mâché* mask, but Annelore appeared with the whole nine yards. After some judicious cutting and stitching, she reduced the nine yards to something that would fit. I wore my gold-embroidered outfit complete with scarlet cape, hat, and sword on a single night of trick-or-treating, but I'll never forget the time Annelore took for me. When my mother asked her why she had gone to so much trouble, Annelore quoted a German proverb, "Begging your pardon, Frau Eisiminger, but a shroud has no pockets."

On another occasion, I casually mentioned that the human heart resembled a valentine. She promptly disabused me of that naïve assumption by taking me on her day off to the University of Heidelberg to see a plaster cast of a human heart as well as a student production of *Carmen*! I like to think that the seeds of her interests took root in me.

Whether I was captivated by bullfighting or anatomy, my curiosity has served me well over the years keeping my mind irrigated through seasons of drought. I've long loved to read outside my field much to the despair of department heads who have labeled me a generalist in a profession that prefers specialists. Long before I had a boss, however, I favored Aristolochus's rangy fox, which knew many things, and a bias against his coiled hedgehog, which knew one thing thoroughly. After a six-year stint as the assistant editor of *The Nathaniel Hawthorne Review*, I decided that if I ever had to read another essay on *The Scarlet Letter*, it would be too soon. Hawthorne, however, still holds my interest, but it's a book of non-fiction this fox reads with greatest interest today.

Mario Livio's book *The Golden Ratio* is one that has recently renewed my confidence that humans do have an overarching purpose, and that our existence is part of a complex if opaque design. Livio, an astrophysicist, makes the astonishing point that the shape of the human inner ear follows the same logarithmic curve that pinecones, pineapples, chambered nautiluses, spiral nebulas, and countless other animate and inanimate things follow. Surely, that similarity is no coincidence. The creator has to be a mathematician, and while there are mad scientists, the force or spirit responsible for the Big Bang did create the universe we all share. After all, He, She, It, or They could have left it a colossal void. Instead, the "desert bloomed." Such creative generosity should be a purposeful inspiration to us all regardless of our faith.

In *The View from a Distant Planet*, another favorite, Harlow Shapley notes that nitrogen, like carbon and water, is essential to life. Moreover, each breath we draw contains a few atoms of this finite resource that Jesus and Mohammed drew into their righteous lungs. Each breath! That notion alone ought to impress everyone with our mutual dependence on the planet's finite resources. The air each of us depends on is the much-recycled breath that our grandchildren and their children will have to breathe for the rest of their lives.

Following the news of scientific research, especially the explorations of space by rocket and telescope, has made many of us more purposeful. I've never been beyond the troposphere myself, but having seen the disturbing pictures of our planet framed in black, I'm convinced that the heightened awareness of civilization's vulnerability is the program's greatest value. Many have understood this point staring in slack-jawed wonder at that blue and white gem displayed against the black velvet of space. Near my desk, I keep a picture taken by Voyager 1 of Earth as seen from beyond Pluto as the spacecraft departed the "snug" confines of our solar system in 1990. Needless to say, one must squint to see us. Now that's perspective!

I realized in college that God inspired Copernicus and Galileo as surely as He inspired Moses and Matthew. Indeed, the deity has inspired every one of us who has expressed the truth of experience in words, paint, marble, or music. Reading Philip Roth's short story "Defender of the Faith," for example, I was impressed by the inspired characterization of his protagonist, Sergeant Nathan Marx, a Jewish infantryman in World War II. After the war when he finally has a moment to reflect, Marx realizes that he had somehow managed to deny himself, as he says, "the posture of the conqueror—the swagger that I, as a Jew, might well have worn as my boots whacked against the rubble of Wesel, Münster, and Braunschweig."

I thought that trio of German cities sounded familiar, so I called my father, a veteran of Sgt. Marx's war. Indeed, Wesel is where Dad crossed the Rhine, was nearly killed, and won a Bronze Star. He survived, however, to lead his 660 black combat engineers through Münster and Braunschweig without losing a single man. Though thousands of men in the Ninth Army fought through those three cities, Dad never permitted himself or his men, including two Jewish officers, the "posture of a conqueror." When two of his men raped a British homemaker before the battalion crossed the Channel, Dad caught and surrendered the suspects to the local authorities, who, after a trial had confirmed their guilt, hanged them. When the *Stars and Stripes* reported the executions, Dad promised his men that anyone who perpetrated a war crime would be prosecuted regardless of which side of the Channel it occurred. On his watch at least, no German women were raped and very few war souvenirs were collected. As he often has said, "We had a job to do, and we did it the best way we could."

Peace, however, did not end his commitment to the "job." In 1946, he volunteered to return to Germany, this time with his family, to rebuild much of what he and his fellows had destroyed. From 1948 to 1949, he helped build Berlin's Tegel Airfield to assist his former foes during the famed airlift. The love that I hold for my parents has only inspired purpose. With the legacy that I've inherited, how can I feel anything but pride and a determination not to disappoint?

Though Dad maintains he was just doing his job, I'm convinced that he was acting on the universal principle of "doing for others." My father never was much of a churchgoer, and his parents were guarded Midwesterners put off by the merest whiff of the didactic. Nevertheless by some moral osmosis, the result of being part of a large family in a loving home, he learned this most basic of lessons: until we know otherwise, the other person deserves our respect, or, as Desmond Tutu once put it, "Whether you are Christian, Muslim, or Jew, the God in me greets the God in you."

My own optimistic sense of purpose was buoyed long ago by reading that every major religion in the world shares the same Golden Rule. What a stunning and hopeful agreement! Emerson, I suppose, would say that each inspired founder tapped into the mind of God where absolute truth resides. I figure if Confucius, Buddha, Rabbi Hillel, Zoraster, Jesus, Mohammed, Emerson, and my parents did it, the rest of us can too.

CREATION MYTH

Long ago and far away,
a young insurgent
stole into a print shop
and placed a nuclear bomb
beneath the type cabinet.

Mirabile dictu!

Some thirteen billion years later,
colons, commas, and letters in all cases
settled heavily back to earth
from *A* to *zyxt*,
and Oxford's great dictionary
was set.

THE PRESUMPTION OF OPTIMISM
"Hell's bells and all is well." Tom Stoppard

A couple of years ago, I was glossing Philip Larkin's "The Wedding Wind," a poem about a country bride trying to understand her buoyant emotions the morning after she'd married. I explained to my class of Clemson juniors that a storm had dropped several inches of rain on the couple's farm during the "honeymoon" forcing the husband to go and shut the barn doors pried opened by the wind. Early the following morning, he leaves again to survey the storm damage while she undertakes a problem over her breakfast coffee in what Jeremy Bentham might call "felicific calculus." Imagining the looming duties of a farmer's wife like beads on the frayed strings of an abacus, she wonders how long the euphoria that runs through her every capillary will continue to pulse?

After an awkward silence, I volunteered to answer that question for the class, "Not forever, of course, but judging from the few details provided, the prognosis for a successful marriage is good. The couple apparently enjoys 'the basic six': good health, a common religion, freedom, a measure of financial security, congenial work, and reciprocated love. Surely at some point he's going to suffer some prostate trouble; one year at least a drought will wipe out the corn crop, and the seven-year itch may strain their trust, but the odds are strong that this couple will succeed," I predicted. Paraphrasing Wayne Booth, I said, "Rather than doubt what you cannot prove, assent to what is probable." That's been my thinking if not my syntax for as long as I can remember. If jurors are told to presume the defendant is innocent, I think the rest of us have a similar obligation to assume the best until we know otherwise. I call this duty the presumption of optimism.

A student, however, troubled by the storm thought that Larkin was implying an unstable start for the newly weds. I said the law of science is that whatever rises must fall, but the law of faith holds that whatever falls must rise. "Something is usually lost in the transition," I added, "but something is usually gained as well. Ask any divorcee five years after the papers are signed if things haven't worked out for the best, and most will tell you they have. The great majority of us, I suspect, deserve a trophy inscribed, 'Better than anyone expected.'" "Whatever made you so optimistic, Dr E?" said the student as the bell rang. There was a paper due the next class and an examination after that, so I never got back to the question. I figure it's about time to answer even at the risk of getting my spiritual boxers in a metaphysical knot.

First, I'd say that I have been lucky. I have a plastic diptych on my desk at home showing my father in full combat uniform and me on the left standing by his duffel bag in August of 1944, the day he left home for the war in Europe. I wasn't quite three, but I knew something significant was up, and my shy smile partly obscured by one hand reveals that. On the right is a photograph of my father heaving me skyward the day he returned from combat in September of 1945. I'm just a blur rising toward heaven, but surely my face wears a smile as broad as my father's. Little did I know that there were boys and girls in Europe and Asia, including my future wife, wearing a very different expression that day, but I was smiling as if Zeus was tossing me into the arms of Aeolus. History has been kind to me, for I surely would have had a very different life if Andreas Eisenmenger had not moved his family to America in 1751 or if Gen. Eisenhower had not been successful on D-Day.

But my optimism was not entirely handed to me on a platinum platter. Early on my parents insisted that I "make the desert bloom." Consequently whether I was earning a merit badge in Boy Scouts, diagramming homework sentences, raking leaves, delivering newspapers, painting the family home, or moving fourteen times before finishing high school, I learned Candide's famous lesson for myself. After searching the world over for happiness and finding a bog of misery, Candide finally decides to stop his wandering, gather his loved ones around him, and cultivate his garden. Voltaire stops there, but extrapolating from my own wanderings and sweaty cultivations, I'd say that one day he awoke and quietly realized the gnawing in his stomach was gone. Contentment, good health, and a full larder make up much of the sweat equity Candide's labors earned for him, and the interest such productive work yields is compounded daily. A few of my students have argued that Candide tumbled into a rut at the novel's end; I'd say he made a congenial structure. At least he had some vine-ripened tomatoes to show for his efforts, and gardening was his choice, not Pangloss's.

Freedom and physical activity, then, are vital to happiness; no one has ever found it for long in a beer can, a pill, or lying on the couch watching television. One does something, and if the activity is such that it fully engages the mind, happiness is a secondary result the way that flat-panel TV screens and automatic insulin pumps were byproducts of man's going to the moon. Space travel involves considerable risks, yet astronauts seem very willing to assume them. I suspect they know something most earth-bound folk will never know, namely that risk is one ingredient that can make an ordinary meal into a *cordon bleu* masterwork. I'll never forget hiking north of Tucson one spring morning with my wife and my eighty-year-old father. We were returning from Finger Peak, and I was leading the descent when I rounded a bend and saw a rattlesnake coiled in my path. It clearly had felt or heard me coming, but I was deaf to his rattle. Had I taken the step my momentum was urging me toward, I would have come down squarely on its spine. For once, my ego, id, and superego agreed: taking the next step as planned was ill advised. So I raised my leading leg, pushed off with my trailing leg, and with a surge of adrenaline worthy of the Roadrunner, leapt over this creature whose tail was all aquiver. Dad seeing my leap and hearing my yelp cleverly deduced what was around the bend. Coming to a quick stop, he picked up a large stone and threw it between the snake and me. Realizing that this was a shot fired across its bow, the serpent slithered off the trail into a grove of yuccas. Though the threat was gone, I found myself leaping in place as if the earth had become a trampoline and my knees belonged to my chest. Like a man possessed, I leapt skyward repeatedly laughing as I rose and fell. When I finally settled down, my wife threw a pebble at the back of my legs and yelled, "Snake!" Once more, I launched myself toward some invisible sky haven while she and Dad shared a laugh. I can't remember a happier time in my life in which sex played no role. Our children's weddings, the births of our three grandchildren, graduating from college—not one of these milestones holds a candle to hurdling that snake and laughing our way down the hill.

Risk or no risk, I learned as a child that happiness is subject to term limits. December 26 was always that dark day when Christmas lost its luster and the realization sank in that I had a year to wait for the next potlatch. But even if the bluebird of happiness is a lame duck, as a comedian once claimed, there are always the cardinals, juncos, and meadowlarks to watch for. "Black as it darkles, a star will sparkle," Mother used to tell me, and I'd go to work on the balsa model I'd found under the tree making "the desert" bloom.

It wasn't the new pogo stick I'd wished for, but it was enough to take my mind off my "poverty" and lift me from the quicksand of self-pity.

Indeed self-pity is an emotion I avoid in others as well, for it dampens my spirit wherever I find it. One reason I have volunteered to teach at-risk students each summer for the last twenty years is the virtual absence of bathos and entitlement among them. With Clemson honors students, I often want to say, "Excuse me, but I can't hear you for the whining." The students in Clemson's "catch-up-in-a-hurry program," however, have been selected because, while their SATs are marginal, they have shown a willingness to work hard and not make excuses. Furthermore, what I have learned from these students, who have every right to blame an education system that has excused them from ever writing an essay, is that the smaller the achievement, the greater the potential. Of course that's Pollyanna speaking, but that's my philosophical approach to these kids, and it appears to work, for their graduation rate is higher than the school average.

One of the things I love about teaching is the way that it teaches the teacher to give more and expect less, not of one's students, of course, but of those with the money. I try not to dwell on the inequities of the system for fear that I'll implode in a cynical black hole from which only a few pathetic x-rays escape. With a hundred students to shepherd each semester, there's little time for wallowing. But then "nothing's hard if you love it," as Albert Einstein observed, even sub-atomic physics. My German mother-in-law once was the sort who if you discovered a flat tire in her presence would say, "But it's only flat on one side." Once her two warring sons agreed to come to see her on her birthday, but before long, they were quarreling again right before her eyes. "You son of a lizard," said one. "You son of an insect," replied the other. She turned to me and said, "It's good to see the boys talking again."

My mother-in-law, who is part of perhaps the last European generation to assume that happiness is survival, never had the luxury of what the Hollywood actor James Cagney called his contractual happiness clause: "If Jimmy isn't happy, Jimmy isn't working." Very few of the globe's six billion inhabitants enjoy such privilege including this tenured professor. Indeed, I once was privy to a coffee-lounge meeting in which our chairman threatened, "I can replace each of you tomorrow with a Harvard Ph. D." Because jobs were scarce in the seventies, not one of us ever called his bluff though one quipped, "But how are you going to live with them?" I've always wished that I'd said, "Wouldn't it be a lot easier to replace you, sir, with an Oxford Ph. D.?"

I've never laid off anyone in my life, but if I had to, I hope I'd tackle the worst case first. I'm not always true to this "worst first" principle, but experience has taught me that if I grade my papers by Friday, the weekend will be a lot more pleasant. I try to remind myself that each year has fifty-two of these calendar sanctuaries and that preserving the sanctity of my time off is vital to not only my well being but the family's. Tackling the worst first usually means having the necessary tools in place when it's time to use them. I'm much more likely to change a flat on my bike, for example, if I know where my tire irons and patch kit are. Many do not share my preemptive need for order; indeed, I know people who will fix a lawnmower and drop their wrenches in the grass. Two weeks later, they'll mow around the tools now lying in ankle-high grass, rusting inexorably back to earth. Personally, I can't imagine that they're happy taking their frustrations out on their tools—can a sadist ever find true happiness if his victim feels nothing?

One reason I'm careful with my tools is that our family never had so much that we took the replacement of lost or broken items for granted. Consequently, I have some tools that are close to a century old, including planes, chisels, and punches I inherited from my father-in-law and grandfather. I take great pleasure wiping them with an oily rag occasionally or sharpening their blades. I inherited these tools in superb condition, and I intend to pass them on in the same condition.

At the age of sixty-four, I have just about every tool and gizmo I've ever wanted. I was surprised recently reading a United Nations' report that all a person in the Third World needs of a material nature is an AM radio, a bicycle, and some kitchen utensils. The U.N. assumes, of course, a water-tight house with electricity and enough income to feed, clothe, and afford medical care. So, let me see if I have this right: a radio, a bike, and a stewpot are all that it takes to make people in the Congo or Amazon Basin happy? Just wait until they reach Johannesburg or Rio. It is interesting, though no surprise, that the very poor (those without a roof or a radio, I suppose) report that they are "very unhappy." Yet the very rich are not, they say, "very happy." Indeed, they claim to be about as happy as middle-class folks say they are.

The wisdom of the blues has long been "mo' money, mo' problems." For a long time I believed that because like most blues singers I could not see myself becoming rich, so I joined the chorus critical of prodigal wealth. "If you can't have it, scorn it," was our refrain. Then the Clemson Alumni Association asked me to guide a group of twenty-five Clemson graduates and their spouses to Europe. They gave me a thousand dollars in "pocket money" to spend as I saw fit on these folks in the belief that money fertilizes the money tree. One grand hardly qualifies as obscene, but it was the most money this frugal soul has ever squandered. Whether that tree has borne fruit as a result of my fertilizing, I don't know. What my spending meant in immediate terms to me, however, was unqualified pleasure. After a meal, I'd order another round of wine for everybody, or I'd pick up the tab for lunch, or pay for a trip down the Grand Canal. I felt like Croesus throwing money to his admiring subjects. Giving money away especially someone else's is delightful, and if my mutuals ever make me a Gatesian-size fortune, I'll do like Bill Gates and give most of it away. For despite the blues, "No money, bigger problems." And few things make one feel better than solving someone else's problem with a little seed money. "It's just money after all," says Bill Gates, and, "You can't take it with you," says every pharaoh including Tut we've ever exhumed.

Why archeology hasn't made realists of more people, I don't know. I'm sure it has a lot to do with religion being hammered into our bones from birth or before in the case of fundamentalist mothers who play hymns for their children in the womb. With sedulous scouring, however, about all the religion that's left in me is a belief in the Creator, the divine mathematician and architect of the universe. I find it oddly comforting, for example, that the Fibonacci sequence governs the order of things from pineapples to spiral nebulas. God may play dice with the universe, but He has a fool-proof system for betting.

I also believe that "the Kingdom of heaven lies within," as Jesus stated, so I think of myself as spiritual but without the dogma. Wallace Stevens felt the need for some "imperishable bliss," but for me bliss is suspect. Has anyone ever wanted a roller coaster ride or an orgasm to last forever? Many pagans have it right: they don't fret much about death and wring their hands over sin for fear they'll overlook the joys of life at hand. My

Aunt Clarice, I now realize, was something of a Druid. A lapsed Baptist, she told me once after Billy, her only son, died in a diving accident that "church" for her meant taking a Sunday morning walk along the beautiful stream that carved the granite margins of her farm. When one of her Baptist "friends" implied that Billy might have passport problems at heaven's gate because he was not "born of the blood," Clarice stopped attending her friend's church and began her peripatetic devotionals. She told me, "After every judgment I hear pronounced, I pause and say, 'and yet....' This little phrase has saved me an awful lot of rash miscalculations. It's amazing how little is written in stone including the Ten Commandments—what is it, 'Thou shalt not kill,' or 'Thou shalt not murder'?"

As a celebrator of life, she said, "Everyone brings something to the party—some bring their own bottle, some their own Bible." Working as an elementary school teacher in rural South Georgia, she volunteered to teach the first black children to attend a white school in Harris County. Many of her Baptist neighbors and colleagues reviled her for that choice, but her faith in herself and her decision never wavered. Like William James, she felt life was worth living, and her belief in that worth made her own life worthwhile.

My beliefs are admittedly unorthodox perhaps because unlike many believers especially fundamentalists, I place considerable faith in science. Scientists tell me that the atoms comprising my body are 13.7 billion years old. They were born in the Big Bang along with everything else and should enjoy millions more years of usefulness. They remind me of the brass bells of Europe. Cast originally as bells, they were melted into cannons. When the war ended, they were recast as bells, and so the cycle has continued for centuries in some cases. The atoms in my body, I'm confident, have many roles to play before the electrons stop orbiting their nuclei, and the quarks are finally understood.

Science, however, is helpless against the cynic. Perhaps it has always been this way, but an alarming number of aging Americans disparage any music that isn't Benny Goodman's or writing that isn't by Hemingway. A curmudgeonly art historian told me a few months ago, "I've read a hundred new books since retiring, and every one was cheap and pornographic." When I suggested some books I thought he might enjoy and that perhaps he needed to stop and smell the roses, he said, "What, and inhale an aphid?" Academics with one foot in the grave like this fellow unhappily assume that the majority of present-day students, administrators, and politicians are stupid, lazy, or crooked. I used to try to disabuse them of their suspicions, but I've finally realized the truth of Lincoln's famous observation, "People are about as happy as they make up their minds to be." When I spot one of these misanthropes in the grocery or pharmacy, I make a beeline for the checkout because they usually succeed in bringing me down, not vice versa.

The fact of the matter is most cynics are mistaken. The amateur social scientist and professional journalist Steven Brill did us all a valuable service when he pretended to be a well-heeled foreigner lost in New York City. He and his wife hailed twelve cabs in the course of his research for *New York* magazine to see how they would fare in what many take to be the shark's maw of Western civilization. Plump as Brill's minnow was, only two sharks took the bait and overcharged the couple. One cabby even walked them to a point where they could see their destination and told them they didn't need a cab for such a short trip. Had I been presented with a hypothetical scenario based on Brill's experiment, I would have guessed one in four or five would take advantage of them, so 17% is an excellent report card for the human race since 83% of our fellows can be trusted.

Is America "a vast conspiracy to make us happy," as John Updike once wrote? Hardly. Nor is socialistic Scandinavia where the "conspiracy" is even wider since their blond bureaucrats try even harder than Uncle Sam's blue-eyed boys. Our Constitution only guarantees Americans the "pursuit of happiness," an opportunity, nothing more. Attainment, the Founding Fathers understood, is ultimately the responsibility of the individual. For myself, I hope to die as happy as a clam in the henhouse, but it's up to me to devise some means of getting in there. I can't expect the winds and tides to drop me where I want to be.

The Helplessness of Fathers

As Homer tells it in the *Iliad*,
Sarpedon was the half-breed son of Zeus
and Laodamia his human mother.
His demigod status made him reckless,
and he challenged Patroclus, Achilles'
strong friend, to combat on the plains of Troy.

Sarpedon's spear sailed harmlessly over
his foe's shoulder, but the brazen weapon
of spear-famed Patroclus was well thrown.

Freezing the action for a moment,
Zeus turned to his wife Hera, and asked
if he should snatch his son from harm's way.
Not sharing the same emotional stake
in the lad as her faithless husband, she said,
"The boy is fated; do not help him."
Zeus sadly agreed that he was no match
for destiny and unfroze the action.

Over his son's dying body, the father
shed tears of blood as Sarpedon cried,
"Father, why have you forsaken me?"
Hearing this, Zeus chose Olympian silence.
"Take this cup of suffering from me."
When there was still no response, the son said,
"It's done; in your hands I place my spirit."

As dark clouds formed, Zeus spoke to Apollo,
begged him to retrieve the mangled body,
wash, anoint, and dress the mortal remains,
and place them in the hands of Sleep and Death.

THE VICE AND VERSA OF PAIN

Call me spoiled, but I've never been much for pain. I'm not sure where I learned my preference for pleasure, but I remember when some fellow Boy Scouts were "frogging" the sides of our shelters at Camp Indian Head, I had no stomach for this pastime. "Though the frogs were thrown in sport," said our Presbyterian scoutmaster chastising the culprits, "they surely died in earnest." I also recall reading with horror an article on the filming of *Lord of the Flies*. On a remote Caribbean island, some of the unsupervised child actors had collected lizards and were secretly observed by their chaperone tossing them lazily into their tent's electric fan. Though a sadistic nanny might have altered the Epicurean outcome for me, I can't imagine that dicing lizards on the fly would have entertained me at any age. Growing up, I was more like our grandson who apologizes to the branches he pushes from his path when we walk in the woods.

Nevertheless, one of the best things we ever did for our daughter was to encourage her to work one summer at Camp Burnt Gin, a state-run camp for the mentally retarded and physically handicapped. For the able bodied, it was a boot camp in suffering with merit badges awarded for pain shared. Feeding, dressing, washing, and diapering mostly adolescents who could not perform these functions for themselves amounted to a forced lesson in empathy though I suppose it could have ended in disgust. The closed sphere of self-involvement in which she had orbited for sixteen years suddenly became an arc resembling two open arms.

The sensitive but self-absorbed character of Laura in Katherine Mansfield's fine story "The Garden Party" used to remind me of our daughter before that summer at Burnt Gin. Laura's world consisted of a tightly laced social circle at the center of which was an aristocratic family outside of whose protective embrace she had rarely traveled. True, she had learned from the family servants that the classes spoke different dialects. And she had noticed the "little rags and shreds of smoke so unlike the great silvery plumes that uncurled from the chimneys" of the wealthy. But her chief occupations were what to wear, how not to appear foolish, and where to place that tent ordered for the garden party. One afternoon just minutes before another gay fete, an elaborate and expensive ploy to escape the boredom of manor life, word comes of a tragic accident in the village just beyond the circumference of her world: a young father has been killed when thrown from his horse. Daringly but naively, Laura volunteers to take some party leftovers to the grieving family. Approaching the death vigil and seeing how unobtrusively the other mourners are dressed, she feels uncomfortable in her lace frock and velvet-ribboned hat. Mansfield subtly implies that the closer Laura comes to the open casket, the wider the aperture of her world opens. Finally she sees the dead man's serenely beautiful face, and in a stunning epiphany, she realizes she cannot return to the artifice of a world where "kisses, voices, tinkling spoons, laughter, and the smell of crushed grass" reign among life's higher priorities.

Teaching Mansfield's story recently in an introduction to literature course, I asked if Laura's self-inflicted discomfort had been instructive. One student volunteered that Laura reminded him of Job even if his tribulations were greater. Acceptance of matters over which humans have little or no control such as this accidental death in the neighborhood was Mansfield's message, the student argued Indeed, most of Job's readers will tell you that the message is one of stoic resignation. But I enjoy rattling their shutters by claiming that as much as God would like to help His suffering servant, He can't. He cannot any more than He can influence the outcome of the wager with Satan that opens the tale because He granted His servant free will at the creation, and He's not about to revoke it now. I remind classes of how in *The Iliad*, all-knowing Zeus is unable to save his mortal son Sarpedon because fate is greater than the gods. Like "sex in heaven," as Lily Tomlin observed, suffering is there as well; "we just don't feel it." Needless to say, few fundamentalists are persuaded by Tomlin's argument, Homer's, or mine.

After "The Garden Party," the class turned to Matthew's account of the crucifixion. Since I was having trouble getting them to respond, I required them to write a question for homework—anything, major or minor—as long as it dealt with Jesus' death. A couple of students wondered whether God is a sadist forcing his son to undergo such torture before he can return home. I apologized for God and myself saying I did not have an answer. Frankly, I'd never thought of the Creator as bloodthirsty, but then I try to distinguish between Him and Jehovah. By the same token since every thesis has its antithesis, I'd never thought of Jesus as a masochist or even a joyless ascetic. I reminded the class of the description in Matthew where Jesus "came eating and drinking [wine]." For his lightsome efforts, Jesus is condemned as a glutton though there's no indication he ever overindulges. John the Baptist, on the other hand, who is far more self-denying than Jesus, abstains from alcohol and is accused of harboring a demon for his efforts.

The question, however, that interested me most came from a forthright but anonymous student who asked, "Why did Jesus only survive nine hours on the cross when others made it a week or two? Did he take the easy way out, and if so what does this say about his resolve as opposed to later martyrs who suffered worse and longer deaths? As an example of how to live and weather pain, should he not have lasted a little longer?" In thirty years of teaching, I don't think I've received a more original or more troubling question from a student. Biting my tongue, I drew out the correct length of time Jesus lived on the cross—six, not nine hours. I added that it's true some Roman victims did die from the initial shock of being nailed to the cross while others lingered for days; weeks, however, seemed an exaggeration. Sadistic as the Romans could be, they were not Nazis; if they kept records on which of their victims survived the longest, we don't have them. With only an hourglass and sundial to keep time in the first century, accurate measurements were impossible anyway.

But then I could not restrain myself any longer, and without any more segue than a brief pause, I said, "If you need a kidney to live, and your brother donates one but dies in the process, does it matter whether he lingered one day or two? Isn't your debt to him the same?" Unfortunately Anon was absent the day I read his or her question, but I still recall members of the class looking nervously about for any clues that might disclose an identity. Still the discussion was lively though no one including myself understood where the question had originated.

The "knee-worn floors" of Matthew Arnold's "Grand Chartreuse," the next item on the syllabus, led us naturally into a discussion of self-mortification. One Catholic student said her aunt was a nun who was "trying to master the art of doing nothing except praying." She said her aunt had read Jesus' implicit challenge in Matthew 19 and decided very young that she was one "who could take it." And while she had not cut off her breasts as some Russian women had, she'd borne no children and remained a virgin. I said that just because Jesus had spent six hours of his thirty-some years on the cross, there is no compelling reason for people to duplicate the crucifixion every day of their lives literally or figuratively. I said I respected people like this student's aunt, but I had more respect for ascetics who invested their lives directly and concretely in the salvation of the world, people like St. Francis and Mother Teresa. I recalled a story Buddha had told about a monk who'd spent most of his life learning to walk on water. Buddha chastised the monk's waste of time saying that for a penny he could have taken the ferry. I wonder if most extreme ascetics don't live to regret the sacrifices they have made based on the shaky assumption that God is impressed by epic displays of self-denial. Nature's lesson, of course, is propagate!

Not long after this class discussion, Mel Gibson's film *The Passion of the Christ* opened in theaters everywhere in March of 2004, and this was followed by a spate of good and bad reviews in the national press. But the reaction that most captured my attention appeared in the local paper, *The Greenville News*. The author, a middle-aged Christian woman, admitted that while she personally had no qualms about the film, some reviewers had seen the torture of Jesus leading up to the crucifixion as "pornographic" in its excess. What occupies three sentences in four gospels mushrooms to take up ten minutes in the film. Realize that no Christian artist carved or painted Jesus on the cross for four hundred years after the church's founding. Such a death was for criminals, so the early Christians, preoccupied with increasing their numbers, were not of a mind to broadcast the way their messiah died. Many missionaries even today take down their altar crucifix when they see their apprentices's faces. As one young African animist put it, "If this is the way God treats His son, imagine what's in store for us?"

The exaggerations of Jesus' suffering began in the fifteenth century when the church recognized that by placing more emphasis on what came to be known as the Stations of the Cross, it could draw more converts to its plague-depleted congregations. But instead of obscene violence and distortions of the record, the *Greenville News'* reviewer saw "God's grace and love...revealed in the suffering and sacrificial death of the Son of God. [Gibson's violence] helps explain," she wrote, "why Christ's followers consider that his teachings and earthly example would be meaningless had they not been followed by his suffering and death...."

Since this editorial was followed by the author's email address, I accepted the implied invitation and wrote. "Dear Susan: Can't say that I enjoyed your review of Gibson's *Passion*.... As for your rationalizations concerning Jesus' suffering, I fail to see how 'God's grace and love are revealed in the suffering...of the Son of God.' Consider if Jesus had died instantly from a blow to the head delivered by a deranged legionnaire somewhere along the Via Dolorosa. And suppose Jesus had risen miraculously from his rock-solid grave the following Sunday. Wouldn't the history of Christianity read much the same from the resurrection on? I have to think it would. Why did Peter and the rest, who ran away and thus saw none of the scourging nor the crucifixion, risk or give their lives to propagate Jesus' radical though illegal theology? Guilt surely had a lot to do with it, but mainly, I suspect, it was the miraculous reappearance of a scarred but otherwise healthy man who had just stepped from his grave.

"Paul is another case entirely. He never knew Jesus and so could not have witnessed any of the violence done to him, yet because he had once persecuted Christians, guilt probably was a motive. But more than guilt, I suspect it was Paul's realization that the paradox at the core of Jesus' teaching is not a contradiction. Counterintuitive as it is to economic theory, individual accounts are increased by frequent expenditures, not by sealing the vault. Truth and reason, after all, have a momentum of their own, and, as I see it, they swept Paul along with Peter and the rest."

A few days later the journalist replied. "Dear Dr. Eisiminger: Thank you for your comments. I wrote from the standpoint of a believer. From my perspective, the life and death of Jesus would have made him little more than a great teacher who died a brutal death if those events had not been followed by the resurrection. Sincerely, Susan" Clearly she'd missed my point, so I wrote back. "Dear Susan, You missed the point. My point has to do with the film's exaggeration of Jesus' suffering, not the resurrection. Do you really think that Jesus' teachings on love would have been diminished if Jesus had not suffered so terribly before and on the cross? If Hitler had been captured by the Russians in 1945 and tortured to death, I grant you there'd be more Neo-Nazis today, but it would not have made his Final Solution any more acceptable. When it comes to the legitimacy of an argument, the degree of suffering is a non-issue."

I never received an answer to this query, and I don't expect I ever will. I must say, however, I was pleased that Mel Gibson apparently agreed with me: he cut some six minutes of the more violent scenes and reissued the film under the title "The Passion Recut" in March of 2005. "By softening some of its more wrenching aspects," Gibson wrote, "I hope to make my film and its message of love available to a wider audience." If my journalistic correspondent ever does respond, I shall remind her of Gibson's decision to edit. I shall also tell her that Buddha, Muhammad, Confucius, Zoraster, and Moses are all thought to have died natural deaths; not one was tortured or crucified. Yet each of these men founded a religion which has adherents some three thousand years later. Something similar can be said for Plato, Aristotle, and a host of other moral philosophers, yet not one of these men or their followers ever used suffering as a bullhorn to call people to God the way some Christian apologists trumpet Jesus' pain. As I once asked a Sunday-school class, if my mother dies in a house fire and my father is killed by a drive-by shooter, do I owe my mother any more because she suffered longer? If the duration and intensity of suffering are indicators of the truth, shouldn't we all be Jews? Yet as many tears as I have shed watching *Schindler's List* and reading Elie Wiesel, I have never been tempted to convert. The suffering of others has made me sympathetic and appreciative, but rarely has it changed my mind.

Notice that I wrote *rarely*, not *never*. In the departmental coffee lounge a few years ago, a friend asked me if the verb *to boast* had any positive connotations. I said that I recalled reading travel brochures that used the word to promote an area's tourist potential. A mountain resort might "boast" of its panoramic view, for example. My friend said the reason he asked was that the Bible text chosen by his minister the day before had used *boast* in an odd way: good Christians, according to Paul, should "boast in their sufferings because suffering yields endurance; endurance yields character, and character yields hope." Another colleague who overheard this said, "Bullshit! Suffering produces bitterness; bitterness produces anger; anger produces violence, pain, misery, and hopelessness! What's to boast about?"

I don't know whether this fellow had been reading Somerset Maugham, but Maugham says something similar in *The Summing Up*: "I knew that suffering did not ennoble; it degraded. It made men selfish, mean, petty, and suspicious. It absorbed them in small things…it made them less than men….” This thought led me back to Jesus’ suffering and the more instructive pain of Gandhi some two thousand years later. Jesus, once the Romans took custody of him, was a helpless voodoo doll, stuck with pins whenever and wherever the soldiers’ sadistic spirits took them. That’s the sort of suffering that makes me look away from the screen or the page, sympathetic as I may be with the victim. Gandhi, on the other hand, freely defied the British monopoly by making salt and daring the colonial authorities to arrest him. When they foolishly took his proffered bait, Gandhi went on a prolonged hunger strike, but which garnered sympathy for his cause, the independence of India from Great Britain Here then is a case where suffering clearly did change minds perhaps faster than Gandhi’s writings or speeches could. “I can sympathize with everything except suffering” writes Oscar Wilde in *The Picture of Dorian Gray*, yet millions of Indians did sympathize with Gandhi, and many joined him in his jailhouse fast. Had I been there, I fancy I would have joined them.

Yet when people change their minds because others have suffered, the paradigm most of us look to isn’t Jesus or Gandhi; it’s a relative or friend. Several years ago, a student of mine (I’ll call her Mary), was racing back to campus one Sunday at dusk with her best friend and roommate riding shotgun. Fatally overconfident in the joy of the moment, neither was wearing a seatbelt. The narrow, winding country road was one Mary knew well since it was the shortest route between her home and school. At a notorious crossroads, the setting sun directly in her eyes, Mary sped through a stop sign she evidently did not see. Midway through the intersection, Mary’s older sedan was struck on the driver’s side by a large pickup pulling a boat. Police estimated that both vehicles were traveling about 50 mph in a 35 mph zone. The force of the impact threw Mary across the front seat directly into the body of her friend who absorbed the lion’s share of Mary’s momentum, saving Mary, but killing her friend. The driver of the truck was saved by his airbag, a relatively new technology at the time. A year later when Mary was well enough to return to school, she changed her major from English to nursing saying she wanted to spend the rest of her life “absorbing the pain of others.”

While the suffering of others may change the way we live and think, usually all it changes is the way we feel. My wife of forty years has had four surgeries in the last fifteen years including a mastectomy and a spinal-disk operation. During this time, my feelings for her have deepened as I have seen her pain and contemplated the void without her. However, as much as I love her, I have never considered changing my opposition to the death penalty, which she supports. And she’s smart enough not to want me to either, at least not on the “evidence” of her suffering.

Martin Luther King apparently read Paul’s observation that “the sufferings of the present are nothing compared to the glory to come” and decided that “suffering is redemptive.” (Imagine all the whipped slaves, battered wives, and Jews in heaven if King is right!) Though Catholics have argued for centuries that good works are the key to salvation, and Protestants have countered that faith is the key, Elbert Hubbard said it’s neither: “God will be looking for our scars, not our medals and degrees.” To both Hubbard and King, suffering is a down payment on a bungalow in heaven. This rationalization strikes me as seriously misguided theology. But given such a rationale, Christian ministers for two millennia have told mistreated servants, children, and wives to go home and “turn the other cheek.” It is appalling that ministers of God have been partners in prolonging suffering, but ultimately the fault lies with Jesus in failing to define just when we should offer that other cheek. The insult Jesus felt when he saw money being exchanged in the temple, for example, did not lead him to walk away; instead, he responded with a manic display of righteous indignation. Clearly then, turning the other cheek was not a categorical imperative for him, and it shouldn't be for us. If the Austrians did the right thing inviting Hitler to assume power, should the Poles have followed suit? Unfortunately, the Sermon on the Mount stops well short of defining any limits that would help his followers decide.

According to a poll reported in the June 2001 *Harper's*, a large segment of the "seriously ill" in America hopes to be "at peace with God" when death finally comes, but a larger segment says that "being pain free" is a higher priority. When it comes to a choice between pain relief and God, most of us find the relaxation of pain to be more compelling. I would modify Bertold Brecht's famous dictum "First bread, then ethics," to "First morphine, then religion." On his death bed, my uncle Bob once told me that if I wanted to lift my spirits, I should raise a tumbler of Jack Daniels to my lips. Indeed, after a few ounces of his "Kentucky sacrament," he departed this world feeling immortal and invisible, and now he is.

SCALES, FEATHERS, AND SKIN

Above a reef of pine,
a roiling swarm of birds
schools like shad—

hundreds banking as one
above a child in a tree beside a pond
who follows dolphin through the fleece—
an exaltation of minnow
soaring in a cloud.

A cloud whose margins
are lobed and undulating
as the human brain,

or, for that matter,
Michelangelo's fluttering drapery
that floats the Creator, Eve,
and a shoal of angels,
all hovering in amazement,
away from rock-bound Adam.

AN EMBARRASSMENT OF SUFFERING:
ON MAKING LIFE A HANGOVER WITHOUT THE BUZZ

I have long been fascinated by ascetics who live near a mountain top, meditate for hours in a drafty cave, sleep on a bed of nails, and allow themselves to be buried alive. I've read that the Buddhist monks who chant their prayers in Himalayan caves have learned to raise their core body temperature to 112^0 F to fight off hypothermia though a fever has never made me more comfortable when the air conditioning is set too high. I have no desire to duplicate such feats, but I still find them interesting in the abstract. I observe the fakir and the hermit the way I watch rugby: I enjoy watching the game but really have no interest in joining the scrum.

Interested as I am in ascetic athleticism, I took the introductory course in Transcendental Meditation in 1973 to get a taste of what I was reading about. While TM eventually provides its practitioners with a personal and secret mantra, other gurus I was reading suggested the koan or quizzical paradox as a meditative focal point. By concentrating on this "point," adepts could rid themselves of desire and the attendant stress that unfulfilled longing creates. The tip of one's nose, a mandala, the navel, or a lotus blossom is a popular substitute if a koan is not available. Before I had acquired my personal mantra, therefore, I tried to solve the ancient puzzle of one hand clapping beyond the obvious answer, silence. Seated in the recommended lotus position, I thought long and hard about the conundrum with no success; the answer simply would not come by repeatedly asking the question. And even though I was supposed to remain still, I decided to move one hand as rapidly as I could and listen intently to its "applause." It's vaguely like checking the answer in the math book's appendix and working backward to determine the method the author used to get that result. Some would call this cheating; I call it research. I discovered that if I moved my flailing hand close to my ear, I could hear a faint "woosh" or "woom." I had it then: the answer to the 3000-year-old puzzle is "woom!" As my excitement faded, I tried to settle into a meditative void, and though nothingness was my goal, my brain was restless from having discovered something where for so long there had been nothing. What would the sound of one hand clapping be, I wondered, if the hand were moving at the speed of sound? A sonic boom! The koan's answer depends on the speed of the moving hand. I believe that for a second or more I rose above the rubber mat I had been sitting crosslegged on. And the TM people said it would be many weeks and dollars ere I levitated! I could barely contain myself, but I settled back into my trance and pondered further. How relative was this answer? What would the sound be if I moved my hand at the speed of light? An atomic explosion! Silence, woom, boom, bang! I'm not sure what the decibel level of my "big bang" would be, but certainly higher than a Twisted Sister concert on the tarmac at JFK. All I can say with certainty (thanks to Albert Einstein) is that the explosion would produce the energy equivalent to the mass of my right arm multiplied by the speed of light squared. Of course, I would be vaporized in the process and much of South Carolina's Piedmont along with me, but nothingness after all was my goal, not the stigmata.

Ascetics and mystics often make much of the fact that the universe was created out of nothing. For this reason among others, nothingness has become a kind of womb they long to return to. (Is "woom" an echo of "womb"?) The Koran states that Allah could have left the universe a vacuum, but He didn't; the evidence is all around us. Paul Valery concurs, but he argues that "despite the artistry of creation, the nothingness still shows through." Whether we came from nothing or will return to nothing is beyond my ken though not my imagination; I worry more about what we should do with ourselves between these theoretical voids. Should one "master the art of doing nothing," as many ascetics have argued, or, "achieve the void and be made whole," as the Tao states? I answer both questions with the Brooklyn Bridge. It would not, of course, have been built by ascetics, and I for one love that bridge, both its practicality and its aesthetic uselessness. As for its utility, in the 1950s, our family lived in Brooklyn, and I could walk or bike freely across the bridge's wooden walkway to Manhattan as motorized vehicles whizzed by below. The bridge was and remains a practical solution benefiting thousands who work in Manhattan but cannot afford to live there or pay the ferryman twice a day. As for aesthetics, John Roebling, the bridge's designer, included two graceful Gothic arches at either end that could just as easily have been rectangular openings to lighten the structure. But this solution would not have been nearly as satisfying to this aging medievalist who thinks Chartres Cathedral is one of the finest structures on the planet.

An old story, possibly apocryphal, involves an American tourist in Palermo, Sicily who heard some voices coming from an ancient sanctuary while he and his wife were exploring the town. Curious, the retired theology professor asked his wife if she'd like to accompany him, and when she declined, he ducked inside alone. When his eyes had adjusted to the dim light, he saw a shimmering crystal carved in the shape of a zero ringed by sputtering candles on the altar. Overhead was a satin banner with the Latin *Nihil*, "nothing," embroidered in gold filigree. The traveler's knowledge of the local dialect was limited, but with his dictionary, he soon understood that the small chorus of monks, the only others in the church, was intoning praise to "The Blessed Cipher." Walking out into the light of day, his waiting wife asked him what he'd seen. Said he, "My dear, is nothing sacred?"

Indeed nothingness may be holy to some, but thirty minutes of silence is not music, nor is a blank canvas or an empty page art, nor is any of these deserving of worship in my opinion. The white spaces and the musical silences are indeed functional, but if I blow continuously into a flute with no modulation, that monotone or noise depending on how long it lasts is no more music than utter silence. If I cover this page with print so dense there is no white space left, have I communicated anything? Have I touched a cold heart? Is it art? Not to me. For starters, there has to be a mix of white and black, sound and silence for there to be meaning or art. And just as a hectic life is relieved by peace and quiet, so is boredom relieved by a concerned human voice, music, or the bustle of small children.

Skeptical as I am of the value of nothingness, I have been nevertheless drawn to the ascetic ideal like the time in the 1970s when I dreamed of joining that secular monastic order called the Peace Corps. The problem was I had a family to support. Doubtless the complexities of that responsibility led to a longing for a simpler life, for the contact I have had with my gurus whether face to face or on the printed page has generally been rewarding. Learning to focus on my breathing and to empty my head of stray or obsessive thoughts, for example, taught me to relax; indeed, it put me to sleep. But the gurus all agree that a nap is not what the ascetic is seeking. Frankly, I'm grateful for any nap even one of five minutes duration because the renewal of energy is immediately felt. Though the ascetic may scorn bed rest, there's no question that midday sleep works for the domesticated feline. But for all its independence, the cat is no ascetic. After its nap, the cat likes nothing better than to go out honkytonking. Indeed cats remind me of Gandhi's observation that it requires a lot of money to support people like him living in poverty

Meditation doesn't always put me to sleep, but it helps. After urinating at three in the morning, all my body wants to do is go back to sleep, but my brain often wants to review some road-rage incident like a cracked CD. Though it's not foolproof, what helps me is a single-minded concentration on my nasal hairs. Yes, I focus as intently as I can with eyes shut in my most comfortable supine position, not too hot, not too cold, and "see" the hairs of my nostrils being blown out and then being sucked back in like a wheat field in a shifting wind. Blown out, sucked in; blown out, sucked in until I can put the road rage out of my conscious mind long enough to fall asleep.

As a tenured academic, I spend about forty hours a week on the eighth floor of Strode Tower in my "tree-house" office ninety feet up overlooking Lake Hartwell and the Clemson Forest. Up there in the clouds some might argue that I have achieved the ascetic ideal of withdrawal. But I'm not a pillar saint, and I'm not ready to share my Buck knife just yet. Okay, you can peel your orange with it, but I want it back clean and sharp, and I want it known that it is mine. You'll notice my initials engraved on its handle. And I don't want anyone to use it without asking me first. I know that I can't take it with me, so I've told my oldest grandson, Edgar, that he may have it when I am no more. The last thing I want is for "Buck" to rust back to earth with my mortal remains. I may have issues with the material world, but I try not to be fanatical or ascetic in that regard.

Nor am I ready to beg for my supper like some mendicant monk any more than I'm willing to share ownership of the half-acre lot which is all the land I can lay claim to on earth. I'm too proud and fussy a capitalist to "dive" dumpsters for food, and Lord knows that at 6' 4" and 215 pounds I could not survive long on what Sister Wendy Beckett and many like her live on: a cup of coffee for breakfast, a few crackers and two potato chips for lunch, and a glass of milk for supper. I for one feel a patriotic obligation to keep American agri-business solvent. Imagine the farmers who'd lose their jobs if we learned to survive on even 1000 calories a day. I like to think of the 3000 calories that I selflessly consume each day as fuel for the engine of our economy because every time I try to lose weight, the Dow plummets.

Nevertheless, as a poet and essayist who plucks hair from his ears while musing the void, I am a quasi-hermit. It comes with the territory the way despair haunts the salesperson. I've learned that my muse is a shy sort, who emerges only when there is peace and solitude. Sometimes I'll receive a glimmer from her in a crowd or a classroom, but for anything sustained, I need to withdraw to the "knee-worn floors" of my basement "cave" or my office "tree house." Apparently she likes to go for long slow bike rides and walks, for she often speaks most clearly on those monkish perambulations. In the last decade or so, I have tried to tease her out when I am driving. When I feel myself succumbing to road rage, I begin chanting "ohm" in traffic to help when I'm on Atlanta's I-285, for example, and there is an eighteen wheeler in front of me, another behind, one on either side, and we're all going so fast in the rain I don't dare take my eyes off the road to check our speed. Indeed, at tense moments like this, it's probably best not to know how flagrantly I am breaking the law. If the cops were to stop me, it would be a welcome respite on the shoulder, but how can they ticket me if I am nothing to them?

I used to chew my tongue as I approached one of several four-way stops on campus where I do the majority of my driving, but if I can remember to chant "I'm a Zen driver" as I approach these busy and confusing intersections, I can usually pass through unscathed. A big part of my success has to do with yielding; ascetics have historically submitted without a fight though many have been civilly disobedient. If there is any question about which car among the four of us goes next, I will motion for some other driver to go first. He waves, I smile, and we all drive on seraphically. True, I've lost five seconds from my lunch hour by yielding when I could have charged forward, but my life expectancy has increased by ten seconds. Now if I could just work on reducing that spike of blood pressure when a line jumper appears. I have no qualms about telling the offender, "Excuse me, but the line forms in the rear!" but I cannot do it *and* remain calm like the Zen cops I admire. These paragons, I've read, may fall asleep while undergoing a root canal or being hauled off to jail. I suspect they are closet narcoleptics, but that may be just a sour-grape fantasy.

In the early 90s, a group of musicians called the Kodo drummers came through Greenville, SC where quite by chance my wife and I happened to hear a performance. This small but dedicated Zen Buddhist sect lives on a tiny island off the coast of Japan, rises with the sun, dresses in natural fibers, runs twenty-four miles every day, returns for a meal of kelp, and then spends the rest of the day drumming on the beach. On stage, their hard brown bodies produce what might be described as rhythmic, hypnotic meditations using drums and an occasional flute, but it's very loud, minimal, and a steady diet of it must be trying. However, they do give something back to an audience in their recordings and public performances unlike so many ascetics who disappear into the desert to polish their souls to perfection and are never seen again. As most musicians go, the Zen drummers are relatively tight-fisted: just a month of each year is spent touring and performing for the unenlightened. Compare that to the rock drummer Ringo Starr, the jazz drummer Joe Morello, the big band drummer Gene Krupa and the decades of music they eagerly and profitably gave their audiences.

The average contemporary Christian ascetic, on the other hand, is seldom so athletic or musically talented as these Japanese drummers. Instead, he or she is often one who reads the New Testament and decides the best way to honor Jesus' sacrifice is to re-enact Good Friday forever—one bad day out of thirty-three years. As often as I have read the gospels, I have yet to find the verses which have led so many to "crucify" themselves repeatedly like Kafka's "hunger artist," a man so fixated on the spirit that he abandoned his humanity. How any ascetic, Christian or otherwise, decides that life should be a repudiation of all pleasure is an enigma, but there are many who have done it thinking pleasure is a sin that must one day be atoned for. What follows is a short list of extremists, immoderate ascetics of many faiths. The Jains will eat no honey because, they reason, bees have spent a lifetime laboring to make it. Fakir Agastiya, a Hindu ascetic, held his arm over head until a bird built its nest on it. St. Simeon, one of the pillar saints, discovered that a maggot on his leg had fallen away from the wound. Said Simeon obligingly to the parasite as he replaced it, "Take, eat what God has given you!" Catherine of Sienna drank the pus from the breast-cancer sores of a woman she was nursing. Nuns at the Roman Catholic convent at Lisieux are reported to have eaten lepers' scabs and drunken tubercular sputum as evidence of their faith. St. Thomas More wore a hairshirt for years beneath his robes which left the skin an open wound of festering sores and crawling lice. Maritza Tamao, a French yoga enthusist, survived fifty-four hours nailed to a cross, fifteen of them with the cross upright. Hindu sadhus often tie stones weighing up to eighteen pounds to their penises to help control lust. And Jagdish Chandler, another Hindu holy man, crawled 870 miles to honor the goddess Mata. Thus the list ends in utter exhaustion.

I am reminded by all this "wheel spinning" that when Buddha met a man who'd spent twenty-five years learning to walk on water, the master said, "But the ferry only costs a penny." If Buddha had met the dehorned sadhus lugging their stones in the unconventional manner described above, he might have said, "With all due respect, sirs, but a cold shower in the rain is free and much less taxing."

Of course asceticism's critics have railed against the extremists since the start. In India where institionalized self-denial probably began, the Hindu *Gitas,* in fact, condemn the "terrible austerities" of the yogis. In the last century, Freud agreed charging that such austerity didn't promote "the development of energetic independent men of action.... It develops well-behaved weaklings who are subsequently lost in the great multitude." Oscar Wilde, another sharp critic, graphically described extreme penance as the "shining sore on the leprous body of Christianity." Similarly, the Catholic travel writer and critic Barbara Grizutti Harrison calls self-mortification a "reproach to joy." And the American novelist John Barth claims that "it is often pleasant to stone a martyr." By "martyr," I assume that Barth is referring to those who deny themselves as an end in itself. Martyrdom as a means to a greater good such as Dietrich Bonhöffer's is another matter altogether.

My own critical questions focus on the facile assumption that repudiating nature will somehow impress nature's creator. Asking such questions has led to the formulation of what I immodestly call Eisiminger's Law: the more ascetic an organization is (though not an individual like Gandhi), the less its influence on society will be. Alas, the celibate Shakers are down to their last couple of members in 2006, yet the Amish and Mennonites who permit marriage are holding their own. The Quakers, however, the least ascetic of these four sects and the most socially involved, continue to exert a disproportionately positive influence in the treatment of prisoners (Amnesty International was founded by Quakers), insuring the rights of women and children, lobbying for gun control and the cause of peace worldwide. The reverse of the law is also true: the more self-indulgent a group is (think of the myriad and short-lived hippie communes of the 1960s), the quicker its demise will be.

Perhaps the last word on asceticism is found in the churches of the world where golden reliquaries containing the bones of those who so scrupulously avoided wealth while alive are now studded with jewels in perpetuity. If at the resurrection the Christian saints return to claim their bodies, they are going to have a difficult time getting to their feet with all that gold on their backs, but then the church has always preferred us on our knees.

As I said at the outset, I have no desire to test the thesis that "less is more" on the connubial couch. As my wife and I approach our fortieth-fifth year of married life together, I know that sex after a week's abstinence is better than sex after a day's leave, and sex after two weeks is better still but not by much. I've yet to try a three-week hiatus. Generally two weeks of self-denial means that I've overlooked an opportunity sometime in the last fortnight. Ascetics, on the other hand, seem to be of the opinion that no sex will make their salvation an explosive orgasm. Personally, I'll take the breast in the hand over that murky bush any day.

Smokin' and Drinkin' and Such

I once had a bumper sticker that read, "If you're smokin' in this car, you'd better be on fire." I haven't always been so intemperate, but these days about the only thing I smoke is a turkey breast for Thanksgiving. I grew up in a two-smoker, four-packs a day household, and most of my parents' friends and relatives were satisfied consumers of everything from cigars to snuff. Though it was second-and-third-hand smoke that I breathed, I was a four-packs-a-day man from the day I was born in 1941 until the day I left for college in 1959. As rumors of tobacco's hazards circulated, Charles Harper, Chairman of Reynolds Tobacco, reassured the public, "[Second-hand smoke is not a problem.] If children don't like to be in a smoky room, they'll leave. [As for infants,]...at some point, they'll crawl." The Surgeon's General Report of 1964 dispelled the industry's smoke screen with solid science and led my parents to quit the carcinogenic habit. My father quit smoking over one weekend; my mother weaned herself over a few years.

I recall thinking as a child that the index and middle fingers must naturally yellow as people get older and that all homes were filled with a faint blue fog. I don't recall that the smoke ever really bothered me, but I do know that when a gym and health teacher had us run a few laps in the ninth grade, he asked me as I gasped supine in the infield how many packs a day I was smoking. I was too winded to respond, but at that time unknown to my teacher, I had never smoked an entire cigarette in my life. Occasionally I would draw a mouthful of smoke from one of my father's neglected cigarettes to fill a cellophane pack cover. With the wrapper pulled back a couple of inches and a hole burned through it, a good imitation of a smoking locomotive could be produced by gently tapping the smoke-filled container. The gym teacher, a prematurely militant anti-smoker (this was the mid 50s after all), told the class, "If God had intended for humans to smoke, He would have set them on fire!"

While my teachers and reformed parents did have an influence on my decision not to smoke, I think a pair of photographs in *Life* did more to seal the covenant. Sometime in the mid to late 50s, *Life* juxtaposed two full-page pictures of human lungs removed in autopsies. One pair, taken from a man who had never smoked, was sanguine as a cut of free-range sirloin. The other excised from the chest of a lifetime smoker was black as a tar bucket mop. I was mesmerized by the contrast, and as the blue fog cleared from my parents' home, my own lungs responded well to air devoid of tar and nicotine. In my junior year, I made the track team as a high jumper, quarter miler, and mile-relay man. I never set any school records, but every time I trained, I saw those two sets of lungs hanging before me like misbegotten carrots.

Despite the power of these evocative images, my will did buckle a few times when I was in the service. On maneuvers in southern Germany once, I opened some C rations and discovered a small pack of Lucky Strikes dressed in its WWII colors—the four cigarettes were nearly twenty years old! More out of the boredom of guard duty than any desire to smoke, I lit one up. The tobacco, however, was so dry that when I inhaled, some loose strands of tobacco were sucked into my lungs with the smoke. I commenced with wild gyrations to hack and spit up something resembling pale green slugs. It was so bad that the soldier who relieved me told me to report to sickbay; indeed, I was as green as the pack I had drawn my Lucky Strike from. My pulmonary convulsions, I thought, would strengthen my resolve, but I was mistaken. A few months later, I was visiting an Army friend who had rented a room in town where he spent his off-duty hours. As I entered, I immediately caught the manly smell from an open humidor of Cavendish Black Cherry pipe tobacco. My friend then filled the bowl of his pipe, tamped it just so, lit the tobacco with a lacquered lighter, and took a long satisfied draft from this small work of art. I admired the ceremoniousness of the procedure, and the aroma was intoxicating. On leaving, I went straight to the Post Exchange and purchased a pipe and a tin of tobacco. At the first opportunity, I lit up, inhaled profoundly, and drew a half inch of orange flame across my naive tongue. By the time it had healed, the cool factor of smoking had dropped to zero. Since then I have been clean.

Well, almost. Like Bill Clinton, I have been passed a few marijuana joints at parties. Some of these I have simply passed on; others I have taken a puff from but did not inhale. Many would say that this is the equivalent of sleeping with Marilyn Monroe and nothing more, but by the 70s, I knew that an unfiltered reefer had four times more tar than a Lucky Strike. Every time I saw a joint being lit, I fancied that I heard it cough. President Clinton was widely ridiculed for saying he never inhaled pot, but I believed him because I had the same desire to look cool and be accepted by my peers while at the same time fearing marijuana would turn my lungs blacker than that cadaver's lung in *Life*.

Beer drinking was another problem altogether. I'd had my obligatory first beer at seventeen and pretended to be stoned after a few swigs. One Friday night, three of my high school friends and I had gone out to get a pizza with the one fellow who had a driver's license. In his trunk were four tepid beers filched from his father's "wine cellar." I'm sure my drunk act wasn't very convincing, but I passed the initiation, and that was all that mattered. My father's bar in the den was always well stocked, but for some reason I had no desire to sample his scotch. Occasionally if I was the first out of bed after one of my parents' cocktail parties, I'd eat the gin-soaked cherries in the empty Tom Collins glasses scattered around the den and kitchen, but the forbidden fruit never produced much of a rush. I preferred to sneak the unadulterated cherries and marble-size onions straight from their refrigerated bottles when I was in my snack mode, which was pretty much the duration of my adolescence. An olive without the gin and vermouth is a "diet Martini," but I was not dieting just yet.

It wasn't until I dropped out of college and was shipped off to Germany by the U.S. Army that I came to know the "revenge of the hops." (Wine gives me a wall-banging headache, so I have only a passing acquaintanceship with "the wrath of the grape.") Drunkenness was my Esperanto when I was stationed in Germany; with a few drinks in me, I could have set Goethe straight if he had rematerialized and wandered into the Kajüte or the Florida Bar, two of the several dives I patronized in the small border town where I was stationed. (When sober, I had a facility with German comparable to a four-year-old.) Bob DiBerardino, a friend of mine, explained that a bartender was just a "pharmacist with a limited inventory." That analogy lent an almost scientific respectability to the German "guest houses" we inhabited in our off-duty time and helped me overcome any misgivings I might have had about rebuilding the post-war German economy with American dollars.

I'll never forget the first real bender I went on in a village outside of Kassel just prior to going on the Wintershield maneuvers. Our team chief Bill Perry drove us to "The

Oblivion Lounge" (Bill's name for it) which turned out to be something of a shrine to Elvis—there were posters of him on all the walls, and the jukebox, it seemed, played nothing but "*Danke Shane*" and "*Muss-ee-den.*" (As I said, my German was limited.) After a few shots of *Jagermeister*, (a potent liquor that went down like rusty roofing nails), chased with mugs of *Kulminator* (11.8% alcohol!), I was as fluent as Elvis. This lethal combination, however, allowed one to pass from sobriety to hangover without ever being pleasantly high. I had been drinking the 3.5% American brew at the enlisted mens' club and thought myself a capacious boozehound. When some pretty *Fräulein* asked me to dance, I quickly learned otherwise. My head felt like the bar's whirling disco ball shimmering unnaturally in the black light. I stumbled around the dance floor, which for some reason my "date" thought was an inventive new American step, but our "dancing" was short lived. Soon she was leading me out back where we both vomited in the outhouse. Good times! My ride, I discovered, had gone off with a "date" of his own, so my newly acquired admirer offered to let me crash in her living room a few blocks away. We helped each other to her family's medieval abode, and I passed out on the floor after failing to mount the bucking couch. Actually, the entire room seemed to be convulsing which quenched the last embers of my libido. Early the next morning, I awoke with a start on the linoleum when I heard angry parents yelling at their hung-over daughter. I got up as quickly as my head with the self-inflicted wound would tolerate, ran my hand through my hair, made my apologies, got some directions, said "*Auf Wiedersehen*" and "*Danke Shane,*" and walked back to where all this tawdry business began. At least I understood what my father meant when he told me, "If you hoot with the owls, you won't soar with the eagles." Fortunately, when I reached the bar, Bill was driving around looking for remnants of the team he was supposed to lead on maneuvers.

Generally, I was a happy drunk who loved to climb things when high, but the logical connection between climbing and getting high was something I could never explain when sober. One night I staggered out of the Kajüte and promptly climbed a thirty-foot linden in front of the bar. A buddy tempted me down like a cat with some tuna by daring me to climb aboard a passing horse-drawn hay wagon. I took the bait, ran to catch the wagon, and climbed aboard. I have forgotten how I got back to the base, but when I did, I decided that at last I was going to climb the mineshaft tower that stood just beyond the gates. I climbed a chain-link fence and began my unsteady ascent of the seventy-foot steel tower. As I approached the top, a gust of cold wind off the North Sea began to sober me up even as it tried to break my grip, so cautiously, I made my way back to earth. I was reminded of that dumb stunt recently reading about a Furman University pre-med student who had too much to drink and challenged his friends to a spit-for-distance contest. Determined to win, he climbed up on the dormitory porch railing thirty feet above the ground to gain some mythical leverage, lost his grip, and fell to his death. It could just as easily have been me forty years ago trying to expectorate on East Germany.

It didn't take me long to realize that there was a military conspiracy to make all enlisted men alcoholics so we'd re-enlist for the cheap hooch. At the Heidwinkel base Swing Club, for example, beer was free on Monday nights and mixed drinks were a dime on Fridays. In the middle of the week, we were left to our own devices, and these usually involved some competitive drinking game like Categories, Buzz, or Twenty-One. Categories was the most popular because it is so easy to learn but hard to master especially after losing a few rounds. A roll of the dice decides who starts the game, and once chosen, the leader calls a category like "cars." As soon as the subject is chosen, the contestant sitting to the leader's left names an automobile brand after the leader's fist strikes the table twice. If an acceptable answer is provided (no repeats are permitted), the leader's fist strikes the table two more times, and the next player names a car. The rhythm has to be maintained; anyone who speaks too soon or late is required to drink a small glass of beer or a shot of bourbon depending on how seriously drunk the group wants to become. After a few rounds, I generally lost all sense of rhythm and found that even with a category like "Items of Apparel You Are Currently Wearing" I got flustered and had to swallow the loss. One of the funniest games that I recall concerned the category of condom brands. It went something like this: "Condoms, thump, thump, Trojans, thump, thump, Sheiks, thump, thump, Pennies, thump...."

"Pennies?" the leader asked, "What's that?"

"It's for the guy who wants to come into some money." We all doubled over in laughter and decided that while there is no such brand name, the name was too good to be penalized.

I believe it was after one such game of Categories that B.J. Smith passed out on the club floor. Someone went to get a razor and shaving cream, and when B.J. awoke, the only facial hair he had left was the right half of his handlebar mustache and his left eyebrow. I was luckier: when I came to, I had two eyebrows divided in the middle, and I've never been a unibrow since. The deepest state of alcohol-induced unconsciousness that I have ever visited, however, was the duchy occupied by John Hammond. John actually made it back to his top bunk after a night of Categories, but he soon grew stiff as an I-beam as he spontaneously arose from his mattress supported only by his forehead and toes. A four-inch crevice slowly opened between him and the mattress extending the length of his body. Someone who witnessed this feat of comatose strength wondered if John wasn't dead and showing early signs of rigor mortis. Before his pulse could be located, however, John's midsection shivered then sagged, and he was pronounced well enough to ignore. Such indulgence is one of the reasons the world consumes roughly five tons of aspirin a day!

A low threshold of pain, a wife and two children, and a job which requires speaking coherently in public, change many things, and there's no question that my attitudes toward alcohol changed after I left the service. I have the evidence in my journal. Back in the 60s, I wrote a little ditty called "To the Right Brothers" which goes as follows:

> Here's to the brothers
> who helped us to fly—
> may the two Gallos
> never go dry.

Compare that gladsome toast to "Sunday-Morning Bender Analysis" that I wrote in the mid 80s:

> Awake at three
> with the postmortem blues,
> Jim studies a death
> without any clues.

The Jim of that last crotchet, as I call my "four-line couplets," is the poet and novel-ist James Dickey, who directed my dissertation at the University of South Carolina in the early 70s. Even though Jim possessed an athlete's body and one of the finest minds of his generation, he was unable to stop his own right hand from delivering the poison that made his life and family miserable and hastened his death. Jim thought of himself as the George Burns of the vodka bottle: Jim thought he could drink vodka the way Burns smoked a half million cigars and still live to reach a hundred. Jim missed his goal by twenty-six years, but he may have emptied a million jiggers of booze. Close to the end of his life, he admitted that he'd been drunk for the better part of twenty-five years. After reading the biographies of Henry Hart and Dickey's son Chris, I think the better part of fifty years is more candid.

I first saw Dickey in 1970 when he came to Clemson where he'd been a freshman in 1942 before leaving to join the Army Air Corps. Dickey was scheduled to read one after-noon for about forty-five minutes and then field questions from the student body for the remainder of the hour for a thousand-dollar-plus stipend. I would estimate that he read fifteen minutes and then staggered off stage on a drunken slur. I heard later that he'd been given a fifth of bourbon the night before by one of his old Clemson football teammates as he left a party in his honor. When Dick Calhoun, a colleague in the English Department, went to get Dickey at The Clemson House about an hour before he was scheduled to read, he found his idol in a stupor. Dick called Dr. Bill Hunter who rushed over with a B-12 shot, some pure oxygen, and a respirator. Hunter revived his bearish patient to the point that Dickey thought he was sober, but his 2 PM performance proved to five hundred people in the auditorium that he wasn't. A year later when I asked him about the Clemson "reading," Jim said, "I don't understand why the Clemson people are still so upset; my recollection is that I read for the full hour." Perhaps he had—in dog hours.

Shortly after the Clemson disaster, I read in an interview Dickey gave *Southern Living* that he was "on the wagon." In the fall of 1973 when I took the first of four courses from the writer at USC, I was naively expecting to see a rare bird, a reformed alcoholic. I was disap-pointed, for I smelled alcohol on his breath almost every time I spoke to him. After one class, however, he flattered me by inviting me to join him for a beer at a bar just off campus. I was torn between the opportunity to sit at the feet of the master for a few minutes, and abetting demon rum. Selfishly, I chose to go to the bar with him, but I know now that if I had not accompanied him, he'd have gone alone or with some other student in the class. I say this because many in the bar recognized him calling him "Jim" or "Jimbo."

Having seen my mentor drunk was enough to reform my drinking excesses. It wasn't many years after our children were born that I unilaterally decided that they were going to be non-smoking teetotalers. When my German mother-in-law sent us some brandy-filled chocolates for Christmas once, Shane, our son, had no desire to try them, which greatly pleased his parents. It did not please me, however, that he took a dozen of the innocent-looking bonbons to school one day and sold them to a classmate.

Two years later when Shane was in the tenth grade, I helped him order some spider eggs that he planned to use in a science-fair project. When the eggs arrived, we placed them in some glass cages and watched for signs of life. When the tiny creatures hatched, one group was given tobacco smoke to breathe, another received gin to drink, another beer, a fourth strong coffee, and a fifth, the control group, received fresh air and water.

All five had stale bread on which to feed. When the spiders spun out their entrails, only the group on bread, water, and fresh air spun symmetrical webs; the rest lacked all sense of concentricity.

Something about those charmingly wacky webs may have tempted our son to try some marijuana at Myrtle Beach the next summer. One of his friends had "scored some good weed," as he told us later when my wife discovered some finely minced leaves and seeds in an old prescription bottle. When I asked him why he'd want to live in a semi-comatose state, he replied that it was no different than the beer I drank after a jog. It was his generation's "drug of choice." I said it robs your attention span, stunts development, makes you psychologically dependent, and leaves your lungs with four times the tar that a cigarette does. I longed for a copy of those pictures in *Life* to no avail.

When Shane went off to college, I expected the worst, and in 1987, it happened. He was driving back to school at USC when he saw a sign as he approached an exit that read, "Drug Check Two Miles Ahead." So with an ounce of marijuana under his seat, he decided he'd foil the cops and leave the Interstate immediately. He did and ran straight into the cops' dragnet. The contraband was soon discovered, and after a night in jail, the judge fined and sentenced him to attend Narcotics Anonymous for six months. Frightened by the whole experience, Shane decided to take the NA meetings seriously, but the death of an acquaintance, I think, had more impact than anything I or any of his peers at the meetings said.

Shane didn't know Daniel well because the latter was a couple of years ahead of him in high school, but they liked many of the same local bands and frequently showed up at the same concerts. In 1988, the Grateful Dead came to Atlanta. Shane's boss at the restaurant where he was busing tables refused to give him the night off, so Shane could not attend without risking his job, which paid him a pittance but fed him all the ribs he cared to eat. Shortly after the Atlanta concert began, a Deadhead passed Daniel some white powder that he thoughtlessly ingested. Unfortunately he suffered a violently allergic reaction to the drug (later identified as LSD), ran out of the Omni, roughly accosted several pedestrians, tried to open the door of a passing vehicle, and then at a full sprint, dived seventy-five feet to his death off a freeway overpass. Shane attended the funeral, and his grief was as palpable as his life was altered.

Our daughter, Anja, on the other hand, joined the "Dare to Say No to Drugs" Club after witnessing her brother's debacle, but she developed a taste for the microbrews when she moved to New York to work after graduation. When I questioned her about her vow not to "desecrate the temple," she said she'd seen the pictures of her mother drunk at New Years in an old scrapbook. I should know; I took the pictures and helped to find her when she dashed laughing into a blizzard shortly after midnight. Anja, however, never had the problems with controlled substances that our son did. An old boy friend of hers who later became an MD told her of smokers he'd met at the hospital where he'd volunteered who after losing their larynx to throat cancer stuffed two or three cigarettes in their tracheotomy hole. Others breathing pure oxygen, he said with more moral authority than I could muster, routinely turned off their supply tank just long enough to smoke without risking an explosion. Such are the sagas that do more than logic, science, and parents can to save the children.

With the profit margin on cocaine running 17,000 to 1, with drug pushers so determined to succeed that they build multi-million-dollar submarines to ferry their product, and with addictions so powerful some have snorted a million dollars into the black holes of their nostrils, controlled substances are not going away any time soon. We might as well try to legislate the weather. So rather than attempting to interdict lightning, as I tell students when I'm riding this hobby horse, it's best to seek a haven from the storm. This means learning the consequences of a zillion volts coursing through the body and locating shelters before the thunder starts. Finally, I tell any, who are still listening, that every wall built to keep out drugs is a Maginot Line. After explaining the allusion to students who only dimly recall the 1991 Gulf War, I conclude by saying the Great Wall of China extends some 1,500 miles, and the perimeter of the fifty American states is roughly 20,000 miles. I'm not saying a 20,000 mile long wall can't be constructed (a hundred million dollars should do it), but if it is built, how do we expect to get to the Bahamas, much less Staten Island?

Though several of my army friends liked to quote the old saw: "In wine is wisdom; in beer, strength; in water, bacteria," I never came close to confusing a six-pack with a support group. Nor did I ever consider draining a lava lamp and drinking its contents the way one lifer sergeant did when the Swing Club was closed for repairs, and the Berlin crisis in 1961 meant everyone was confined to base. When I graduated from college, I had a 3.5—grade-point average, that is, not blood-alcohol level. I can honestly say that while I was in school I spent more money on books and recordings than alcohol. I wish all students could make the same claim, but I know that whether it's alcohol, tobacco, marijuana or something stronger still, virtually everyone is going to experiment with some mind-expanding, inhibition-lowering substance, legal or otherwise, before leaving this life. Benjamin Franklin argued that beer is proof that God loves us. And the Vatican has assigned St. Bibiana the hapless task of comforting hung-over Catholics. No extraterrestrial support for smokers is available that I'm aware of. I still can't say for sure, but I'm willing to bet that God is a moderate drinker and a non-smoker. I'll send up a smoke signal when I know.

COAST CURE
For Anja

If tired of the din
and gloom is chronic,
the sea is gin,
her wind's a tonic.

Robert Louis Stevenson's father used to fine his son a penny for each slang word that passed his lips. My father did no such thing, but he did charge me a nickel whenever both of my hands appeared above the table at the same time unless I was cutting my steak or buttering my bread. Consequently, my manners are impeccable, and slang does not intimidate me. In fact, I fear no word regardless of which side of the tracks it calls home. This is due in a circuitous way to Mrs. Thigpen, my sixth-grade English teacher, who advised our class to place a checkmark beside every word we looked up. If a check was already there, we were honor bound to cut off a finger joint. We had twenty-eight chances, therefore, to acquire a good vocabulary; after that we had to fall on a sword. Fortunately my fingers are whole, not because I have a good memory, but because I was blessed with an appreciation of hyperbole and irony.

The Congolese say that the beginning of wisdom is the acquisition of a roof. The Chinese argue that wisdom comes when you learn to call things by the right name. Now I was born with a roof over my head, but I've had a lot of names to learn, and these have sometimes swollen my head as I shall illustrate.

Once one of the young secretaries in the English department was astonished that I could spell the word *twelve* without the assistance of a dictionary. Since then whenever someone calls the department with a word question, she transfers the call to me. One morning a rather urgent call came in before I arrived, so the secretary told the caller to ring back during my office hour later that morning. When I walked into the English office to check my mail, the young woman handed me the following message: "Expect a call about 10 AM from a lady in Seneca who wants to know the other word in English beside *hungry* and *angry* that ends in *-gry*." Standing at her desk, I ran through the alphabet (*angry, bangry, cangry,...*) with no success and then went to my office where I located Paul Dickson's *Word Treasury*. I had a vague recollection that Dickson had something to say about this very question, being one that for some reason the editors at Merriam-Webster often field. Fortunately I found *anhungry* (an archaic synonym for *hungry*) without too much difficulty, but the more I thought about the inanity of the caller's question, the more I wanted to do more than just tell her the answer. Minutes after I located the word, the phone rang, and my mysterious inquisitor shyly asked if I knew "that other word in English that ends in *-gry*." "Indeed I do, Madam," I harumphed in my best academic manner. "It's *anhungry*. Shakespeare used it once, and it can be found on page eighty-five of *Webster's Third International Dictionary*." For a long time there was only silence on the line from Seneca. Finally I heard a stunned voice say, "Thank you" before the receiver fell weakly back into its cradle. I did not tell her that I was given the question in advance the way Charles Van Doren of *The $64,000 Question* was. For days I fondly imagined this woman telling her husband and friends of the English professor at Clemson who not only knew the word *anhungry* but had counted its frequency and memorized the pagination of an unabridged dictionary! To my credit I must say, I did not tell her that there are a half dozen other English words that end in *-gry*.

Indeed, most of my word triumphs have been of the fraudulent variety though I have never been investigated by a House subcommittee. One weekend after struggling mightily with the morning crossword, I was forced to consult *The New York Times Crossword*

Puzzle Dictionary. With a ragged feather in my cap, I drove to the school's gymnasium to conquer the twenty-five-meter natatorium. As I picked up a towel at the desk, I noticed that the student-clerk was doing the morning crossword that I'd just completed, and from the looks of his knitted brow, he was struggling mightily. My heart leapt.

"Finish it?" I asked as innocently as I could even with victory at my lips.

"Nah.... Where's Creighton?" the clerk asked.

"Omaha," I said a nanosecond too quickly I feared.

"That fits," said the clerk apparently without suspecting anything. "Who's the Babylonian deity?"

"Three letters or four?" I asked with slow if false deliberation.

"Three and it ends in a 'u.'"

"Anu," I pounced, unable to restrain myself any longer.

"Wow, thanks mister."

I walked off swinging my towel, basking in the warmth of the clerk's gaze.

My efforts aren't always so warmly appreciated. Once near Christmas, I was seated in the reference section of the Barnes and Noble bookstore in Greenville. The espresso fumes and the aroma of an *Oxford Shorter Edition* in my lap had wafted me into a pleasurable trance. Suddenly my aromatic dream state was interrupted by a young man who came up behind me, reached over and took down a volume identified by him to the young woman he was with as "the book that won me $50 at the office."

"Really," she said, not quite believing him. "How did you do that?"

"I told this guy one day in the men's room that a man named John invented the flush toilet. He bet me $50 bucks that I was wrong, so I brought this book in to prove my case."

Unable to resist, I said, "Uh, excuse me, but I thought Thomas Crapper invented the flush toilet?"

"I really don't remember the details now; it's been a long time," the amateur wordsmith said nervously reshelving the book. Without a word of thanks for my emendation, he hustled his puzzled lady friend off toward the espresso bar.

Now the use of *crapper* to mean "toilet" surely was influenced by the nineteenth-century sanitary engineer Thomas Crapper, despite what Tony Thorne says in *The Dictionary of Contemporary Slang,* a copy of which lay beside me. *John,* however, is more problematic. The most plausible guess is that it derives from John Adams, the first American president to enjoy indoor plumbing in the White House. But the biggest mystery was how this careless fellow had won $50 with a wrong answer. Had he bet his colleague that a man named Crapper invented the flush toilet and forgotten the details; had he bet that a president named John had the first White House crapper, or was he making the whole story up to impress his girl friend? Now I must admit that I too wooed my future wife with word lore, but I tried to be accurate lest she look a word up for herself. I imagine the young man's girl friend looked the word up after leaving, but the truth is that I have no idea how the episode played itself out, and that is why I prefer to be a more central player in the word operas in which fate casts me.

The role of spoiler is my favorite in these miniature melodramas. On a 1995 trip to Germany, for example, a pompous young man was showing me his new Volkswagen Pink-Floyd-Edition Rabbit. When he began telling me how much better German cars are than the Japanese Toyota I drive, I asked him if he knew what "pink Floyd" meant in American slang.

"It's a British rock group that took their name from two American blues musicians," he said.

"Yes, I know," I replied, "but what male body part does 'pink Floyd' refer to?"

"I give up. What?" he asked.

"A white man's reproductive organ," I said, marveling at how rapidly his crest fell.

Another word-melodrama in which I played a slightly different role involved a colleague of mine from the Clemson Speech Section. She had left academe and moved to California to pursue a job in television, which she found about the same time that she married. I heard from her every second or third Christmas, so I was surprised when she called one Sunday afternoon and said that her husband had recently left her and a thief had stolen $2500 worth of her belongings including her computer. But the real reason she had called was that she had a word question for me. My heart leapt.

"I'm looking to leave California," she explained, "and so I have sent my résumé all over the English-speaking world. A few days ago I heard from a station manager in Southampton, England, isn't that great? I'm very excited by his interest, but I don't understand one word of his letter."

"What is it written in," I asked jealously, "Klingon?"

"No," she said. "There's just one word that I don't understand even after looking it up. Do you mind if I read it to you?"

"Of course not, Debbie," I said pontiff-like. "It always helps to hear a word in its fullest context."

"OK," he says, "Yada, yada, yada, could you please amplify the penultimate paragraph." Now I've shown this sentence to four people at the station, and the best guess is that the manager thinks life is like an essay, so he wants me to explain what I want to do before I retire, retirement being the ultimate paragraph. Do you think this is right, Skip? I'm at a loss."

Savoring an imminent triumph, I paused and trying my best not to patronize, said, "I do not think so, Debbie. I fear that your friend at the station is over ingenious. "Do you have a copy of the letter that you sent to England? I think that's what the station manager is referring to, not a forecast of your life. What was in the next to the last paragraph of your cover letter?"

"Oh, my God, of course, you're right," Debbie said with a mixture of amazement and exasperation.

"Of course, I am," I said, "but what did you write him? You did save a copy, didn't you?"

"Oh, no!" she shouted in despair. "My cover letter was on my hard drive that was stolen last week."

Gradually, however, her letter came back to her with the full realization of her false assumption. She had assumed that anyone who could use *penultimate* must be learned and complex, and so the most Byzantine interpretation of the text had seemed most plausible to her and her station friends.

"Debbie, Debbie, Debbie," I said, fully patronizing her at last. "When there are multiple solutions, always seize the simplest one."

I have no idea where that pompous oversimplification came from, but it sounded

Solomonic at the time. Of course, like most home-grown prophets and proverbs, they're usually untrustworthy. Many complex solutions are preferable to simple ones simply because they work. The best solution, therefore, is not necessarily the simplest or the most complex, but the one that gets the job done.

Nevertheless, sometimes the best solution *is* the simplest, but it may be the most difficult to locate. In the early nineties, a colleague brought me a movie review with an observation by the reviewer that the film in question was "a Merchant-Ivory production." The context provided no further clues, and so ignoring the capital letters, I began to search for a discussion of relative ivory grades. My guess was that "merchant-ivory" was a cracked tusk that superficially had been made to look good for rapid sale. If Roman marble merchants had waxed inferior-grade Carrara to unload it on the unwary, why not unscrupulous ivory dealers? Though I never found anything to support my explanation, I confidently presented this etymology to my colleague. He, however, had had the good sense to walk down the hall to a woman who teaches film, and from her he learned to my everlasting regret that Messrs. Merchant and Ivory are two prominent British film producers who specialize in grandiose, Edwardian-era reproductions. Accepting defeat with dignity is easier when you realize that you're completely outgunned, outmanned, outmaneuvered, and wrong.

Indeed, this was the case on April 28, 1995 when thirty-five people stood up to prove my error. It seems that for years one of my closest friends and colleagues, Dr. John Idol from Boone, North Carolina, and a word-haunted man himself, had been calling a ski or knit cap a toboggan. I told him on several occasions with the confidence of Adam that a toboggan was a sled, not a cap, though you might wear one riding a toboggan. Unfortunately I never bothered to look up the word, violating my first rule of maintaining vocabulary one-upmanship.

On the occasion of John's retirement after I had roasted and toasted my friend to a fare-thee-well, John rose, pulled from his brief case a ludicrous, orange-tasseled knit cap, tugged it down to his ears, and explained our running feud over *toboggan*. He then asked anyone in the audience to stand if they had ever heard *toboggan* used for "this thing that I have on my head." I did a cervix-snapping double-take when I turned around and saw thirty-five of his Tar Heeled relatives standing behind me in a fine show of familial solidarity. I was had. These people had been forewarned, for they had risen as one. I laughed with the rest, but I was stung.

As soon as I could, I made tracks to the library's dialect dictionaries and found the following entry in *The Dictionary of American English*, "**toboggan**...A long-tasseled stocking cap, in full *toboggan cap.*" The phrase "in full" brought a smile to my face, but in the list of citations, there was the following quotation from a 1948 issue of *Pacific Spectator:* "He had on faded overalls with new blue patches on the knees, a sweater under the overalls, and a knitted blue toboggan on his head against the cold." The definition was some comfort, but the quotation proved that the single word *toboggan* had made it into the dictionary in the sense that my North Carolina friend had been using it all of his life.

As E. E. Cummings wrote in his Sonnet 39:

> all ignorance toboggans into know
> and trudges up to ignorance again....

Whenever I picture ignorance now, I imagine a boy like Bill Watterson's cartoon charac-ter Calvin oscillating between dumb and smart, riding a toboggan and wearing one too.

☙

I have illustrated how language may be used to puncture pretensions, deceive, trump a rival, and patronize a friend. For my linguistic sins, it is only fair that I have been made to eat the rump of crow. Though I have frequently been guilty of playing light and loose with words, I recognize that language is a matter of the utmost gravity. Let me conclude, therefore, with two anecdotes of a different stripe.

When I was a Young Pioneer at the First Presbyterian Church in Columbus, Georgia, Rev. Thomas (the kids called him "Doubting") taught us that "in the beginning was the Word." "The Word," of course, was God's word which had the force of creation itself. After the dust settled, "the Word" was the Bible, which Rev. Thomas read and freely interpreted, I now realize, with our class's help. We laughed crudely when Ehud killed the evil King Eglon and caused his bowels to run. We gaped as only adolescent boys can at the image of King Solomon climbing the palm tree of his bride-to-be and "squeezing her coconuts," as Rev. Thomas said. We booed when Elisha whistled for a bear to kill forty boys like our-selves because they called him "Baldy." We debated whether the Red Sea might have been the Reed Sea that anyone could part and elude an army in. We scorned in virtual unison the Bible's stand on capital punishment, the role of women, slavery, and a host of other social issues. When word leaked to the church elders what the Young Pioneers were up to, however, Rev. Thomas "received a call" from the University of Georgia Graduate School. He moved north to work on his Ph. D. in history, and I never read anything the same way again. When I discovered the word *piss* in 2 Kings 18:27, for example, I decided that if a prophet of God could use crude language then no word in and of itself was intrinsically bad or sacred. I still remember two of my friends cheering me at fourteen when I spoke my first *damn* with conviction. If God and His people, I reasoned, used obscenity, wit, and metaphor, then I could too. If God's people expressed indignation, sensuality, and love in language, then this was a model for us all.

The human soul or self, in fact, is as much a product of language as it is a gift of nature. Until a human infant learns to speak, that child has only the most rudimentary of identities or personalities. A friend of our family is a woman of thirty-five years now who was born brain damaged. For fifteen years she had no speech and could not write, yet the flicker in her eyes and a thousand ways of smiling and frowning suggested there was much more lurking below the surface of her facial expressions. Finally, she gained enough control over her neck muscles, even as her arms and legs continued to flail, so that with a strapped-on helmet equipped with a rubber-tipped pointer curving down to about twelve inches before her nose, she could type. Almost immediately, a torrent of words came from her Sears Electric and with them a truly complex and intelligent self emerged from the darkness. As she typed herself into existence, into a full-blown being, her parents and friends discovered who this person really was whom they had fed, bathed, and loved for over a decade without fully knowing because there was for the most part only her physical self to know.

"The limits of my language," Wittgenstein said, "are the limits of my world." Without limits to language acquisition and expression, I would add, the self can develop infinitely. Fine words butter no parsnips, Southerners like to remind those who speak with more eloquence than they do, but without language man might as well be a boiled parsnip. Words then have a gravity and a gravitational force of their own; indeed, as I once wrote:

> A hawk cannot soar
> and ask itself why—
> words are too heavy
> for hawks to fly.
>
> Weighted as we are
> with all of our words,
> our feathered language
> lifts us like birds.

ACCEPTING RESPONSIBILITY

> Shoulder your small part
> with a fragrant grace—
> every rose petal
> holds the world in place.

A Continual Allegory: Some Thoughts on Literalmindedness

Marianne Moore urged writers to become "literalists of the imagination," but it's the literalists without imagination who fascinate and frustrate me. I once read a letter to a newspaper editor from a woman who argued that the Bible is without error and often anticipates the findings of science. The prophet Amos, she said, predicted the discovery of the seventh star in the Pleiades. However, modern astronomers think that Amos may have seen a seventh star in that tiny constellation because in the eighth century B.C. the Pleiades briefly contained a supernova. In fact, astronomers now number close to five hundred stars in that cluster, a number that Amos clearly did not predict. Furthermore, Isaiah, the letter writer opined, anticipated the discovery that the earth is a sphere when he spoke of the "circle of the earth." But, in truth, neither the King James' "circle" nor the Revised Standard Version's "vault" necessarily implies that our planet is an oblate spheroid, which it is, or even a sphere. Isaiah, like Homer, may have been thinking of a round, flat disk like a hockey puck floating in space covered by a "sky dome." At any rate, I sent my objections to the editor of the newspaper who had printed the woman's letter, and he wrote to inform me that there was "no space."

But if writers as accomplished as Charles Dickens and F. Scott Fitzgerald with "real toads in their imaginary gardens," as Miss Moore desired, misuse *literally*, perhaps there is no help for any of us. Dickens, for example, has a character "literally feasting his eyes...," and Fitzgerald creates someone who "literally glowed...." Of course it is a far cry from being literal-minded to misusing *literally*, especially when *Webster's Dictionary of English Usage* lamely argues that *literally* may be used as a simple intensifier like *really* or *actually*. Webster's good name notwithstanding, this acceptance strikes me as paradoxical and contrary to the ethic of prose clarity. I prefer to reserve, for example, "literally glowed" for those who swallow an isotope of radium, and I wish to save "figuratively glowed" for those proud folk who *seem* to have swallowed the isotope. I propose that we save "literally climbed the walls" and "literally died" for those who climb and die respectively, not those who feel like it. Vladimir Nabokov has a character in *Invitation to a Beheading* whose "eyes literally scoured the corners of the cell." My presumptuous advice to this master prose stylist is to drop the word *literally* to make the metaphor subtly more effective and economical.

The word *literal*, incidentally, comes from the Latin *litteralis* meaning "by the letter" and "suggests the influence of the letter as a measure of strictness and rightness," according to the *Oxford Companion to the English Language*. As a poet myself whose legal tender is the figure of speech, I recognize that the phrase "fishers of men," for example, can only be understood figuratively, that the phrase "pearls before swine" may be literal or figurative, and that the phrase "God and Mammon" must be figurative unless the reader is polytheistic. When the Bible uses contradictory figures as in the two births of Eve (first, created "in our image," says Jehovah, and a chapter later created from Adam's rib), some literalists say that the problem would be resolved if we had the ur-text of Genesis, but that is like wishing for a video tape of Australopithecus!

Perhaps because as a teacher my livelihood depends upon an endless supply of *tabula rasas*, I find it much easier to forgive a student's literal-mindedness than a graduate's. One of my college sophomores once told me and his class that he would not be celebrating Easter because his church (part of a small Baptist sect in the Carolinas) recognized that Jesus did not rise from the dead in "three days and three nights."

"But didn't he?" I asked. "He was crucified on Friday and was seen alive on Sunday. Friday, Saturday, Sunday—three days!"

"On the contrary, professor," he said. "A day is twenty-four hours, the creation took 144 hours, and Christ was dead only about forty hours, not seventy-two as he promised. Easter, therefore, is a fraud!"

"You, sir, drive a hard bargain," I said figuratively.

As I recall, this young man did pass the course, but he had a difficult time with poetry, and he thought that Shirley Jackson's famed short story "The Lottery" was about the annual Puritan practice of stoning a person to death to help the corn grow. He argued out of class, I was told, that Superman could not fly "faster than a speeding bullet" because given his size and weight he'd spawn a tornado every time he launched himself out of the window of the Daily Planet. It occurs to me that this young man, a product of a "segregation academy" incidentally, might be one of the stunted victims that I privately predicted in 1983 when the Bob Jones University Press published the *Christian Student Dictionary*. The premise underlying this work is that if you deny the existence of labels like *cigarette, abortion, atheism, puberty*, and *Santa Claus* maybe the packages themselves will go away. None of these words is contained in the *CSD*. But on second thought, literalists must have a word to start with; it's what lies beyond the word that escapes them. Perhaps the thinking is that if you deny children a word, when they finally locate it, they'll be satisfied with it alone and look no further. When one Bob Jones student, according to a story circulating in these parts, transferred to a state university to take some engineering courses, he received an invitation to a new-student mixer. At the bottom of his invitation were the following abbreviations, "RSVP BYOB." On the prescribed evening having made his prospects of attending known to his mysterious host, he showed up at a bacchic blowout complete with a mosh pit clutching a Bible instead of a bottle. Such are the pitfalls of knowing French but not that a letter is multifaceted.

Once students leave the portals of academe whether their literal-mindedness is deliberate or inadvertent, they are expected to apply what they have learned in the laboratory. Some are evidently not paying attention. One high school graduate went to his doctor complaining of pain in his right ear. The doctor, who later wrote up this case in the *American Medical News*, issued the patient a prescription for ear-drops which, it must be stated, was filled a bit carelessly. The druggist wrote that the patient should apply three drops to his "rear" instead of his "r. ear." For three days the patient whose ear was still aching took the ear-dropper and dutifully followed the letter of the absurd directions as faithfully as the Nazi subaltern who gassed himself when he located a Jew in the fallen leaves of his family tree. What kind of person was the patient or the subaltern? Howard Nemerov answered that question in the following poem:

> Just so you shouldn't have to ask again,
> He was the kind of guy that if you said
> Something and you were the kind of guy that said,
> "You can say that again," he'd say it again.

The Nazi, I must confess, is a fiction, but it wouldn't surprise me if he weren't, for the insane are often revealed by their literal-mindedness. One mentally-ill man used what was evidently his last shred of sanity to request mental-health care. When his request was denied, he walked into an industrial-arts woodshop and coolly ran his right hand through a power saw. After the hand was successfully reattached over his objections, he explained that as an adolescent he had tattooed "666" on the knuckles of his right hand to show his allegiance to Satan. Later when his tattoo offended him, he took the Bible's injunction literally and cut off his hand. Like a child, this disturbed individual could only understand "cut off thy hand" in concrete terms. It probably never occurred to him that a confession, penance, and a ruby-laser treatment might have erased the offense and spared his hand. Shakespeare reminds us in *The Merchant of Venice* that literalists can have their pound of flesh, but woe betide them who shed a drop of blood!

Autistic individuals have similar problems with figurative language. Dr. Temple Grandin, a professor of animal science at Colorado State University despite her autism, admits in her autobiography that symbolism, irony, and metaphor are often lost on her. For this reason and her empathy with animals, she chose a career in science where the language usually is literal, and cattle being led to slaughter, her specialty, do not kid around. When she hears a proverb as common as "a rolling stone gathers no moss," for instance, she has to "run a video of the rock rolling and getting that moss off" before she understands. But even with her mental video, she gets the maxim wrong, for the rolling stone is not shedding moss; it never acquires any in the first place—it crushes those moss spores before they can attach themselves and germinate.

With the perils of literal-mindedness in mind, the founders of many of the world's religions have taken pains to warn the faithful. Paul in the Christian Bible warns that "the letter killeth, but the spirit giveth life." Likewise Allah states that the Koran "was sent to earth in seven dialects, and in every one of its sentences there is an outer and inner meaning." Similarly, the Hindu Gitas urge readers to "study the words ... but look behind them to the thought they indicate, and having found it, throw the words away as chaff when you have sifted out the grain." Each of these three warnings is, of course, daringly couched in figurative language.

Countless faithful commentators, furthermore, have reiterated the admonitions of the gods they worship. Martin Luther, for example, whose followers were smashing "graven images" in Northern Europe regardless of their artistic value, told his anti-Catholic following that Jehovah's second commandment notwithstanding, it is not necessary "to swallow the Holy Ghost feathers and all." A thousand years before Luther, St. Augustine had cautioned, "We must be on guard against giving interpretations of Scripture that are farfetched or opposed to science and so exposing the word of God to the ridicule of unbelievers." Yet when Galileo offered to let his inquisitors see for themselves the moons of Jupiter, one cardinal, who subscribed to the doctrine of correspondences, is reported to have said, "There are seven days in a week, seven orifices in the body; therefore, there are seven heavenly planets. I don't need to look."

This failure to look and to accept something on the basis of a few words and a casual observation (Aren't pores orifices? Are ears?) has had and continues to have dire results. After all, 38% of Americans think that the Bible is literally true. Because Eve sinned, for example, women still cannot enter the Roman Catholic clergy. Because the Old Testament gives the diameter of a bronze tub as 10 cubits and the circumference as 30 cubits, some fundamentalists assign a value of 3.0 to pi. Because Mark says that the faithful "shall take up serpents ... and drink any deadly thing," some believers sip strychnine and fondle live rattlesnakes in their worship ceremonies. Because Jehovah divided the light from the dark in the first chapter of Genesis, Bob Jones Jr. once argued for racial segregation. Because God divided the land from the sea, Jones also felt that space and undersea exploration were sacrileges.

Because Jesus told Peter that he would build his church upon "this rock," the basilica of St. Peter's is built over Peter's stony tomb. (Jesus was joking, for heaven's sake! Peter's name means "the rock.") Because Luke says, "blessed are the barren," the male members of the Skoptzies, a Russian Orthodox sect, cut off their testicles, and the women cut off their breasts. Because Paul writes in Acts that the faithful should "abstain ... from blood," Jehovah's Witnesses will to this day refuse a blood transfusion. (Modern translators now render this passage as "eat not blood" or "rare meat.") Because St. John the Divine describes an angel standing at each of earth's four corners, some fundamentalists believe the earth is flat and square. And finally because an angel in Revelations says "take the book and eat it up," King Menelik II of Ethiopia attempted to eat the First and Second Book of Kings. The toxic dyes were more than his stomach and colon could tolerate, for he died in the twenty-fifth chapter.

If a sacred text must be interpreted by man or a priesthood of believers before it can be understood, literalists argue that this gives too much glory to man and detracts from the sovereignty of the deity, who speaks boldly without equivocation. I suspect, however, that some Christian bibliolaters have been misled by the famous opening lines of John's gospel, "In the beginning was the word," and, as a result, they have begun to worship the word rather than the creator. However, if one reads John's entire first chapter, it is clear that John intends for "the word" to represent Jesus who was present with God and the Holy Spirit from the creation. Too many literalists, it seems, read "the word" or *logos* as the fourth member of the Trinity, and in doing so, they have created a radical worship. They have selected a few verses and carved these in stone in order, I suspect, to further a narrow agenda or to seize some power and distinction in a world they feel alienated from.

One would think that Jesus' habit of making a moral point via the parable would be sufficient to make readers of the Bible wary of too literal an interpretation, but the 38% figure cited earlier shows the folly of that observation. In addition to the parables scattered throughout the Bible, there are passages such as, "You are the salt ... [and] I am the vine," which demand a figurative reading. In Genesis, for example, Jehovah warns Adam that he will "die the same day" in the King James translation if he eats of the tree of knowledge of good and evil. Later, of course, Adam does sample the forbidden fruit, but Genesis reports that he died, not that day but centuries later at the age of 930! And in Luke, to cite a New Testament example, Jesus calls Herod Antipas "that fox." Herod is one of the few people mentioned in the Bible whose existence can be verified by objective historians, and while he was a shrewd king, he was not a carnivorous mammal with a pointed snout and a bushy tail.

As I've suggested, literalists often insist on eating their cake and having it whole as well. The old argument that if Jesus made and drank wine it must be acceptable for mere mortals is often countered with the "grape-juice argument." The apostle John didn't mean wine, so this argument goes; he meant grape juice because there was not sufficient time for the wine to ferment. But if Superman can fly, why can't he have x-ray vision? (Incidentally in the Inuit Bible, Jesus turns water into blubber.)

The arch-Biblical literalist Josh McDowell has a similar problem with the rediscovery of Tyre even though the Old Testament prophet Ezekiel predicted that the city would be destroyed and "never found again." Indeed, Tyre was destroyed by Nebuchadnezzar, but its ruins have never been lost, for there has been some sort of human habitation there on that Mediterranean island/peninsula for close to five thousand years. McDowell acknowledges the "rediscovery" of the city, but he adds that "a better interpretation" of "never found again" is, "Tyre will never be found again in such wealth and splendor as it origi-nally enjoyed." To this selective literalist, the prediction in Ezekiel is a Rorschach meaning anything that doesn't contradict the facts. But McDowell places words in the prophet's mouth that we have no way of knowing if he intended.

ഏ

When the film *E.T.* was all the rage, I took our children to see it. In the scene when Elliot and his extraterrestrial friend launch their bicycle from a hilltop and fly gloriously across the face of a full moon, a woman seated a few rows in front of us suddenly stood up. Securing a child with one hand and her purse with the other, she looked up at the screen, snorted "I'm sure!" and stormed out of the theater.

Like many literalists, this woman has been short-changed. The education that she received limited her as surely as an innocent person sent to prison. But what seems odd to me is that freeing these people from Blake's "mind-forged manacles" is so rare when the Bible itself shows how change is possible.

Leviticus, for example, sets the stage. The author states unequivocally that the oc-casional slaughter of live animals on a consecrated altar is a righteous duty of the faithful. We know that for thousands of years such slaughter was so routine that Abraham with-out question or hesitation was prepared to kill his own son when Jehovah ordered it. A millennium later, Paul writing to the Hebrews essentially said, "Enough! Jesus made the ultimate sacrifice on the cross. Any further shedding of blood in God's name demeans the son's gift." Remarkably the ancient tradition ended though the "God-breathed words" of Leviticus are still printed between the same covers as Paul's letter to the Hebrews.

The heart of "Biblical inerrancy" lies in II Timothy 3:16: "All scripture is given by inspiration of God...." However, there is a huge difference between God's word and the author, just as there's a difference between inspiring a book and writing it. People should not hold God responsible for what God-inspired authors and His translators write. As I have shown, God and His son use figurative language throughout the Bible; why should man created in God's image do any less?

John Keats argued that "a man's life of any worth is a continual allegory," for indeed every life regardless of how base or brief has something to teach the rest of us. The literalist often chooses to study a single life and neglects billions of others. Certainly such simplic-ity is appealing, but like a self-restricted diet, the perils are real. In a poem of my own, I have a hidebound Scotch Presbyterian say:

> "Eat a potato?
> That is a libel.
> No where is that word
> in my Bible."

> To which I reply:
> You've searched the Word
> for a wink from Jesus,
> but you have a friend
> in exegesis.

THE LONG AND SHORT OF BREVITY: FACT AND SPECULATION

Because "Dr. Eisiminger" is a six-syllable mouthful, I have long encouraged students to call me "Dr. E" to lessen the anxiety attached to speaking in class. It seems I am not alone: in 2000 according to the files of the Social Security Administration, there were 221 Americans with single-letter surnames and at least one for each letter of the alphabet. "A" is the most popular with twenty-four of us carrying that surname at the top of phone book listings and class rolls. "N," "Q," and "X," are the least popular, there being only two people for each of these. However, in Myanmar, hundreds of families are named "U"; while in Korea, there are thousands who answer to "O" once the transliterations are completed. A German proverb states, "In brevity is the spice," yet Germans have no apparent compunction compounding words like *Oberdonaudampfschifffahrtsgesellschaftskapitän* for a river-boat captain employed by the Upper-Danube Steam Boat Company—nine English morsels crammed into one fat *Wurst*. In fact, a syllable count of the Gospel of Mark made by Walter Kirkconnell reveals that German uses 32,650 syllables to express what English conveys in a mere 29,000. (Incidentally, according to Robert MacNeil, English has a vocabulary of about half a million words while German limps along on 185,000.) French needs 36,000 syllables to express Mark's Greek, Russian 36,500, Italian 40,500, and Bengali 43,100. Of all the great modern languages, English with arguably the largest vocabulary is surely the most economical though comparisons with ideographic languages like Chinese are admittedly difficult. But the economy of English, may be part of what makes its speakers impatient with our more prolix neighbors. It may also account for the way we rush through lunch and sex. Could the American "working vacation" be a reflection of our no-nonsense language? Just a thought.

As a native-born speaker of English, I come by my preference for brevity naturally. Nearly fifty of my English teachers over two decades beat the drum of language economy as steadily as any other. The poet and novelist James Dickey once told a class that I was part of to go home and write a thousand heroic couplets. A professor had given him the same advice years earlier along with "Don't fall" and "Get up," which Dickey claimed had done him a world of good. He said he had no interest in reading our "millenary couplets," as he put it, but we'd be better human beings if we did. Instructions to begin, as I trust our current President now realizes, should always include an exit strategy: with close to three thousand couplets under my belt and Dickey dead for nearly a decade, I don't know how to stop! In fact as I sit here wondering where this essay is going, I have doodled in the margin:

Detouring around Robin Hood's barn
makes for a very tedious yarn.
The circumlocutionary route
may lead you places you can't get out.

Although a few syllables shy of the heroic, these couplets are meant to imply that windy locutions are the written and oral equivalents of manure.

It is often observed that this nation's most cherished prose is succinct without being ungracious. We declared our independence from England in 1322 words; Moses gave us an account of creation in 794 words and spelled out the Ten Commandments in 297; Lincoln dedicated the Gettysburg Cemetery in 268 words, and in reciting the Lord's Prayer, we utter only fifty-six. Indeed, the very brevity of these timeless expressions is what has made them such fertile soil for our allusions. "To be brief," said Santayana, "is almost a condition of being inspired."

Nevertheless, a great many of us, especially English teachers, have a tendency to reward length over concision, cogency, and content. For over twenty years, I served as a reader and table leader for the Educational Testing Service on SAT II and AP essay examinations. It quickly became obvious to me and most other readers that "development," as the ETS likes to call length, is a virtue. One reader admitted that he read the first and last sentence of a paper to see if any red flags were unfurled, appraised the readability of the handwriting, checked the length, and placed a grade on the paper. He claimed that in ten years of reading, he was never off by more than one grade.

One place, however, where concision usually wins is in comedy, which follows a variation of the Law of Parsimony, for brevity, as various writers have told us, is the soul of wit, wisdom, and lingerie. "Punch it up," to a comedy writer usually means using the rasp and file on some wooden prose to give it a sharper comic "edge." Minimalist architects like to say "less is more; more's a bore," and generally the same advice applies to comedy. Indeed, some of the very best *New Yorker* cartoons have no caption at all. One of my favorite Saul Steinberg drawings shows a "J. Alfred Prufrock-style" social gathering with four abstractions intent on one another ("talking of Michelangelo") while the dark coil of a solitary guest sits daydreaming about "swelling a progress" and frolicking with mermaids.

For several months now in 2006, I have joined tens of thousands of *New Yorker* readers in submitting a caption for an uncaptioned drawing in a weekly contest. Each week, the editors publish the three best captions submitted, after which readers are asked to go on-line to vote for their favorite. In a very unscientific survey, it seems that the *New Yorker's* readers, while they may have read tens of thousands of words about ketchup, truck driving, and oranges over the years, prefer their cartoons with a rapier's point. One recent cartoon showed a job applicant being interviewed in the foreground as three office workers armed with ax, baseball bat, and pistol chase a hapless co-worker down a corridor. Though it could be argued that the drawing needed no caption, the contest's challenge was to put some words into the job interviewer's mouth. I submitted, "We don't have anything right now, but if you could wait a second...." The winner, submitted by John Maynard of Berkeley, California, was, "How soon can you start?" I was on the right track, but I have to concede that the edge honed by my file is duller than Mr. Maynard's.

In another contest, a priest, a minister, and a rabbi walk into a bar as the bartender is using the phone. I toyed with Rainbow Coalitions, Olympic committees, and global paradigms, but finally my barkeep says, "Hold on, the Ecumenical Council just walked in." However, my thirteen syllables lost to the following seven submitted by Kelly Younger of Los Angeles, "Stop me if you've heard this one." No contest, I concede, spare is fair.

A former colleague of mine used to assign students in his advanced composition classes a thousand-word essay. Once graded, he returned the essays with instructions to rewrite them in five hundred words. Finally they were reduced to a hundred words or less. He claimed this reductive exercise taught a valuable lesson. Probably so, but if I condensed this essay of mine to "Be brief," assuming any editor would accept it, most readers would want their money back. The flamboyant pianist Liberace could perform Chopin's "Minute Waltz" in thirty-seven seconds, but few, I suspect, want to dance much less listen to such a tempo. I suppose it's a lot like lace: if the lace maker fills in all the holes, where's the charm and delicacy?

One of the best light verse writers today is Edmund Conti, author of "Potholes." The poem in its entirety reads, "A void." I tell students that the space between Conti's "A" and his "void" is analogous to a carefully crafted opening, not a tear, in a lace curtain; fill the white space and the filigree beauty of the lace disappears as does the poem if some editor foolishly decides to close that calculated gap.

When I preach the virtues of concision to students, I often use a sentence from one of their peers: "My mother has about two cats." Most students see the problem right away, but then at least one practitioner of instant messaging will submit an ugly paper using "4" for "for" and "w/o" for "without," etc. Once after lecturing on Zipf's Law, the tendency in English to shorten the words we use the most or lengthen those we use the least, one student apologized for something he'd written saying, "My b."

"My b?" I inquired, "what are you saying, son?"

"It's Zip's Law, sir,—'my apologies' became 'my bad,' which has become 'my b.' Do you want me to wordy it up for you?"

Precisely where to draw the line between the tedious and the trenchant is a tough call. In a sentence written by a former student, however, the call was easy: "Brevity occurs when everything is short, concise, and to the point." But if there are two havens, as I like to tell students, like Boston and Plymouth, I don't think there's any question that the former offers a deeper and more sheltered harbor. And if there are three havens (add the Cape Cod Marina in the mix), Boston surely is the safest. But if there is a single haven, please resist the temptation to call it a "safe haven" because any haven or harbor by definition especially for boats and small ships is safer than the open sea. Why that is so hard for the grizzled talking heads of our media to grasp is a mystery, but my best guess is that public speakers are insecure and nervous. I know the first time I used "inchoate" in spoken conversation, I unconsciously followed it by mumbling "in the early stages." I suspect I was reassuring myself as well as my listeners.

As I said, though, the line between too much and too little is difficult to draw. In a *B.C.* strip drawn by Johnny Hart in 2004, one caveman approaches another who has recently entered the business of selling "live bait." Suspecting a tautology in the proprietor's signage, the customer asks, "Do you sell dead bait?"

"Of course not," replies the owner.

Turning to leave, the customer confidently but mysteriously concludes, "The sign is redundant."

Now I've shown this strip to a couple of English teaching colleagues, and the three of us agree that the sign is not redundant. While "edible bait" or "alluring bait" may be tautologies, "live bait" is acceptable as anyone who's ever fished with a plastic worm knows. The not-so-funny joke, therefore, has to be on the customer whose ignorance has been unmasked, and if that's not the point, either all three of us missed the subtlety, or Mr. Hart doesn't fish much.

"Grocery store" is another difficult call, but I prefer to call the store a "grocery" and what is sold there "groceries." However, if you wish to refer to several groceries ("There are three groceries in our small town"), are you speaking of the food stores or the food they sell? It does get sticky.

"When I struggle to be terse," the classical poet Horace wrote, "I end by being obscure." E-mail and IM have only thickened the fog in the last twenty years. At the start of a recent academic year, I sent out an e-mail memorandum asking colleagues for any upper-level humanities proposals they might have in mind for the next year. A recently hired lecturer wrote right back asking if a part-time person such as himself would be eligible to teach one of these plums. Not sure of his status in the hierarchy of personnel, I wrote the department head and asked if he had any objections.

"No way!" he responded *in toto*.

His economy and speed of reply were admirable, but I had no idea what he meant. So I wrote back asking, "Is there 'no way' that you have an objection or 'no way' that Mr. X will teach a 300-level class? Just want to be sure."

Replied my laconic boss, "No objection."

The new poet laureate Donald Hall once wrote that his prose ethic was clarity, and this has guided me for over thirty years whether I'm writing an essay or a couplet. First, I must be understood; second, I must be economical. One has to admire a language where "*El Pueblo de Nuestra Senora la Reina de los Angeles de Porciuncula*" has evolved into "LA"; "Send me some electronic mail" has morphed into "E me," and "OK" has shrunken to "K." No mistaking those clipped masterpieces as long as there's plenty of context!

❧

John Chancellor was once asked if the three-hundred-word limit imposed by NBC on the anchorman's nightly editorials didn't chafe. "Not at all," replied Chancellor. "In Genesis, that gets you into the fourth day." And if one compresses the New Testament as some anonymous wag has done to, "He was born. He lived. He died. He's coming back, and he's not going to be happy," three hundred words places you well into the Apocrypha. Matthew warns us that on the Day of Judgment we'll all be required to justify a lifetime of "idle" words. I take this as a roundabout way of restating Nietzsche's slightly updated observation that the well-turned sound bite is a form of immortality. Few recall any more than that.

TWELVE TOES AND COUNTING:
GLIMPSES OF COLLEGE-STUDENT LIFE AT THE MILLENNIUM

Over a period of fifteen semesters, I have asked students on the first day of class to tell me something about themselves that "you ordinarily wouldn't reveal on a first date." After asking them to write down their name, hometown, major, favorite movies, novels, television shows, career plans, and assuring them that none of this will affect their grades, I say, "Finally, I'd like for you to tell me something more revealing. Whether you brag or confess, describe or analyze, tell me something quirky that sets you apart from the pack, the covey, the herd, and most other students at Clemson; something that might even be unique. For example, one kid told me he had twelve toes; another's feet resembled a hobbit's; another's loft had self-destructed with him in it, a future nurse had diapered more old men than children, and one kid had 'been a byrd [sic?] in a past life.' What you tell me can, of course, be more conventional like some public recognition, a scholarship, a personality trait, a physical attribute, an exotic travel destination, a family connection, indeed, anything that concretely or obliquely contributes to who and what you are." Most students, and I've taught over a thousand in the last five years, tell me that they are the first in their family to attend college, that they were named Miss Congeniality in a Goose Creek beauty pageant, that their grandfather was a halfback here in the 40s, or that they "have a great sense of humor," which is fine, but it's not what I'm fishing for. I'm trolling for the epiphanic details like the hobbit's feet, the compulsive's "rainbow closet," and the former "byrd" that are so sweet it would be a shame not to record them.

Inevitably, a few students at the start of every semester are experiencing a "major crisis"—that is, a radical change of heart concerning their course of study. Their successful uncles advised them when they were twelve to go into economics, and now they can't bear the thought of another accounting course. Furthermore, their parents had cut up their credit cards between semesters when word came that their GPR had plummeted to 2.0, which is the equivalent these days of 8000 on the Dow-Jones. One career-conflicted student said that she was a political science major but had not registered to vote. A nursing major revealed that she hated needles. An electrical engineer confessed she was terrified of electricity. A tourism major said he'd "been all over but didn't remember most of it." More English majors than I care to recall have admitted that they dislike reading. This disconnect is probably why few students receive their degree in the major they declared as freshmen. And this is as it should be; it's a lot easier to change majors than careers.

Often students, especially freshmen confident of their majors, are still basking in the glow of their high school successes. Said one, "I've never made below an 'A' in English—hint, hint." Another bragged, "I maintained perfect attendance K through 12," yet over the course of the semester he took all the cuts I permitted. He was a quick study. Another, who has me, an old Army brat, beat, wrote, "I've attended fifteen schools, and I'm a long way from finished." (I attended fourteen.) Occasionally Clemson, South Carolina's visibly-secular, land-grant university, gets a Roman Catholic kid who escaped from New Jersey. One such apostate wrote, "I survived twelve years of parochial school, but I still panic when I see a nun." Since I always ask if any of my students are on scholarship, quite a few tell me that they are the recipient of a Piggly Wiggly Scholarship, or the Heavenly

Ham Scholarship, or the York County Scholarship for the Children of Peach Growers. I am often amazed at how narrow the recipient base must be for many of these financial awards. One student said he'd received a scholarship because he had a semi-functional colon. His friends dubbed him the winner of the "Half-Ass Scholarship," but I'll bet his debt-ridden parents didn't care what it was called.

It shouldn't be surprising that many students are homesick on the first day of class and take, therefore, the small opportunity I give them to commemorate their families: "I'm distantly related to Bonnie Parker and Blackbeard!" "My granddad is the only man to KO me." "My great, great grandfather was the mayor of Dublin." "My grandfather married Mel Brooks' sister." "Hoagie Carmichael is my 4th cousin." "I'm an African-American descendant of Alexander Hamilton." "My dad dated Elvis's first girl friend." "The thin Mama from the Mamas and the Papas held me when I was a baby." And, "My uncle owns a nightclub where Tom Petty, Billy Joel and the Rolling Stones once played," are typical. Distant and strained as they might be, most family references are positive, and it almost seems like students are grasping for connections as if they were empty life jackets floating away from the Titanic. One lonesome young lady said she had seven brothers and forty-one first cousins and not one of them attended Clemson. Another, a test-tube baby, was an only child but had grown accustomed to the solitude.

A small minority of family references, however, are negative: "My Dad's a butcher, and I'm a vegetarian." "My mother's dead, and I don't speak to my father." "My folks are members of the 'frozen chosen'—they're neo-Calvinist Presbyterians." "My grandfather had connections to the Chicago mob." [I assume that's negative; I chose not to inquire.] Another said, "My entire family looks and acts like farmers; I try not to." It's sad when eighteen year olds are so self-righteous they cannot appreciate the opportunity their folks have worked hard to give them. These parents and others like them know they are farmers or mill workers, and it would break their hearts to know their kids are ashamed of any part of them. My personal favorites are the grateful children who brag, "My parents are still married, and I love them for it." Or the twenty year old, who looks thirty, who quietly vows, "I'm the single parent of a three-year-old daughter, and I promise you she's not going through the hell I've been through." As much as I admire the impulses of this single mother, I also know how difficult it is to protect children from themselves.

Second only to the parents and often first in students' affections are the significant others that many openly confess they came to Clemson to meet. "It's raining men!" one woman exclaimed. Most students are happy with the person they're dating though several express implicit reservations: "I'm dating a Hooter's girl." [No reservations here!] "I'm dating a street chemist." "I'm dating a guy whose head hurts when he misses a Simpson episode." "I'm dating a city girl who thinks all snakes come in two pieces." "I'm dating a Mormon who disapproves of everything I do for fun." "I'm dating a McCoy—should I be worried?" And, "I'm dating a Polish boy whose first name is fifteen letters long, mostly consonants, and I haven't learned to spell it yet." Saddest are the adolescent lovelorn: "My parents had my marriage annulled when I was sixteen." "I'm a nineteen-year-old single mom." "I haven't had a boy friend in three years." And, "I have a girl friend that I met on the Internet, but she won't tell me where she lives. I sympathized, but she may have known something I didn't.

Just as college students may be separated from their boy friends and girl friends, so are they divorced from the pets they raised. Since the university doesn't allow animals in the dormitories, students are frequently homesick for those feathered and furry creatures they left behind. "I have dog named Toto," said a girl from Kansas. "I have a pet wolf, and I miss him," wrote another. "My Quaker parrot can whistle the theme from Andy Griffith," wrote a kid from North Carolina. And, "I have a pet giraffe named Oscar, who's only six feet tall," said a tall, skinny freshman. When students move off campus, which Clemson permits them to do when they are sophomores, they often bring their pets along or buy new ones. "I live with three guys and fifty gerbils," wrote one free-spirited young lady. A small minority of students, however, are zoophobic. One such wrote that her roommate had a cat, but she was "terrified of the beast." Another confessed to a fear of aquariums without explaining whether it was the guppy-eating fish contained therein or the possibility of the glass breaking across the lower bunk that frightened her. I have no idea what one young man meant by, "I used to show sheep, but no one knew it." Did he show them at night or out of town and never told anyone about his hobby, or were the judges not paying attention?

Clemson is only thirty-five miles from the ragged nail hole of the Bible belt (Bob Jones University), so it is not surprising that many of our students are Christian fundamentalists. Typical of the comments that reflect student religious concerns are: "I read a lot of sermons." "I was baptized in the Georgia Dome by Billy Graham in front of 40,000 people." "I was called to the ministry at the age of twenty." "I was voted 'Most Christ-like' by my church youth group." And, "I don't believe in dinosaurs," said one kid who might have been a creationist or just opposed to science and the fossil record in general. He dropped the class before I could find out. A small number of Wiccans, Deists, and New Agers show up each semester vastly outnumbered by the Baptists but determined, nevertheless, to defend their beliefs. "I have a medieval Celtic soul," wrote one young lady who later submitted a superb essay on Stonehenge. She'd been raised in a commune in northern California where she learned to "self-medicate" herself with crystals and "herbs." A very small number of Clemson students haven't been touched by religion at all. I remember one woman telling me that she had never read any part of the Bible before, felt no guilt whatsoever at this lacuna in her education, and wanted "to have more than one husband, all famous actors or rock musicians." I gave her high marks for candor if not fidelity.

A sizeable percentage of students wear their accomplishments on their sleeve. Quite a few of these "badges" honor their cars and trucks, which are either gifts of their parents or purchased with the meager incomes of after-school jobs. One lucky student, however, wrote, "I won a Honda in a Pepsi Bottle-Cap Game!" Many choose to tell me of their driving skills or the absence thereof: "I've driven a car for three years but have never earned a license." A young man with NASCAR ambitions wrote, "I've never lost a race on the street and never received a speeding ticket either." Another was a bit more modest: "I've never received a speeding ticket though I deserved a few." One young lady admitted that she'd paid Clemson Parking Services more than $1700 in fines over three years. As a consequence, she was banned from driving on campus until she graduated. I'm surprised by how many tell me of their wrecks: "I've been in thirteen auto accidents; two on the same day." "I've had two accidents, both in the commuter parking lot at Clemson." And, "I totaled two cars in two weeks. Fortunately, I'm fairly impervious to pain."

Physical prowess gives many of the young males something to brag about: "I can kick a football fifty yards." "I'm an ambidextrous ping pong player." "I jump from tall obstacles and return to write about it." "I kill wounded ducks by crushing their skulls in my teeth. It's a Louisiana thing." "I have hitchhikers' thumbs." "I can make my eyeballs twitch by squeezing my abs." And, "I can cross one eye without crossing the other." As if to warn me, one cautioned, "My jaw comes out of joint when I yawn." A wiry fellow, who apparently aspires to his own show on the Animal Planet channel, wrote, "I've been bitten by a snake four times and killed a possum with my bare hands." A hulking fellow said, "I once carried five college-aged girls on my shoulders without compressing any vertebrae." I'll never forget the fellow who boasted, "I can do a good imitation of a Sumo wrestler." I was expecting a defensive lineman, but the young fellow weighed less than Don Knotts in a Speedo and didn't appear to know a barbell from a dumbbell.

Even in the occasional honors class, few students boast in writing at least of their academic accomplishments. Some, however, cannot resist: "I'm an autodidact." "I have a 4.0 and intend to keep it." "Some of my photographs have been exhibited at the Corcoran Gallery in Washington." And, "I enjoy watching The Learning Channel." However, Clemson students are usually modest when bragging: "I won a faux-Charlie-Chaplin Contest when I was six," is fairly typical, or, "I'm weirdly normal," or, "Though I made the President's list last semester, I failed the entry exam at IHOP," and, "I pay more in monthly bills than my parents do." I wanted to tell him to lose his $56 per month cell phone, but I thought that might be presumptuous.

Hand in hand with the academic boast is the guilty confession: one self-aware young man said that though he was his class valedictorian, "I don't spell so good." And another admitted that she'd made over $600 in royalties on an Advanced Placement English paper she'd written three years earlier. Some term-paper web site had paid her $250, and every time some student bought a copy of her essay, she received $5.

It's remarkable what some students are willing to talk about on the first day of the semester. Several students have told me, a total stranger (in most cases) old enough to be their grandfather, that they sleep naked or they're still virgins. More surprising are those who admit right after I tell them how much I expect of them that they're lazy or lack ambition! Representative are: "I seldom get up before 3 PM." "I'm in a coma." "I've been here almost six years and don't want to leave." And, "I'm a tenured senior and scared of growing up." After these, I'm happy to contemplate a semester with the kid who tells me, "I can't sit still" I trusted that meant he was curious and energetic, not a quivering bundle of omnidirectional protoplasm. I was wrong. But having said that, despite all those Ritalin-addicted kids in the public schools I've read about, I've yet to have a really serious discipline problem in over thirty years of college teaching. One girl balanced her checkbook right under my nose, and another took a cell-phone call in the back of the class, but the worst rudeness is the occasional kid who leaves unannounced in the middle of class—just fishes up his book bag and departs.

Many students these days have a tattoo or body piercing, and few are shy about discussing it: "I have a gold lightning bolt through each nipple," said one gay fellow. "I have three tattoos—a rose, a barbed-wire arm band, and a skull," said a woman who'd spent a lot of time on a motorcycle. "I have a $1000 worth of tattoos," said one shy fellow who wore long sleeves on the warmest days. "I have eleven piercings, but I'm still a virgin," said a junior chastely. A few, however, are having second thoughts about their investments: "I have two tattoos only one of which I regret." And some are frankly terrified their parents will discover the permanent marks they have had needled beneath their skin: "I have three tattoos, and my daddy doesn't know about any of them."

Food issues are quite common among college women. The following were all written by young females: "I'm the only woman in the world who hates chocolate." "I can't get through the day without a Diet Coke." "I wish I didn't love pepperoni pizza!" "I gained fifteen pounds last semester!" "I only eat with plastic—metal makes me gain weight." And, "I got addicted to chocolate trying to quit smoking." Occasionally males too will speak of food but usually without the guilt: "I can eat a whole IHOP waffle in one bite." "I love bacon!" "I once drank a full container of maple syrup at the Awful Waffle." "Ben and Jerry's Phish rocks." And, "I eat a lot; in fact, I'm hungry right now."

Despite the over and under indulgences, I'm always surprised at how many serious health problems late adolescents have. Hernia and appendix operations, scoped knees, abortions, breast augmentations and reductions, asthma, diabetes, mononucleosis, depression, anxiety attacks, attempted suicide, even kidney stones may fill up their dance cards before they are twenty-one. One kid said that after a heat stroke the previous summer he could not smell or taste anything. Another said he'd lost much of his hearing when he fell from a cliff he was scaling. Risky behavior is second nature to most adolescents, of course, which accounts for their willingness to sample controlled substances like Ecstasy, crack cocaine, and angel dust. Aware of the legal consequences, however, very few talk openly about their experiments, but one student defiantly said, "I got fired from a grocery back home for failing a drug test. Legalize pot!" A few weeks later, the same fellow came to the office to make up a test; when he left, there were marijuana seeds, leaves, and stems scattered across the desk top. Was he careless with his stash, or was he leaving me a vegetable bribe? I never found out His essay read like something composed aboard the Beetles' yellow submarine: "I was borne in Sugar Tits, Tennesea to a wooman named Butercup who still calls me Swetcheks." I had no choice but to fail the paper, and he soon dropped the class.

In closing, let me sample the contributions of a single sophomore literature class to disabuse anyone of the notion if I haven't already done so that the modern college classroom is not already "diverse." In the front row sits, "I'm a horandle speler," beside, "I want to be the Oprah Winfrey of the Carolinas," beside, "I hate all bare feet except my own," beside "I can chug three beers in nine seconds," beside, "My granddaddy owns Candle, Alaska," and, "I milk goats and write poems, but not at the same time." The second row is comprised of: "I have the biggest room on campus," beside, "I'm a Tri-Delt pledge," beside, "I've lost as many as twenty straight hands of blackjack," beside, "I can eat an entire bag of double-stuff Oreos," beside, "I have a bad habit of humming all the time," and, "When I eat a banana, I wear the sticker on my forehead." In the third row are: "I sleep between Garfield sheets with a Pound Puppy named Whiskers," beside, "My daddy's going to buy me a car," beside, "I'd like to patton [patent?] my own slang," beside, "My daddy's a Baptist minister, and I'm gay," beside, "We live in a geodesic dome built by my ex-hippy mom and dad," and, "Once I sore [saw?] a blimp." In the fourth row are, "I've driven 12,000 miles in the past four months for no apparent reason," beside, "I've saved my sister twice from suicide," beside, "My friends call me 'the apostle,'" beside, "I can shotgun a six-pack of beer at one sitting," and, "I'm a stall mucker." And closing out the back row are, "I milk cows six hours a day," beside, "I'm a minor-league mascot back home," beside, "Some think me insane," beside, "I won $10,000 in a radio contest," beside, "You taught my parents in 1974," and, "I wear a kilt and shoot at people for fun on the weekends." No, this wasn't a Scottish drive-by killer; he was a young man of Scotch-Irish extraction whose hobby is Revolutionary War re-enactments.

And people wonder why I don't want to retire.

WHEN THE TEACHER'S WRONG

O nce when Socrates finished a lesson, Plato and the other kids took out their cigarette lighters and waved them overhead in unison. What?! There were no lighters four hundred years before Jesus, you say. Well, perhaps not, nor were there any cigarettes. The fact is that good as Socrates was, he wasn't Mr. Chips or Yoda every day. Indeed there was the time when Plato himself complained, "Master, you're killing us." To which Socrates sharply replied, "Then you'll die educated, Grasshopper." And he did.

Almost everyone has a bad-teacher story to tell. I've sat before well over a hundred teachers and professors in my day, and so has most everyone else with a college diploma. Why then are we surprised by the few bad apples in the vast barrel of golden delicious? Still the variety of diseases that infect the harvest is astonishing: The first-grade teacher who smells something foul and orders the young fellow she suspects to drop his pants before the entire class. The alien physics teacher on *Third Rock from the Sun* who announces that he is here "to attach the electrodes of learning to the nipples of ignorance." The seventh-grade physical-education teacher who shows films of his old college basketball games every time it threatens to rain. The Sunday-school teacher who boasts, "I just show up and let the Lord work through me." The Advanced Placement history teacher who reads from the textbook in his 8AM class and plays a tape of his reading for the four classes which follow. The high-school English teacher who has her students memorize and recite *The Gettysburg Address* as she has personally rewritten it. The college English professor who passes wind, belches, and calls the women in class *broads* without apology. The English instructor who turns a sophomore survey of contemporary American literature into an all-Steven-King "seminar." The Romantics professor who gives only multiple-choice examinations because he doesn't want to "waste my eyesight on student essays." The French professor who crams five and a half weeks of summer work into three, so he can take advantage of a time-share in Provence. The professor of Victorian literature who falls asleep himself reading *Sartor Resartus* from the podium. The English professor who plays recordings of Shakespeare to his undergraduates and the same tape (except in stereo) to his graduate students. The English professor who announces on the first day of his seminar that "this is a course with four thousand facts about Spenser—learn them all and you will earn an A." The organic chemistry professor who announces in the first class, "I believe in a bell-curve distribution; therefore, if 10% of you make A's, 10% must fail." Another professor of Shakespeare who orders his class to "discuss Hamlet as Shakespeare's greatest play, and if you don't agree, to what defect in yourself do you attribute this?" And finally, there is the community-college teacher who is teaching five writing classes on-line from her home. When asked what program she uses for line editing, she replies, "Oh, I just add a terminal comment like, 'Your spelling needs improvement,' or, 'too many comma faults.'"

More interesting in my opinion is the teacher who is factually wrong. Many students recall a time when they were right and the teacher wasn't. They may not have realized it at the time, but once the truth dawns, it is seldom forgotten. My wife is reminded of such a time whenever she comes upon "vagabond." She grew up in Germany and had English classes from the fifth grade until she graduated from *Mittelschule*. One day standing before her classmates in the tenth grade and reading a passage from *Lucky Jim*, she was corrected by Herr Brinkmann when she "stumbled" on "vagabond." Her teacher, who had never crossed the English Channel or seen a Rex Harrison movie, snickered self-righteously and said that the word is pronounced "vagabound." Since she was ridiculed publicly, the "correct" pronunciation was engraved on the steel plate of her memory. (Perhaps Herr Brinkmann was thinking of the Middle English "vagabound," but I doubt it. Incidentally, some Englishmen do say "vagabuhnd," today but never "vagabound.") Years later when my wife came to the States, she noticed that people responded with an amused, quizzical look every time she used the word, so she asked me, her husband, how to pronounce the word, and I set her straight with the Shorter Oxford—though I hated to run that charming "vagabound" out of the gypsy camp of her vocabulary. Though I haven't heard her mispronounce the word in thirty years, she still hesitates briefly before speaking it. Such is the lasting insecurity caused by pedagogical misinformation.

A friend of mine tells a similar story about her daughter's third-grade teacher. This tale, however, comes with a tart twist of lemon. The class had just finished a unit on the weather which Amanda, my friend's daughter, felt quite confident about since her father was an atmospheric physicist, and he had been informally "teaching" her meteorology since she was old enough to talk. On a class field trip, she distinguished a cumulus from an altostratus for her teacher who thought those "fluffy things up there" were just clouds. After the unit test, however, Amanda brought home a "B" with a long face besides.

"But you knew the material cold last night—what happened?" her father asked.

"I missed number seven, and Mrs. Lovingood took off ten points," his daughter said handing her father the crumpled test paper.

"Let's see—number seven asks, 'What happens when a cold front meets a warm front?' And you answered, 'It rains.' I don't understand," her father said patting her on the head; "your answer is correct. Perhaps I'd better go see your teacher; I don't think this can be handled over the phone." The next day he called the school, made an appointment, and showed up ready to defend his daughter's answer.

"Dr. Pinckney, it's so nice to see you again," said Mrs. Lovingood, an African-American woman with a great pudding of a bosom. "I can't imagine that Amanda is having trouble," she said as the professor squeezed his six-foot frame into a tiny desk; "she's such a sweet and serious student." The distinguished professor of physics explained why he had come, and the third-grade teacher of general science said she wished that more parents were as involved with their children's education as Dr. Pinckney and his wife. The test, she explained, had been designed by the state which meant that there was a state key. "Let's see now, that was number seven on the weather-unit test, wasn't it? Here it is—'precipitation'; that's the answer on the key, and that's the word I drilled the class on. Not little old 'rain.' I even wrote it on the chalkboard." The professor was in a deep bind now because he knew that "precipitation" was a better answer than "rain" since the former included sleet, snow, and rain not to mention sneet and a host of other recent neologisms. He wondered aloud if some partial credit might be awarded, but he felt like a hypocrite since in his own classes he was a stickler for precise terminology. Unfolding himself from the desk, he made up something about a dentist's appointment, tucked his tail between his legs, and left. Of course, the teacher at fault here was the professor, and neither Amanda nor her parents ever hear the word "precipitation" without thinking of the father's embarrassment.

Timothy Stanley, another friend who is a professor, tells the bitter story of being taught "white superiority" in a West Texas grammar school. He also recalls the flash of atomic explosions coming from White Sands Proving Grounds, but that's another story. As a boy in the 1950s, the professor was bussed to school past Hispanic and Negro children walking to a school across town. Some passed through the shadow of Tim's white school carrying tattered earlier editions of the same books he was studying. He didn't give the matter much thought in the 50s because one of his teachers had explained the "natural inferiority of the darker races," and no one he knew questioned the arrangement. Furthermore, Tim's father was off fighting the "yellow" Japanese at the time, and by 1945, the boy had developed a strong dislike of anything Asian. To this day, he cannot pull up behind a Mitsubishi pick-up at a stop light without wanting to "squeeze off a few rounds" into the tailgate. His father, who survived the war by shooting down half a dozen Zeroes built by Mitsubishi, was a tail gunner in the B-24. After the war, Hollywood and his father's stories of Japanese atrocities placed a permanent barrier between him and the Orient. Fortunately, however, reading Rousseau in graduate school convinced him that at least some "savages" could be "noble."

In fact, my friend is not too different from the thousands of German school children in the 1930s who were taught using a state-approved curriculum that Jews were "vermin" and thus deserving of the Nazi's "rat trap." Had those atomic tests that my friend saw distant flashes of in West Texas failed, or if the Germans had developed nuclear weapons before the Americans did, it's very likely that many classrooms today throughout Europe and North America would be openly teaching racial hatred. Though by the twenty-first century, there might not be many dark-skinned people left to hate.

Even though I opened by stating that most everyone has been mistaught at one time, I can honestly say that except for a choral director whom I will mention shortly, it never happened to me. Sure, some of the information I picked up in my history, geography, and English courses is now wrong or dated, but that's why Britannica, Americana, and other reference tools are updated regularly. The best I can do to get personally involved in this essay is to tell a few stories about myself: the first about me as a father, the second about me as a teacher.

When our son, who'd fallen into the middle-school slump, was registering for the ninth grade, I encouraged him to take wood shop instead of a study hall or some other "easy" elective. I had images of us sitting at a work bench cutting dovetails for a grandchild's cradle. I had loved my shop class at PS 201 in Brooklyn and have kept my hand in woodworking in some small degree ever since I made my father a longhorn tie rack with a spoke shave and a band saw. Despite (or perhaps "because of") the flame-red nostrils and glass-bead eyes, my father never mounted the rack in his closet, but I was not discouraged, and if we had not moved to Georgia at the end of the year, I would have taken Wood Shop II. Anyway six months later after considerable prying, our son revealed that he was going to make a bar stool as his final shop project. Four waist-high legs were to be turned from solid cherry, and the seat, also cherry, would be hollowed by hand to fit his bottom. We already had a full complement of stools around our kitchen bar, but, I said, we could always use a fifth for the occasional guest, so I urged him to deliver us a stool the way that fully-armed Athena sprang from Zeus's forehead. Perhaps I aimed too high.

At term's end, our son came home with his stool in a large plastic shopping bag. As he placed the construct on the tile floor in the kitchen, I noticed that it wobbled even when it was moved to the carpet of the dining room. My disappointment only increased when he pulled off the plastic with mock fanfare as if he were unveiling the lost, bronze *David* by Michelangelo. I was speechless, but my wife filled in seamlessly as I bit my tongue. Not only were the stool's legs uneven, the four horizontal struts rose and fell like a stock-market graph. But worst of all, wood glue had run out of most joints and down the legs where it had dried like snot on a neglected baby's lip.

Finally I spoke: "What did the teacher give you on this?"

"An 'A,'" our son said in the clipped monotone of jaded adolescence.

"Congratulations," I said and retired to the garage to clean the lawnmower's air filter, which I confess did not really need cleaning. The next day without telling our son, I called the school and spoke with his shop teacher. "If what our son brought home is an example of 'A' work," I asked, "what does an 'F' look like?"

"I don't give 'F's', sir. Adolescent egos are far too fragile. I try to encourage them, not stifle them. Don't you recall your first woodworking project?"

"Yes," I said, "it was a bedside lamp in the form of an old-fashioned hand pump. To turn the lamp on or off, you pumped the handle, which had a beaded chain from the socket attached." I hesitated as I launch into the rehearsed portion of my speech. "If I remember correctly, I received a 'C' for my efforts even though I had wiped glue from every joint. That grade was both a reward and an incentive. I knew my pump was not plumb just as my son knows his stool is a lost labor, and neither is he fooled nor consoled by your evaluation. I suppose he appreciates what the 'A' does for his grade-point average, but I haven't noticed any passion for woodworking during the past year. I can promise you that I will not be sending you any more of our offspring."

Indeed, our son has not undertaken a woodworking project since the ninth grade unless you count a few meandering shelves supported by an aluminum frame screwed to his garage wall. Despite the "A," he knew the stool was a personal indictment, and it wasn't because I or my wife told him. Today the cherry bar stool is a low garden stool. When our son married, he left his handiwork in the basement. With his permission, I solved the wobble with a rasp and file after I cut the legs down above the unsightly braces and sanded off the dried glue. It resides in the garden shed between my son and the dovetails he'll never cut. I suspect that it hurts him to look at its muddy feet, but he knows now it serves a practical end; I hope that's some consolation.

The last anecdote dates from my second or third year of teaching; I have over thirty-five now. In 1970, I had taught Frost's "The Road Not Taken" to college sophomores several times without a word of dissent. Indeed the class had laughed at my joke, "I took the road less traveled, and now I need my front-end aligned." I felt confident about what I was telling the class because in high school we had sung a choral version, and the choir director, an ex-Marine, had told us all about the spiritual rewards of choosing the hard path over the easy one, lifting yourself by the bootstraps, and coming up through the ranks. He said, "Imagine that you loved to collect guns and that your father owned a small grocery. Would you rather pursue your passion in guns, or work in the grocery knowing that one day it would be yours?" Of course at seventeen, we all said, "Guns!" not knowing a thing about the staggering odds against becoming a self-supporting arms merchant. Another reason that I felt confident about my interpretation of the poem is that there was a photograph of a leaf-strewn crossroad in the text we were using. One road was wide and inviting; the other was narrow and seemed to peter out in a briar patch. And furthermore, the answer to the question, "Which path in the photograph might Frost have chosen?" was answered in the teacher's manual, "Probably the less traveled, less distinct path." "Probably" had worried me, but I overlooked it.

So after extolling the ascetic virtues of adversity, poverty, and the Peace Corps, I asked if there were any questions. An owl-eyed kid from New Jersey, who seldom spoke but weighed my every word in the balance of his brain, raised his hand and asked, "Why does Frost say in line ten that both those roads were worn 'really about the same'?" I stammered something, reread line ten aloud, and quoted Whitman's, "Do I contradict myself? Very well then...I contradict myself; I am large...I contain multitudes." I said that I would check into the apparent paradox, for clearly the last line says that one road was narrower than the other, "and that has made all the difference." Back in the office I read the poem closely for the first time and realized to my horror that Frost was not extolling the virtues of monastic choices. Instead, he is saying that when adults are asked by the young how they made a difficult decision, they often lie or exaggerate and say they deliberately chose the harder way, not that they flipped a mental coin which is how many, maybe most, tough personal decisions are made. I thought of my own choice as a freshman to change my major from business to English. I was sitting in the library after a stimulating discussion of *Waiting for Godot* and said to myself, "That's what I'd like to do with my life—read, write, and talk about books." So I went to the registrar's office, filled out a change-of-major form, and found two professors willing to sign it. The following day after a stimulating lecture on tax reform, I was ready to change my major back to business, but I didn't, for I was sure that Godot was an English major, and I wanted to be prepared when he arrived. To my credit, I think, I confessed my misreading of Frost to the class and said that I now understood how seven-foot-tall Wilt Chamberlain had felt the first time the shorter, smaller Bill Russell blocked one of his shots—astonished, humbled, and determined to put the ball in the hole the next time.

The former Governor of Texas John Connally once candidly confessed that in the 1920s when the shape of the earth was still an issue in the Bible Belt ("If angels trumpet from 'four corners of the earth,' it must be square.") Connally told a school board which was considering whether to hire him, "I can teach it round, or I can teach it flat." Well, I cannot. If I know the earth is an oblate spheroid, I will resign from teaching before I teach it flat or round. I refuse to be like the botanist who ripped out all the plants in a 100' x 100' plot that he could not identify before his taxonomy class assembled to practice their classification skills. And if a misidentification is called to my attention, I shall research the matter, admit my error if I have made one, and apologize. If this recurs with some regularity, I shall resign my post. It's one sure way of knowing when to retire.

SCARLET WOMEN AND BLUE-EYED BOYS

One reason I wouldn't want to live at 20,000 feet above or below sea level, beside the limited supply of available oxygen, is the absence of color. Like sunlight and rain, color is a free lunch spread by Mother Nature every time her "lemon-yellow" sun rises despite Crayola's retirement of this color in 1990. I have much to be thankful for, and not being color blind, as seven percent of all men are, is one of them. Women are rarely afflicted with such shortsightedness.

I think I was about ten when I realized how sensitive to color I'd become. I was snooping among some folders in my parents' file cabinet while my mother was shopping when I found a copy of my birth certificate. Imagine my surprise when I read under "Complexion" that my skin color was listed as "olive." Now you need to understand that up to that time I'd never eaten or seen anything but ripe black olives, so "olive" to me meant "purplish-black." I wasn't terribly fond of ripe olives especially the ones with the seeds still inside; they were just all that I knew. Mother never bought the unripe variety because (she told me later) they were too salty, and we all hated pimentos, which was the only way they came. Perhaps my consternation had something to do with my father being transferred every couple of years by the Army, twice in war zones, a fact of life that made me a less-than-secure pre-adolescent. So "olive" led me to the conclusion that I'd been adopted: the real Skip Eisiminger had died, and I was called up from the "minors" to fill out the lineup. When Mother returned, I listened to her assurances that she'd never given birth to a child darker than myself and that, indeed, I was the one with an olive complexion. "Olive," she assured me, meant "yellowish-brown" when the word referred to skin tone. In a certain slant of light, I could see that shade on my forearms, but the next time I used my crayons, I noted that the Crayola labeled "olive" was not the shade of my arm; rather it was a stomach-churning green. (But then the crayon labeled "flesh" was far peachier than my arm as well.) Consequently, I was well into adolescence before I was confident I never had an alien sibling.

I grew up with a box of forty-eight Crayola crayons, which I carried about in an old coffee can when the cardboard wore out. After my parents had convinced me that I should not eat them, I used these delicious wax sticks to animate Hopalong Cassidy, Gene Autry, Champion, and a host of other western heroes in my coloring books. A best-left-nameless art teacher in the third grade introduced me to Roy G. Biv. Roy was no match for Hopalong, but he did help me nail down the color spectrum, the primaries, and secondaries. In addition to teaching the fundamentals of color, our teacher introduced the class to art criticism. To this end, she wore a cardboard octagon around her neck, one side red, the other green. When any of her students "drove recklessly," she'd flash them the red of her "traffic" sign; if the class "drove" in an orderly fashion, her "light" flashed green. But she also used the sign in place of any thoughtful commentary: if she liked your fingerpainting, meaning you didn't have it on your clothes, you got the green. If she disapproved of your smear or the place you'd smeared it, you received the red card like a soccer player banished from the field. In this class, "cautionary yellow" wasn't even in the critical lexicon. Art was either "red" or "green." Most of mine was "red" as was that of my two classmates who got into a paint-throwing contest and "failed with flying colors." Even then, I sensed that the teacher's red octagon, which she was waving frantically, was insufficient to describe the misdemeanors of my classmates or the nuances of art.

I was in high school when I read in the *Washington Post* one morning that Crayola was changing "Prussian blue" to "midnight blue." After delivering about seventy-five papers, I often sat outside our garage reading the sports section and the comics before school. The journalist who'd written the piece said that the failure of most students in the 1950s to know either who the Prussians were or that they wore dark-blue uniforms were the reasons for the name change. My father, who worked in the Pentagon at the time, was of another opinion: "Prussian" sounds too much like "Russian," he said, and at the height of the Cold War, no one risked looking like a "Commie-lover" or a "Red." However, when the Russians placed their Sputnik in orbit in 1957, I remember a lot fewer "Reds" and a lot more "Russians" in Dad's remarks as he scanned his morning *Post*. Silently, I wondered whether the Russians referred to us as the "red, white, and blues."

About the time of the Russians' space coup, we purchased our first television set—a black-and-white Dumont in the same dark-brown Bakelite as the kitchen radio. The appliance was the only thing in Mother's kitchen that wasn't white trimmed in chrome; in fact, it may have been the only appliance in any 50s-era American kitchen that wasn't white. I guess that is the period many today think of as "the good old days," but to me achromatic kitchens seemed dull places. Now chocolate brown is not one of my favorite colors, but it was the only color available in the size television we wanted, and it did match the walnut paneling in the den where it took up residence in front of Dad's red-leather easy chair.

Sitting there one afternoon watching Howdy Doody with my sisters and some friends, Carly Hall said that his family now owned a color TV. I'd read of this development in *Popular Science*, but I had no idea these futuristic sets were already available. A few days later, I begged Carly to let me see his "color" set. It must have been a Sunday morning because when he turned the set on, choirs and preachers commanded each of our three channels. The trouble was, each sacred venue was blue on top, red in the middle, and green on the bottom. Carly said the set worked better when an episode of *Daniel Boone* was being broadcast especially when there were some "redskins" in the middleground walking across a green meadow under an azure sky. During the *Camel News Caravan*, which is all his divorced, working mother ever watched, Carly's sheet of plastic came off. His mother was still upset with him for sending $3 to "some damn-fool outfit" for his "color TV."

My mother's love of white kitchens and Carly's mother's distaste for "color television" was my introduction to gender color differences. I became more attuned to the disparity in personal taste a few years later when I told Brenda O'Baugh, my first serious girl friend, what I saw studying her face. A writer in one of my father's *Playboys* had advised, "Don't neglect to compliment a woman's eyes," so I told Brenda that her blue eyes reminded me of my grandmother's Plymouth. As she frowned, I said, "Actually, they are more like Dodger blue." When the furrows deepened, I said recalling her love of nature that her eyes were "the same shade as the blue-bottle fly." I quickly learned that not all "blues" are created equal. I don't suppose that I'd been in the Army more than a couple of months when Brenda wrote me a Dear John; she'd apparently found someone who had the right simile to unlock her heart.

By the time I became a teacher, I was married and a strong advocate of women's rights. Far be it for me to obstruct any woman who wanted to burn her bra regardless of its color. One day I asked a class of freshmen if there was a difference in the way men and women organize their lives, and one young lady volunteered that she had a "rainbow closet," meaning that all her clothes were hung in harmony with the natural order of the spectrum. Not a male in the class including me had ever heard of a "rainbow closet"; most men, it appears, organize their clothes by garment type, not color. To many of us a "rainbow closet" implies a homosexual with a lot of pastel sweaters from Barney's of New York. Indeed a few years ago, I met an obviously gay male at a party sporting a lapel pin with a rainbow arcing from an open door over which were the embossed words, "I'm out!"

Incidentally, this young man is the only person I've ever heard use the word "Isabelline." The word means "brownish-yellow," the color of soiled underpants, and unless you wash a lot of diapers, there aren't many places you can use the word. It's interesting that the word may derive from the Spanish Princess Isabel who publicly vowed not to change her underwear until King Philip's siege of Ostend was successful. How she thought her sacrifice would aid the siege, is not recorded. Since that military endeavor took three years to accomplish, my guess is that the ladies of Isabel's court coined the dainty word, no doubt snickering behind her back when using it. The males of the court, I suspect, probably coined something more vulgar, but it has not survived. In my experience, no straight male has ever used the word: you may recall that when I was discussing "olive" earlier I did not mention it. I'm not surprised that either gender is reluctant to employ it because it would require an explanation that no one would be comfortable with.

The whole sordid affair is reminiscent of "street colors" that several cosmetics manufacturers introduced in the 1990s. "Toxin," "Gangrene," "Urban Decay," "Bruise," "Frost-Bite," and "Roach," among others quickly became popular to almost universal surprise among young white women with a taste for "gangsta rap." The usual explanation for the success of these colors was that the women who chose them were rebelling against the "preppy colors" that had reigned as long as rich whites had oppressed minorities. But this choice was more a class preference than a gender difference and so falls outside my purview. The Sex Pistols may have dabbed a bit of "Bruise" lipstick across their cheeks prior to a performance, but I'll bet it came off before they met their fathers after the show.

Speaking of family, I don't recall my paternal grandmother being especially color sensitive, and Heaven knows she never wore any street colors. She usually dressed in grays, off-whites, and browns. I would not be surprised to learn that she was a stockholder in the Taupe Dye Company. But when I inherited her small journal-notebook a few years after her death, I realized just how attuned to color she was. The very first page of the book that she kept records in for over twenty years was reserved to record the family's automobile purchases. Here's that page in its entirety: "We got our first Auto. April 26, 1924, black. 2nd, Dec. 6, 1928, green. 3rd, Aug 20, 1930, navy blue. 4th, July 27, 1934, maroon. 5th, Feb. 26, 1937, gunmetal. Car stolen Feb. 17, 1938 in front of Barnes Hospital, East St. Louis [Furthermore, it was uninsured, but there was no mention of that!]. 6th, March 8, 1938 gunmetal. 7th, Chevrolet, May 2, 1940." If she kept a diary any later than February 1941, I have not seen it. Of course, what caught my masculine eye as I read this diary page was the fact that she didn't take written notice of any car's make until their seventh purchase! Yet she carefully recorded every car's color except the last. I asked myself if someone inquired about my first car, how would I describe it? I'd say, "1930 Model A convertible with red spoked wheels." The car's blackness would be understood if the inquisitor were male and had a few years on him. If not, I might toss in the fact that it was black, but I would never say, "My first car? It was black." Yet my own flesh and blood, provider of one quarter of my genetic bankroll, described her first car as "black," nothing else. And this was at a time when 95% of all cars were black because it absorbed light faster than other colors, as Henry Ford discovered, and, therefore, dried more quickly. It was purely an economic choice like painting all nineteenth-century barns and schoolhouses red because that was the cheapest color available.

I e-mailed my sister and a distant female cousin with a copy of the list above asking them if they would ever describe a car the way Grandmother Eisiminger had, and their response was an overwhelming "Yes!" My sister said that an old boy friend once had asked her what her fantasy car was, and she began with the car's color. "It drove him batty!" she added, as did her habit of answering questions about the car she drove by saying, "I don't know, but it's orange." Insensitive to her color tunnel-vision, he dumped her shortly afterwards. My cousin's response illustrated the same gender difference. She said that when her husband describes a car he begins with the make and model. However, if he asks her, "What kind of car did Joe have?" her answer would be something like, "White." And in this naked monosyllable, she would be confident she had pinned down the vehicle's identity among the millions of white cars on the road as surely as if she'd provided a teaspoon of the car's DNA and a full set of fingerprints.

Of course, one e-mail deserves another, and so I wrote, "OK, I've given this some thought. Here's my theory of gender and color—color is a female thing. Males of the species (being naturally better endowed with color than females, especially those of us with feathers or hair) are not so concerned with it. The female must be concerned with color lest she acquire or produce a bad egg, if you catch my drift. Furthermore while the Paleolithic male was out hunting wooly mammoths, all the same dull brown, the female was foraging for berries and mushrooms whose color might have meant the difference between living and dying. Consequently, natural selection favored the female with the keenest eye for color. I haven't done a count, but I'll bet the female eye has more of those rods and cones that quiver when red and blue (the color of most ripe berries) are near. All of which leads one to ask why human females generally use more color than the men they are stalking. 'Color-blind' men grade first on the curve, second on the hue!"

Only my cousin rose to the bait. She responded, "Beside being very scientific and no doubt true [had she counted the rods and cones?], this gave me my best laugh of the day, especially the 'grade-on-the-curve' part. Perhaps I should write an exposé for my sisters telling them to give up colors altogether especially in regard to wardrobe and eye-shadow...though I suppose lipstick must stay as there is a biological reason for that altogether, which we shouldn't go into. It's funny that human males are relatively colorless and that nowadays females are attracted more by the color of a man's car than his hair. . . ."

Having some second thoughts about the biological basis of my theory, I replied, "Now I'm not so sure. It may all be cultural rather than genetic as I first so confidently stated. Men, I have learned, are twenty-four times more likely to be color blind than women. This may account for the fact that if I have twenty blue dress-shirts and each is a different shade of blue, every one is 'blue' to me but not my wife. Too, I now realize that women are forced to make decisions between 'wheat' and 'oatmeal,' for example, every day, when any straight male will tell you that they are the same color despite what Calvin Klein might tell you! Calling off-white 'wheat,' is just another way to add 20% to the price of a blouse.

"When we repainted our living room a few years back, Ingrid [my wife] brought home a chart with thirty samples of off-white. Guess who made the final selection? You should know that my choice was made within minutes while Ingrid agonized for days with several of her 'color-gifted' friends. Isn't it interesting that in New York, the fashion capital of this country and perhaps the world, most women prefer black, which technically isn't a color? (Don't they realize that nature prefers white, red, and blue flowers in that order and has never produced a black bloom?) Tease and tint your hair, don a red blouse, paint your nails scarlet, and you are immediately 'from Jersey,' a fashion fate worse than wearing white after Labor Day. In fact, I've heard New Yorkers say that 'the redder the nails, the more bridges she crossed to reach Manhattan.' Unfazed Jersy-ites respond, 'The bigger the hair, the closer to God.'"

To test some of my color ideas, I decided that I would poll my students (average age 20) and a few friends (average age 60). My grandmother inspired the first of eight questions: "Describe in a few words any one of your grandparents' automobiles." Typical of the men were the following: "old brown Cadillac," "black Olds," "Ford with a funny odor," but there were quite a few males who omitted the make such as these: "black and rusted," "ugly and expensive," and, "large, slow, and boring." Women, on the other hand, hardly ever mentioned the make if they'd ever known it. These are typical: "dusty blue 'boat,'" "big, old, and money-green," "little red truck," "grannymobile," and "hoopty."

Second, inspired by my sister's boy friend, I asked respondents to describe in a few words their fantasy car. Many males were quite specific: "Porsche 911," "1955 Mercedes-Benz Gull-Wing," and, "red Plymouth Prowler" are typical. More men than I expected, however, generalized: "anything with a new-car smell," "a sleek, silver SUV," "a pollution-free 8,000,000 mile per gallon candy dispenser," and, "anything sleek and sexy." Women occasionally were very concrete: "black and gold Jeep," "little red Corvette," and, "silver Audi," but of those who mentioned the make, most specified the color as well. More women described their dream car in general terms: "racy red," "big, green, and fast," "sleek and luxurious," "suburban pimp-ride," "red sport-convertible," and, "safe, comfortable car with a 200,000 mile warranty."

Third, I asked for their top three colors. Both men and women liked blue best followed by red. (One male listed his favorite as "red, redder, and reddest.") In third place for men was black. For women, purple and pink tied for third with black and green close behind. And one woman qualified her preference for yellow, "Only if I'm tan."

Fourth, I asked for any colors my respondents detested. Men ranked pink first, purple and yellow tied for second, and brown came in third. Women placed "puke green" first, mustard second, and orange, pink, and brown tied for third. Frankly, I've long been suspicious of color preferences, more so since conducting this poll. "Detroit Announces That Blue Is Number One This Year," is the sort of headline one sees every year or so, but which blue do Americans really prefer? Personally I love a "navy blue," but I loathe "baby blue" especially on the exterior of an automobile. Can you imagine a powder-blue Ferrari? (Yes, but only one driven by a Hollywood ingenue with more money than the GNP of some Central American countries.)

Fifth, I asked, "If you're buying a shirt (male) or blouse (female), do you prefer chromatic hues (red, green, blue, e.g.) or achromatic ones (white, black, gray)?" In general, women preferred chromatics more than men who have a higher tolerance for the achromatics. I was somewhat surprised by this, but then how many men wear a red suit even to a party? Nancy Reagan might, but Ronnie, never.

The sixth question asked for a one- or two-word definition of each of the following: "taupe, cerulean, russet, ocher, and verdant." If I use the questionnaire again, I'll change "russet" because I realize women are more likely to have heard of russet potatoes. Still women didn't do that much better on this item scoring only 52% to the men's dismal 34%. Many knew none of these, and not one knew all five among the sixty-four people who answered the questionnaire. Still the conclusion I draw here is that women have a slightly more sophisticated color vocabulary than their masculine counterparts. Both men and women, scientists say, can distinguish some six million colors; women just have more names for theirs.

Question seven asked respondents to rank "soft colors or pastels" on a scale of 1-10 (with 10 being the best). Women gave pastels a 6.2; men gave them a 4.9. Using the same scale, they were then asked to rank bright colors (this was question eight). Consistent with the results of question five, women ranked bright colors at 7.3 while men gave them a 6.1. I think then it is safe to say that women like a wider range of colors, both bright and pastel.

Briefly to summarize the results: just like my grandmother, women are much more likely to describe a relative's car or their fantasy car solely by color. Men and women prefer blue and red, but after that there is a wide divergence. Surprisingly, there is far less agreement in the colors that the sexes dislike. As a rule women like brighter colors than men do; by a small margin men prefer the achromatics. And finally, women have a broader color vocabulary. As my cousin suggested, American women probably could do with less color because males aren't especially sensitive to it. I doubt that any man has ever gone to bed with a woman because he liked the shade of her lipstick or the color of her dress. In societies where color is less prominent like Saudi Arabia, women appear to have no trouble getting a man's eye even under a heavy black robe and veil. You can bet the mortgage that if the woman is available, she will have used some eye shadow and eyeliner.

The origins of this discussion of gender color differences are rooted in prehistory when European mothers are thought to have first chosen blue for their sons' receiving blanket and pink to swaddle their daughters in. Desmond Morris speculates that the origins are a reflection of the ancient sexist hierarchy that prized boys over girls. Blue was picked because the gods themselves surely protect boys who were dressed in the same color as the sky. And girls wrapped in pink, the natural color of their flesh, tells any spirit intent on doing harm that these undisguised and thus unprotected females are not all that special, or the parents would have done more to guard them. It's a little like giving a child an unflattering name: any child named Oedipus ("swollen foot") Cruikshank ("crippled leg") can't have much going for it, or at least that is what literate demons should conclude. Not much has changed since Oedipus' day: you still won't find blue stockings on a scarlet woman, nor will a blue-eyed boy dress in a pink suit unless his name is Gatsby, but then he's already doomed.

Honk If You Love Voltaire: A Religious Life

My earliest religious memory is being taught to pray by my mother at the age of four:

"Now I lay me down to sleep.
I pray the Lord my soul to keep.
If I should die before I wake,
I pray the Lord my soul to take."

The source of considerable discomfort to me, this prayer is still the source of my occasional insomnia. The reminder of death at bedtime for probably a dozen years before I quit the morbid practice, however, probably led to another prayer in my adolescence, "Lord, make a regular man out of me."

A third prayer that I recall from my grade school years was a self-created desire to be the first in our family to die. The wish originated in a panic when I convinced myself that my parents had left me to the Gypsies, when they were simply reminiscing with some old friends at the hardware store while I waited at home peering through the Venetian blinds. Of course, my prayer was an overreaction to my fear of abandonment, but I requested the favor of an early death for several years before I outgrew this unwholesome practice. Fear, it seems, was a seminal influence on my religious development, and I'm confident that it's an underlying factor in many believers who fear unbelief more than the devil.

My childhood, however, was not entirely morose. I recall Dear, my maternal grandmother, who incidentally owed her nickname to this adoring grandson, telling me one night as we sat on her back porch that the stars were knot holes in heaven's floor. When I awoke once about three in the morning as a fire engine jangled by, I wondered why the heavenly lights were still on so late. Were the angels so extravagant, or did they just sleep during the day? If they slept while the sun was up, who was looking out for our welfare? And couldn't God afford a seamless floor covering? Questions that made a grandmother squirm had much to do with creating my personal brand of nondogmatic spirituality.

I began a more formal religious regimen when my mother enrolled me in a Protestant Sunday school at the age of five in Heidelberg, Germany. (My father was a military officer, so we moved every two or three years.) The start of my religious odyssey, however, was not auspicious. Someone's offering apparently had rolled out on the floor, so I tidied it up and placed it in my pocket. When my mother found the quarter in my coat after church, she accused me of not putting my money in the plate. I tried to explain, but guilt was already my meat, shame my potatoes. Later that summer, I passed out in church when the congregation rose unexpectedly to sing a hymn. My father carried me outside into the shade and tried to comfort me, but I knew that God was punishing a thief. When I took my measure beside Calvin's yardstick, I was a foot shy of salvation.

I convinced myself that the slate was washed clean when we moved to Virginia, and before I knew it, I qualified for a "Hundred Sunday Bible" at the Falls Church Presbyterian Church. When the Army moved us again, I found myself in Brooklyn's P.S. 201, where I was the only Protestant in my seventh-grade class. On Wednesday afternoons when my classmates went to religious training at the corner Catholic church, I sat alone while Miss Munnely graded papers, and I estimated the range of the Pope's authority. When my father heard about these students attending confirmation classes, he surprised everyone by inquiring if the Ft. Hamilton Protestant chaplain would include me in his next class. I suspect he had a notion that some of the material covered would be on the SAT's. Suddenly I found myself memorizing the books of the Bible, the Lord's Prayer, and the Apostles' Creed. The Sunday that I stood confirmed in faith before the congregation was one of the prouder of my first twelve years, made even more significant by my father, who had privately been taking these classes himself, standing with me and a dozen other children. I never have understood why he didn't tell me about his classes, but then we rarely spoke or speak about theological matters, my father being from the John Wayne School of Theology. I was proud that he had joined the church, yet I often wished he would confide his thoughts about Jonah's survival, Mary's virginity, and Jesus's resurrection to me, but then his misgivings (if he had any) were no match for mine.

A year later, the Army sent our family to Norfolk, Virginia where my father attended the Armed Forces Staff College, and I made friends with the base chaplain's son. After Indian baseball on the parade ground one afternoon, we went to the chaplain's quarters to play indoors. As we passed by his parents' open bedroom, I glanced through the dark into the brightly lit bathroom. There the chaplain's wife was just stepping out of the shower and reaching for her towel. She looked up at me, smiled softly, and slowly swung the door shut with her bare, wet foot. I stood there in the hall while something foreign rolled in my groin. It was a religious experience, but I had no name for what I had been converted to.

The Army next moved us back to Ft. Benning, Georgia where my father went through airborne training. The family, however, lived in Columbus within walking distance of my grandparents. Here my grandmother, who had told me about the quaint floor of heaven a decade earlier, predicted that I would become a preacher. She had ten grandchildren, and it was appropriate, she said, that a tithe be returned to the church. I realized even then that I should have never told her about climbing the towering oak in the backyard every time a thunderstorm was cooking on the horizon. Up in that tree as the wind tried to toss me from my mount, I felt closer to the deity, whom I often recognized in violent weather. Yet even on clear days, judging from my shadow, I had begun to notice that the sun seemed to follow me about, so I was sure I had been chosen for something miraculous. At the First Presbyterian, I stretched my arms and let my head sag forward before the cruciform mirror in the choir room. I prayed that God would clarify which spiritual Banzai charge He wanted me to lead, but all I heard was silence, a very good answer I now realize, for at that hormone-conflicted time, I would have nailed myself to a cross like one of those Filipino ascetics if I'd thought He wanted me to. I studied my catechism devoutly, recited my verses each Sunday, and prepared for "sword drill," but when my father was called back to Washington, I was pried from the church kitchen that was fueling the grease fire in my soul. My spirit slumping, I arrived just in time to be chosen to play a mute shepherd in a nativity scene on the Mall within a stone's throw of the White House. After one dispirited performance, I wondered if President Eisenhower ever had the Secret Service drop his son John off at Sunday school, the way my father often did, and then pick him up when it was over.

Even as I stewed over our most recent uprooting and worried about my father's soul, I found myself admitting that what I liked best about church were the hymns and pipe organ. The music of the longhaired organist moved me, made the hair at my nape stand erect while the words of the close-cropped minister brushed them back down. In fact, the mountain-road oratorical manner of the ranting Rev. Valentine was distinctly unpleasant. The man was stone deaf to the whisper's clout. I never understood why he couldn't just speak to the congregation instead of roaring along trying to out-Jehovah Jehovah. I longed for a minister who could talk to me in the rational cadences of Mrs. Cooley, my senior English teacher.

After a brief but abortive attempt to get a degree in civil engineering at Georgia Tech in 1959, I enlisted in the Army for Germany. I honestly had no idea when I was seventeen that one could major in English or history. I figured that my father had studied engineering, so I should study engineering. I realized too late that my tacit acquiescence in the choice of a major was akin to my father's silent drift into confirmation class. In short order, the Army sent me to West Germany to gather electronic intelligence that slipped over the Iron Curtain. I tried attending several German churches, but the language barrier was insuperable. Fortunately, I was stationed with a company of college dropouts like myself, so there was more to off-duty time than carousing at the Enlisted Men's Club. I began reading paperback novels donated by the USO, fighting over the Stars and Stripes crossword puzzles, and going to the free movies in the mess hall. I also took several leaves to England, Italy, and France where I visited some of the great cathedrals, but to me they were marmoreal tombs, more interesting as art and architecture than spiritual havens. I began to wonder about the commitment of those within the church when I saw two nuns in Rome staring intently at wedding gowns in a store window. Wasn't it enough to be a bride of Christ? In Paris, I visited several of the big churches like Sacré-Coeur that reeked of urinous beggars, asleep but upright in the pews. The church custodians allowed people to sit or kneel, but anyone lying down got the bum's rush whether they smelled of vomit or Chanel.

When I returned after three years to the States, I was married and my wife was pregnant. The Army had given me time I never had in high school to read and think, but religion, I feared, in any traditional sense was fading from my life as acne cleared from my face. My German wife and I settled in Columbus, Georgia because my mother's family was there (though my parents and sisters were back in Germany), and several aunts and uncles had offered to help us get established while I returned to school. My maternal grandmother and spiritual mentor, however, had died just six months before we arrived.

Though my wife was nominally Lutheran, I convinced her to go with me to my old church—the First Presbyterian. The Rev. Robert McNeill who'd been an outspoken advocate of desegregation in the mid-50s had lost his job. I did not much care for his replacement, but we did like the assistant pastor and his wife who turned out to be neighbors in the next block. We soon became fast friends and made a special point of attending church when Roger was preaching. Early in 1965, he was embroiled in a battle with the church elders to permit the operation of a day-care center in the church's Sunday school rooms, which stood vacant during the week. Though the church was situated on the edge of a black neighborhood, there wasn't a single African-American in the church membership. Roger preached that the "church exists to give itself away," but the elders and the senior minister ("Beelzebubba," Roger called him), pulled rank on their assistant pastor, and plans for the proposed day-care facility were shelved. Disappointed, Roger and his wife decided to return to school to fix the world a different way—teaching history. In Roger's first letter from the University of Georgia to us, he said he had discovered to his delight that in the Library of Congress cataloguing system, theology books are shelved in the BS section. When the church failed to support Roger on the day-care issue, I thought that the moral authority of the church had become more thunder than lightning. And Roger's veiled scatological joke implied that I had little to fear from the thunder either.

In the newspapers of the late '60s and '70s as I finished my schooling and took a teaching job at Clemson University, I read Dr. Billy Graham's confident measurement of heaven's 1600 square miles and Dr. Bailey Smith's equally confident claim that "God does not hear the prayer of a Jew." Marjoe Gortner, a former child evangelist, revealed how his mother would paint a crucifix on his forehead using a clear liquid chemical before revival meetings and then wait until the perspiration turned the cross a bright red as he worked up a lather "barking like a dog for Jesus." Only then would he pass the offering plate. Just a few miles away in Greenville, SC, the Rev. Bob Jones, III, was denouncing First Lady Betty Ford as "a plain slut." This rude condemnation came after Mrs. Ford candidly admitted to an interviewer on national television that while some of her grown children might have had premarital sex and smoked marijuana without her knowledge or permission, she still loved them. A year earlier, Dr. Jones had applied to the state attorney general for two .45 caliber submachine guns and two .30 caliber Browning automatic rifles because "the school has two thousand young ladies living on campus." The attorney general thought that the school's steel fences, security guards, and locked doors offered reasonable safety. He worried that the mile-plus range of the weapons threatened the well-being of the school's neighbors, and the application was denied. All four of these churchmen, not to mention Swaggart, Bakker, Falwell, and Roberts, left the communion wafer souring on my tongue.

My inability to swallow whole the body of Christ led me deeper into my literary studies. I decided that if God wasn't dead, as *Time* had famously wondered despite Nietzsche's self-assured declaration, then He might well be reading Faulkner or Hemingway. St. Aquinas had warned of the one-book man, a caricature that surely does not include the deity who inspired Mozart, Michelangelo, and Milton as surely as Moses and Matthew. Yet every Christian denomination I've ever sought to join has insisted on the divine status of the Bible despite Abraham's shocking readiness to cut his son's throat, Lot's willingness to sacrifice his daughters, and David's unholy treatment of Bathsheba. I simply refuse to take any book as dogma that argues for slavery, capital punishment, second-class citizenship for women, the tormenting of homosexuals, and the execution of witches.

Nevertheless, if the Bible is man-made literature filled with heroes and anti-heroes rather than a God-dictated white paper, there is room for it on my shelves with a host of others. But like Bertrand Russell, I will place an antidote next to the poison and stand Voltaire beside the Testaments.

To satisfy my spiritual appetite in my twenties and thirties, I sampled fare from a variety of church-picnic tables. I had a brief fling as a Deist after taking a course in eighteenth-century literature because it seemed that the Creator had, indeed, set and wound the sundials rather precisely once and for all. However, like so much standoffish classical architecture, Deism lacked the warm appeal I sought. Nevertheless, when I began teaching American literature at Clemson, I loved to engage my mostly Baptist and Methodist students in discussions of Franklin, Pope, and Dryden's notion that "Whatever is, is right." I would ask, for example, "What good is lightning? Lightning is real, so what makes it right?" Usually a budding forester would offer that lightning starts forest fires which burn out the underbrush allowing new vegetation to sprout for wildlife. An agriculture student might offer that lightning fixes nitrogen in the soil thus providing free fertilizer. And a ham radio operator might recall that after an electrical storm, the airways are freer of static. I then would say, "Well, if the lightning destroys a church full of people, is it still right?" Here's where the discussion became interesting, for most of my students had never considered that, as some wag said, "In the beginning, God said, Ha!"

I'll never forget one free-thinking student telling a class that Jesus might be the Antichrist because the gospels don't rule out the possibility of a breech birth. Furthermore, he said, Easter is a fraud because Christ said he'd rise in three days when, in fact, he rose in about forty hours. A devout classmate, who carried his well-thumbed Bible in a zip-lock bag, said, "Excuse me, please, in Jesus' name. Just because Christ rose from the dead in forty hours doesn't make Jesus or the Resurrection a fraud. He was put to death on a Friday, and he rose on Sunday! That is good enough for me and millions more." I never try to resolve or take sides in such disputes, but the discussion of these matters in and out of class is what college is mainly about. My old college friend Max Langley, who liked to quote Ernst Haeckel's definition of God as a "gaseous vertebrate," told me once in the Columbus College library that every thinking person eventually experiences a crisis of faith. After hearing that, I did everything I could to precipitate my own crisis and generally succeeded. Spiritual crises like runaway buses, it seems, are much easier to handle if you're driving the bus, not riding helplessly in the back seat with your jaw set and eyes shut.

Speaking of former students of a religious bent, the deepest-dip theo-Nazi I ever taught was a math major who argued with a colleague that "X equals Jesus." One day she came to my freshman composition class with the *Christian Student Dictionary* published by Bob Jones University Press. Having never seen this reference work before and being something of a lexiconiphile, I asked if I might look it over while she and her classmates wrote an in-class essay. To my astonishment, her dictionary, published in 1983, did not have definitions for *skepticism, interracial, atheism, puberty, abortion,* or *cigarette.* I suppose the editors thought that if they ignored an embarrassment, it would disappear. After class, I suggested to her that a more complete college dictionary might better serve her writing needs. She begged to differ and reminded me that "Satan's biggest lie is moderation." Not to be outquoted, I mentioned Luther's observation that "it isn't necessary to swallow the Holy Ghost feathers and all." "Yes, but Luther was a Lutheran," she said. She had me there. Her analysis of Richard Wilbur's "Death of a Toad," incidentally, noted that since the poet's use of three, six-line stanzas was a subtle manifestation of the apocalyptic 666, the lawn mower, which had mortally wounded the toad, symbolized satanic technology. I failed the paper and wrote, "You have a friend in exegesis, but you haven't met him yet." The student dropped the class, and I never saw her again, but I can't say that I'm sorry.

As far as organized religion is concerned, I suppose the last straw snapped when my dying uncle sent the Rev. Jim Bakker several thousand dollars to reserve a time-share condominium at what some called "The Christers Theme Park" near Charlotte, North Carolina. Uncle Bill died before the facility was ever built (indeed, it has never been built), but his money was never returned. This uncle, however, was always one to cover his bets. For instance, he once "guaranteed" his winning the Publisher's Clearing House Sweepstakes Award by subscribing to one hundred and twenty magazines, all that were offered. He lost. That's when he put his money on a "red" Jim Bakker, but the number turned up "black."

The next stop at the church picnic table was a dish of asceticism. A powerful concert by the Japanese Kodo drummers, a small sect of Zen Buddhists who run twenty miles a day together, eat nothing but seaweed, and drum for hours on the beach of a small, God-forsaken Pacific island, reignited an old ascetic ideal in me in the early 1990s. I had longed to join the Peace Corps while I was in college in the 60s, but a family of three to support killed that dream. I had also dabbled in Transcendental Meditation for a while, but it proved too stressful in the long-run because I constantly worried whether I had enough time not to worry for forty minutes each day.

One day, a woodworker friend called and asked if I'd help him deliver a new communion table and pulpit to the Poor Clares' convent in Greenville. I leapt at the chance to explore the inside of a place ordinarily shut to those of fluctuating faith. After we had unloaded the new furniture and while the nuns settled their debts, I wandered off in the garden where a nun approached me and asked if I'd like to see the convent's beehives. When I agreed, she produced a veiled hat and a pair of gloves for both of us. As the sister opened the hive, she remarked on the perfect hexagonal cells, not unlike the small, tidy rooms in the dormitory. "The bees are exemplars of cleanliness, organization, industry, and loyalty," she said. "They appear to die in the winter and are reborn in the spring, so they naturally remind us of our Savior whose mercy is sweet yet whose judgment is sharp. We use their wax for candles and sell their honey." Naively I asked, "Don't you save any for yourselves?" "Oh, no, we never sweeten our food or drink." What a reproach to pleasure, I thought. If they could, these nuns would blot out the sun because its warmth feels good. Driving back to Clemson, my friend remembered the story of the Hindu monk who after twenty-five years of hard work and self-denial had taught himself to walk on water. "What a shame and waste of time," said the Buddha on meeting the renown ascetic. "For a penny, you could have taken the ferry." As my sainted grandmother, who loved candied yams as much as her Jesus, liked to say, "Blessed are they who expect nothing, for they will not be disappointed."

I wouldn't call cults a main dish on the church picnic table, but I did pick at one dish when a friend disappeared into the black hole of Eckankar. When I came to Clemson, I was assigned to Professor Bob Cross for mentoring. Bob and I hit it off from the start, but what fascinated me most about Bob was the relationship he had with his wife. The two were inseparable. Fortunately, there were no children, for a Cross child would have found the competition stiff for parental love. At work, they asked for and received one office with facing desks. At home, they read science fiction and took long walks together with their poodle. Perhaps I missed the warning signs, but Bob missed them as well, for we were both stunned when Joan announced, "Earth is the hell for all planets circling Alpha Centauri." She, for one, was moving to California to have her astral shoes "resouled" as the new editor of the *Eckankar Journal*. In her spare time, she and her fellow Eckankar disciples planned to travel to various planes of the Sugmad and serve their Eck master. In 1997, some twenty years later when I read of the thirty-nine Heaven's Gate suicides, I scanned the list of the deceased fully expecting to find Joan's name among those tailing the Hale-Bopp comet. Fortunately, Joan's name was not among the missing. About the only cult that impresses me now is the Frisbeeterian, not to be confused with the Presleyterian, which is interesting to me only in an academic, pop culture sort of way. The former faction believes that when someone dies, the soul goes up on a roof, and no one can retrieve it. It makes as much sense as leaving a devoted husband for the unexplored Sugmad.

I jest in earnest, of course, but where do I stand well past the midpoint of "a religious life"? Outside the church like a flying buttress or inside like a pillar? Both and neither. A few years ago as I prepared to teach a selection from "Matthew" in a humanities class, I decided to paraphrase and edit for myself the "Sermon on the Mount." Here's the result: "Good people are hopeful of a final reward, generous, unassuming, compassionate, modest, and forgiving. They mourn their dead and try their best to place the welfare of others before themselves. They actively seek peace among those who fight. They are aware of their own shortcomings. They're willing to be martyred but only for a *good* cause. They are firm in their faith despite opposition. They swallow their anger (though they may manifest righteous indignation), are not lustful or deceitful, and keep their promises. They build strong families that are seldom split by divorce but recognize that, at times, separation is preferable to union. They pray and perform their charities in private. They suffer *small* offenses with forbearance. They recognize that the health of the spirit is worth more than material wealth. Food and clothing beyond the minimum needs are unimportant. They are not hypocritical or judgmental. Their paradigm is the Good Samaritan and Jesus himself. They believe all people are brothers and sisters."

With regard to the infinite and eternal Creator, I do believe that whatever set all matter in motion has remained in contact with the Earth and humankind, but I do not regard this power as absolute, for that would negate human freedom, which is no more absolute than the deity's is. I see God, His sleeves rolled, as a green-visored dealer in a poker game, shuffling the cards but giving man an opportunity to cut them. God then deals without knowing who is receiving which cards. There are times when God's own hand is so poor that He folds His cards, stands, and walks around the green-felt table. As He makes the rounds without signaling any of His favorites, He sees who holds the highest hand, but He has no way of preventing someone with a weak hand from bluffing and occasionally winning. Nor does He have any way of keeping the player with the potential winning hand from folding. Since He called the game and dealt, He is the most powerful, and since He saw the hands after folding, He is the most knowledgeable, but He is neither all-powerful nor all-knowing. Most humans, on the other hand, are born with four cards of an inside straight and hustle most of their lives trying to fill it.

Finally, some Sunday morning when I'm not eating a Swiss-cheese omelet, reading the comics, or taking an bike ride in the Clemson Forest, I will visit Jerusalem—the Muslim Temple Mount, the Christian Church of the Holy Sepulcher, and the Jewish Wailing Wall. From each, I will take the best that I can. Should all three of these shrines be blown up tomorrow, you will not see me worshipping in any of the craters, for I'm confident they will be filled to capacity with the faithful. Still:

> Without the church, much would rise in smoke.
> I believe in the faith of other folk.

A Sexual Life

How the first molecule reproduced itself is the ultimate mystery. However, according to Arthur Guiterman, the answer is simple if you're a one-cell organism:

> Amoebas at the start
> were not complex;
> they tore themselves apart
> and started sex.

When it came to man, the Greeks believed that a jealous god divided the sexes and dared them to find their better halves before they became infertile. Consequently, man spends nine months struggling to find a way out of the womb and the rest of his life in search of another. His role model appears to be the male green flatworm who permanently resides inside the female. The consequence of these human efforts to return to the womb is "a world shrunken to a heap of hot flesh straining on a bed" in the unromantic view of classical scholar E.R. Dodds. The Hebrews, who suffered from the same epidemic of "mild apoplexy" as Dodds' Greeks, had another idea about reproduction. Six thousand years before the Manhattan Project, Jehovah just "split the Adam."

Today some claim that the only way to tell the sexes apart is with a court order. One anonymous father explained the difference between men and women to his son by saying, "A boy goes with his father to the honeymoon suite, but he goes home with his mother." Another difference many have observed is that while women commonly laugh at male strip shows, men sit glumly trying to stare holes through the women they're ogling. My wife learned this basic difference the hard way while I was attending a summer seminar several years ago. She doused a birthday card with some cheap perfume as a joke and sent it to a single, male friend of ours. The friend, knowing I was out of town, put on a suit, drove three hundred miles, and showed up on our doorstep with a dozen roses expecting my wife to greet him in a negligee. She quickly disabused him of that expectation, sending him back down the Interstate, detumescent. It seems that men need to believe that every woman who mails a jesting card or casts a furtive glance their way is signaling sexual availability. In one study, 75% of the men who were asked by a woman in a bar if they would like to go to bed with her said yes. When a man asked several women the same question, not one woman answered affirmatively. Apparently Mae West, who limited her preference to "foreign and domestic men," was not among the women asked.

Regardless of the sex, however, childhood is a period of intense sexual curiosity. It is also a time when sexual myth and ignorance wax luxuriously. One of the myths of my childhood had to do with saltpeter, a substance, I was told, that had the same shriveling effect on a boy's whizzer as salt has on a slug. It was rumored that saltpeter "cured" a boy's overactive libido and left him sexless as a pig's thigh in the smoke house. One summer at Boy Scout camp, word escaped from the mess hall that the dreaded chemical was in the eggs. Though I was not especially fond of those single-serving boxes of dry cereal, I ate the stuff secure in the knowledge that I was foiling an adult plot to neuter my generation.

Given the sad state of sex education, no one should be ashamed of believing the whispered tales of youth. Da Vinci believed that erections were fed by air from the lungs, and Balzac once feared that a nocturnal emission cost him a novel. Untold thousands have believed that European feudal lords had the right to deflower any virgin in their bailiwick, and history teachers are often asked (after class as a rule) if Catherine the Great really died horsing around with a stallion. Aristotle tried to convince women that if they conceived in a north wind they'd have a boy. If they wished for a girl, they had to wait for the wind to blow from the south. Hippocrates disagreed and advised men to tie a string tightly around the right testicle to produce a boy, and vice versa for a girl. In the mid 90s, I recall a doctor friend of mine laughing as he told me of a patient who used an orange-peel diaphragm and douched with Classic Coke. I laughed right along with him at the time, but a Harvard study published in the late 60s proved that Classic Coke killed 91% of the sperm it contacted, and Diet Coke was fully 100% effective, though not recommended for anything but drinking by the manufacturer.

Given "experts" who advise eating Graham crackers to curb lust and others who judge a person's sex drive by the sensitivity of the "funny bone," who can blame some poor guy in Anchorage who thinks that dried, ground flies from Spain will heat a frigid wife? The fact is:

> Neither Spanish fly
> nor Beefeater gin
> works like the prospect
> of Jesus' foreskin.

Of course, I didn't know that when I was fifteen. Though I had heard of Spanish fly, I had no idea where to find any. My father had bourbon in his liquor cabinet and three kids to his credit, so I figured Ogden Nash knew what he was talking about:

> Candy
> is dandy,
> but liquor
> is quicker.

The first opportunity I got to ply a woman with alcohol, I passed out before she did and awoke with acute crapulence. But I was a wiser man then knowing that one in the hand is often better than two in the bush, especially these days when no one can know what's in the bushes with you.

Indeed, lowering the age of puberty to twelve and raising the average age of marriage to twenty-five surely has increased the number of people who have decided to take matters into their own hands, for masturbation means safe sex in the age of AIDS. But today's nostrum was yesterday's plague. Indeed, the Roman Catholic Church once refused to permit masturbation even to obtain a semen specimen for the detection and cure of gonorrhea. Hilaire Belloc summarized the pre-AIDS attitude toward masturbation as follows:

> The world is full of double beds
> And such delightful maidenheads
> That there is simply no excuse

For sodomy and self-abuse.

Though Mark Twain called masturbation "a majestic diversion," it was not until the sexual revolution of the 1960s that one read whole-hearted endorsements of the practice such as the following, which appeared in *Cosmopolitan* in 1971: "Masturbation...is wholesome, normal, and sound. You are training your body to become a superb instrument of love. Masturbate to your heart's content." Perhaps an answer to the masturbation debate is the "Argonaut solution." If man had a detachable penis like the Argonaut octopus, the Church could lock it up in a Vatican vault until the proper time when it could be checked out like a book on reserve, an hour at a time with heavy fines for tardy returns or abuse. Alas, the ambulatory dildo remains a pipe dream of the Church.

Chastity, in fact, may be more lonely and self-abusive than masturbation. I recall one of my high school English teachers reading Herrick's title "To the Virgins," then pausing for a pregnant moment and bitterly saying, "Thanks for nothing!" Indeed my adolescence was a period of great sexual conflict. In my presence, my mother would ask my sisters, even when they were still "carpenter's dreams," flat as boards, "Who *buys* a cow if the milk is free?" At the same time, the chaplain, who was preparing me for confirmation, was quoting St. Augustine, who before being led off to the monastery, said, "Make me chaste and continent, Lord, but not just yet." The chaplain said this partly in jest, being a hip, married Protestant, but, indeed, the idea that "virtue is an intact hymen" has been the moral advice of the church for centuries. Though the automobile and the birth-control pill seriously wounded chastity, hymen-reconstruction surgery or "revirginization" remains popular in some parts of the world, and in this country about one-fifth of adults say they never have sex and never will. Though the National Chastity Association (NCA) might like to distribute chastity belts and restore the old Austrian Chastity Police to power, the ideal for most Americans these days appears to be, in the words of E.M. Forster, "Less chastity and more delicacy." Indelicate case in point, most of the chastity belts sold today are bought by bondage freaks, not jealous husbands.

Despite the NCA, all of us feel the urge at some point to fly upside down like a barn swallow trying to attract a mate and wing our DNA into the future. But in the age of AIDS, men are urged to "wrap that rascal," and to "vulcanize before you spread her thighs." Men in turn complain that wearing a condom is "like showering in a raincoat," or "smelling a rose through a gas mask." Thirty years ago, an Army buddy of mine decided to "seek the middle ground" in this debate; he wore his ribbed condoms inside out so that his partner didn't receive all the enjoyment. The government of Uganda, however, has apparently given up looking for the middle ground and decided that collective suicide is the best contraceptive of all. In September of 1991, the Ugandan Minister of Information issued a directive to state-supported media ordering them to stop announcements concerning condoms and their role in curbing AIDS. Uganda, incidentally, remains one of the African states worst afflicted by the AIDS pandemic.

I attribute the Ugandan announcement to a resurgence of Victorian colonial prudery, which among other things denied the existence of lesbianism, concluded that foreplay was centered in the neck, and assured women that the female orgasm was a disease. Such excessive propriety is the sort of thing that led CBS in 1955 to change Cole Porter's phrase "four-letter words" to "three-letter words" (to avoid that four-letter word *sex*, I suppose).

We shouldn't feel too smugly superior today, however, for 9% of Americans do not think menstruation is a subject that should be taught in all-girl, sex-education classes.

For a year while my father was studying at New York University, I attended a straight-laced school in Brooklyn which was 99% Catholic. One Wednesday afternoon when everyone except me was excused for religious training, I tagged along playing hooky from study hall and overheard a nun telling some small girls to avoid patent-leather shoes on sunny days lest a reflection of their panties be seen on their shoe tops. That fear, I suppose, accounts for nuns' long, black habits and their sensible shoes. C.P. Sawyer also found the whole business of prudery laughable. Tongue in cheek, he wrote:

> I used to love my garden,
> But now my love is dead,
> For I found a bachelor's button
> In black-eyed Susan's bed.

Alex Comfort, author of *The Joy of Sex* and the last man to worry whether Susan was married, advised, "If you're going to take off your clothes, take off your shell too." But a lot of us, like the shy fellow who placed his foot in the john and peed down his leg so not to offend his wife, have a permanent carapace.

For all the well-intentioned warnings from the Church, such as the nun's above, British social critic Malcolm Muggeridge claimed that "the orgasm has replaced the Cross as the focus of longing and the image of fulfillment." But no Hindu has ever hidden the fact that Krishna seduced 16,000 virgins in a night. And in at least one Hindu sect, sex is virtually worshiped in the form of a stone phallus which is set inside a circular base called a yoni. At the annual Feast of Siva's Marriage, a Hindu priest ceremoniously smears the lingam and yoni with clarified butter and then washes them with milk. Muslims, on the other hand, are about as squeamish when it comes to sex as Christians. The Ayatollah Khomeini once urged men to hold their penises with only two fingers when urinating, and for Allah's sake, not to urinate in the direction of Mecca.

The early Christian church, in fact, labored sedulously to transform sex into sin. With the scalpel of logic firmly in hand, church fathers in the fifth century declared that since sperm and urine issue from the same organ, priests should be celibate. Recommendations for the laity were almost as stringent. According to some medieval church fathers, intercourse should be abstained from on Thursdays, Fridays, Saturdays, Sundays, and Mondays in honor of Christ's arrest, his crucifixion, his mother, his resurrection, and the dead, respectively. That left Tuesdays and Wednesdays, but about half of those days over a year were excluded because of fasts and church festivals. Consequently, "emergent occasions," as intercourse was euphemistically called, was rare indeed. It would not be until the Enlightenment that men were as comfortable with sex as William Byrd of colonial Virginia, who could "roger" his wife or the maid and then relax with a "sermon in Tillotson" before bed. Today's ethos is perhaps best captured by Mae West's famous line, "To err is human, but it feels divine."

That is until you exceed your limits, because promiscuous sex is, I imagine, something like being tickled to the point of pain. My older sister was once propositioned by the unwilting Wilt Chamberlain as she waited for a train in San Francisco. Despite her rejection,

Wilt with 20,000 conquests under his belt looked happy enough, but Don Juan's diaries after a mere one thousand sexual victories tell a story of bitterness and disillusionment, of compulsively plotting pathways of ascent even as he panted in decline. The promiscuous among us "hear America swinging," but their heads are caught in their zippers, and sex on the brain, as Malcolm Muggeridge reminds us, is a very unsatisfactory place to have it.

In the late 70s an Army buddy of mine and his wife paid a visit to Plato's Retreat in New York City, where despite the name, all the love was not above the neck. After four hours in the "mat room" with a half dozen unwashed strangers, my friend longed to escape from a man everyone called "the human tripod" and a woman who had "sweet thang" tattooed in her pubic hairs. After swimming, dancing, drinking, and playing pool in the buff, all he wanted was his pants, his wife, and a way out. Malcolm Bradbury wrote that, "If God had wanted us to have group sex, He'd have given us more organs." Voltaire, I suspect, would have agreed. After an orgy, Voltaire was asked if he would like to attend another. "Once is a philosopher," the author said. "Twice is a pervert."

On April 9, 1984, the orgies ended when *Time* announced that due to herpes (which until the late 70s was often diagnosed as psoriasis) and an uncertain economy, the sexual revolution was over. For all its virtues, democracy when applied to love and sex is a vice. For despite Erica Jong's rhapsodic defense, there are no "zipless fucks" or "Teflon liaisons." As Harry Stein, the former *Esquire* ethicist wrote:

> It's impossible to compartmentalize our lives, to keep a single aspect of our existence under lock and key yet be blissfully open about the rest.... When it comes to infidelity [even in a mat room with your spouse present] we have seven millennia of human history to draw upon, and the evidence appears conclusive: duplicity no matter how it's dressed up generally makes everyone feel rotten.

My Army friend and his wife split up, in fact, long before the revolution ended.

The fantastic women who, in Yeats' words, "offer to love's play [their] dark declivities," exist mostly in the dank air between men's ears. The Duchess of Marlborough, however, may have been an exception. She wrote in her diary, "The Duke returned from the wars today and did pleasure me in his top boots." And dozens of British women did give a bare-breasted greeting on the Southampton docks to their men returning from the Falklands War. But the Duchess and the British "war widows" were offering their declivities, as it were, to one man only, not the regiment or the fleet. The rule is that men want women more than women want men, most of whom are as discriminating as pollen in a gale. In their defiance of the natural law, men in their desperation remind me of the mule:

> A sterile member
> hasn't stopped the mule
> from seeking exceptions
> to hard-fast rules.

One of the exceptions is Lucille's Clifton's magical woman who puts a spell on a man and spins him like a helicopter blade on her loins. Another is the woman whose smile draws the purse strings of a man's scrotum tight and whose tongue can tie wet noodles in knots. Male-oriented fiction is filled with women like these, but the non-fiction woman is far different. Yes, according to Gershon Legman's computations, there are about fourteen million sexual positions, but each one makes another unwanted pregnancy possible in a country where 15% are illegitimate and adolescent mothers without husbands are the core of the poverty problem. Yes, humans have some two hundred sex-related thoughts each day, but an orgasm burns only 150 calories (a beer's worth), and the sexual organs are really only modified mucus membranes and sweat glands. Few of us, however, and that includes physicians, think of the genitals in such clinical terms.

Especially among married couples, the reality of sex may vary from the Victorian woman who closed her eyes, opened her legs, and thought of England, to the wife of a Klansman who claimed her husband was a "wizard between the sheets." It ranges from one couple whose idea of sexual compatibility is a night when both have headaches, to a couple who warms up watching home videos of themselves in heat oblivious to ringing doorbells and telephones. It ranges from Rodney Dangerfield, who would have no sex if not for pickpockets, to the wife of a former colleague who regards herself as the "priestess of the fuzzy oracle." The ideal, however, exists somewhere between these real limits.

The ideal, however, is faceted, not smooth. One facet as someone put it is "not the length of the ship, but the courtesy to stay in port until all have gotten off." Another facet is the knowledge that unless pleasure is mutual, it's no fun for either. The ideal is not a divine mandate to populate the wilderness; instead, it's a responsibility to bring into the world no more children than you can provide for and love. The ideal is a flexible cultural notion that once permitted Chinese men to think kissing a three-inch bound foot was the pinnacle of eroticism. And it is the knowledge that sex is not a male or heterosexual need, but a universal human right. To achieve the ideal:

> Espalier desire
> well before the show—
> left wild or cut back
> means nothing can grow.

Only when there is a domestic florescence can the "earth move" for all and, as Lear said, "copulation thrive."

But with age, the ideal is increasingly difficult to attain. The stereotype of the aging Lothario is a man with a closed mind and an open fly, open either because he's a horny old goat or because he forgets to close it. The male reality is:

> After a while
> he may start to wheeze,
> but the antique rat
> still loves the cheese.

The female reality is a woman organist with many good tunes left in her pipes.

Once a rake, however, always a rake, for old habits are slow to die. Just before Hugh Hefner retired from his position with *Playboy,* but while he still had the run of the Playboy

Mansion with all its attendant voyeuristic opportunities, he is reported to have walked the streets of Chicago past midnight hoping to see a woman undressing before an open window. It's true that once-supple limbs turn stiff with age, and limbs that once were stiff turn disconsolately limp, but humans rust out, as Franklin said, faster than they wear out. And while love does tarnish with age, so does sterling silver, but that doesn't diminish its value. It may even enhance it, for a fine patina has a luster all its own.

While frigidity is sometimes a problem in a woman's post-menopausal years, the bane of aging males is impotence. Cary Grant denied it was a problem at all. His advice to men was to confess it up front, for "no woman can wait to disprove it." A few years ago after my wife had a mastectomy, I found that when the major appeared it was hard for my soldier to come to attention. In despair I wrote:

> The surgeon who cut
> Jill's cancerous breast
> also cut Jack but
> there's no scar on his chest.

I felt myself to be "incompotent," but I wasn't laughing at the word play. I wrote to my closest friend:

> My only hope
> for another erection
> is *rigor mortis*
> or the Resurrection.

He replied advising me to see if my problem was psychological or physiological. To this end he said to wrap my penis before going to bed with a ring of one-cent stamps. In the morning if the perforations were torn, my problem was psychological and just to give myself some time.

Through all of this, my wife has been enormously understanding and sympathetic. She reminded me of something we both had noticed years ago in London's White Chapel Tower. Henry the Eighth, who left six wives unhappy, had the largest codpiece in the armor collection. Her story helped me to recall that while Anne Boleyn, Henry's second wife, had an extra nipple ("a witch's teat"), she gladly would have traded it for her head on the executioner's scaffold.

The connection between sex and death has long been recognized. The French are fond of noting that man, unlike the crowing rooster, grieves after sex, for an orgasm is a "little death," and a drop of semen is equivalent to a drop of blood. Zoologists and botanists also have noted the phenomenon called semelparity, or procreation after a lifetime of preparation. This, I imagine, is the ultimate sex, explosively ecstatic even as it is self-destructive. Examples of semelparity include the Pacific salmon, which after as long as nine years at sea, spawn a few days before their death. And some bamboos briefly flower after 120 years of preparation and then perish. It's as if a celibate priest ejaculated seventy years worth of semen and fell dead in his coffin-bed. Theologians, on the other hand, like to remind us that life is a loan and ultimately we owe God a death for all the pleasures we have enjoyed. Personally, I wish there were some other currency acceptable in the settle-ment of this debt. Lily Tomlin likes to reassure her audiences that "there is sex after death. We just won't be able to feel it." Lauren Bacall's tender gesture was more comforting. At Humphrey Bogart's funeral, she placed in her old friend's coffin a gold whistle that was engraved, "If you need anything just whistle." I shudder to think, however, that Bogart ever used the thing.

In the Army, I recall that one favorite bull-session topic was whether a man, who ejaculates when hanged, feels it. Thirty years later, I still do not know if dead men whistle or what the dying feel, but I feel certain that the whip-tail lizard, which reproduces with-out sex, does not have the answer either. I'm satisfied that death is a successful return to the earthen womb from which humans departed a lifetime ago and where they lie await-ing the spring.

A Grammarian Considers the Deity

OK, so it's decided—
God's a verb, not a noun,
but is It active or passive?
Did It make the light,
or was the light made by It?

Gerund, participle, or infinitive?
Is It damning or to damn?

Transitive or intransitive?
Does Its blessing cross Its verb?

Indicative, imperative, or subjunctive?
Does it act as a tour guide,
despot, or hypothesis?

Progressive or emphatic?
Is It watching or does It watch?

Past, present, or future?
Was It, or is It still to be?

A Feel for the Ball

S port is a microcosm, a stitched, leather globe that I can almost get my hand completely around. As the slippery spheres of politics, economics, and science slip from my grasp, sport is a smooth ball with three holes conveniently drilled or with a pebbled grain that I can firmly grip on those rare occasions when I cannot get the entire thing in my hand. Only the medicine ball requires two hands, but its days have been numbered by the Universal weight machine and other technological innovations. Sport, like life, then, is ephemeral; a baseball, for example, takes eleven minutes to hand-stitch but lasts on average five pitches in the major leagues. The ball lasts just long enough for a player or a fan to feel its seams and stitches. Every dimple or protrusion on the ball's surface is a facet of life, an idea that fingers press hard against before the ball flies off into the dugout or space.

One of the first seams on the sporting "ball" that I could get a grip on was its language. I grew up reading Shirley Povich in the *Washington Post* and later Jim Murray in the *Los Angeles Times*, whom James Dickey has praised as "America's greatest poet who never published a poem." I still aspire to describe Rickey Henderson's "strike zone as the size of Hitler's heart," the Indianapolis 500 as "a run for the lilies," or the Chicago Cubs as "the Ursa Minors."

The word *sport* itself is a clipped form of *disport,* and ever since I could read, I have loved to disport myself in the language of athletes. Among the first words to dazzle my eye were the marvelous alliterative monikers like the Sultan of Swat and the Splendid Splinter. About the same time, I began using *can of corn, Texas leaguer,* and *southpaw* on the neighborhood sandlots. Years later, I discovered that life itself can be described as a ball game. (Indeed, the precedent for such metaphorical usage is very old: Genesis begins, "In the big inning."). Hardly anyone scores right off the bat fresh from the bush leagues, but if you keep your eye on the ball, you might get to first base. Should you fail, you can always take a rain check or go into extra innings. Eventually even those out in left field hit a home run. The trick is to know the score and touch all the bases. Unless you're sent to the showers, you're home free.

The trouble is that for many, perhaps the majority of men, talking sports may be as close as they can come to intimacy. One summer I worked for a Georgia foreman to whom masculine intimacy was an alien concept, who urged his laborers on by saying, "Hunker down, you hairy dawgs." Men who don't follow the sports page are left with only power tools to kindle the flame of manly conversation. Too often men at a social gathering are left feeling like Lefty Driesell's Maryland basketball team visiting the civilized confines of the neo-gothic Duke campus. Lefty's rag-tag, playground-style team was greeted by a sign that read, "Ain't no steel nets here."

Another "stitch on the ball" is the telling number or statistic. I do not have Ty Cobb's .367 lifetime batting average or Cy Young's 511 lifetime victories in mind, though these are meaningful numbers—ideals for the young to strive toward the way Hank Aaron spent a career chasing home run number 715. For mere mortals, who do hundred sit-ups every morning in order to swing a softball bat *and* mow the yard on the same weekend, I'm referring to numbers more mundane but still dazzling and true: running 526 consecutive pool balls, sinking 499 straight free-throws, or doing 37,350 pushups, each in twenty-four hours or less.

Related to the numerical "stitches" on the sporting ball are the mythic feats that may change lives. In high school I spent the better part of two years trying to exceed my personal best of 5' 4" in the high jump. I never succeeded, but when I read of the one-legged high jumper Arnie Boldt soaring over 6' 8", I vowed never to high jump again. Call it the "anxiety of influence." Feats such as Mantle's 565' home run, Ruth's throwing two balls simultaneously from one hand both for strikes, and Abebe Bilika's two barefooted victories in the Olympic marathon may have ended more athletic careers than we will ever know. But as any coach will tell you, quitting just because your golf partner hit a 170 yard drive into the cup without a bounce or a roll, or pulling your team off the field just because the opposition has a pitcher, who when his right arm tires, pitches left-handed, is flagrant defeatism.

Some athletic feats, such as hitting a double and stealing first on a pitch to the next batter, are simply foolish. Others are not so much inane as they are excessive, for zeal is another of the ball's "stitches." A softball teammate of mine, for instance, was playing in a weekend tournament when a call came from his nine-month pregnant wife. My friend, who was in the on-deck circle when he received the word, told the excited messenger, "Tell her to wait until I hit." Such zeal breeds odd excesses that are as grotesque as the lumpy tureen called the America's Cup. Into this pot one might place the entire "sport" of body building, the Hawaiian Ironman Triathalon, and Jack La Lanne's towing seventy dinghies loaded with seventy people one mile on his seventieth birthday. Also deserving of inclusion are the financial excesses of sport: baseball hitters who average $30,000 a hit, pitchers who get $1,500 a pitch, and Honus Wagner baseball cards selling for $100,000 apiece. One of these rare items was crumpled recently and immediately lost $40,000 of its value. Don't get me wrong; I'm all for a free market, but I don't think the team owners or the state should receive all that money. What I object to is the mad excess of sport—what one critic of Olympic swimming was referring to when he said, "All a swimmer's youth evaporates in the pool." But at least a swimmer finishes his or her competitive career with a healthy body; the zealous footballer, on the other hand, may finish his with the zippered, arthritic knees of a Joe Namath. As Merle Kessler wrote, "Football players, like prostitutes, are in the business of ruining their bodies for the pleasure of strangers."

Nevertheless, I remain hopeful of change, for nowhere is change more evident than in the sporting microcosm. The winner of the first automobile race in history, for example, in 1894 averaged eleven miles per hour; today's Indianapolis 500 winners average close to 200. The Matterhorn, which was not climbed until 1865, now has thousands who have claimed its summit. Johnny Weissmuller, who won five Olympic medals in the 1920s, could not make a good college swim team if he were in his prime today. Sadly, much change such as the proposals for thumbless gloves and head protection for boxers has been resisted in the name of "box-office." Doubtless many of the approximately five hundred boxers who have died in the ring since 1918 would have lived if these innovations had been adopted. Some critics of sports like James Brady blame the "corruption" of sport on "aluminum bats, Technicolor tennis shirts, and double-knit fabrics." But personally I've never been much of a purist. I like the designated hitter, the video-taped review, the Fosbury Flop, and soccer-style field-goal kickers because they've all made their respective sports fairer or more interesting. It's hard to believe that before the jump shot was invented by Hank Lusetti in the mid-1940s, the flatfooted, two-handed set shot prevailed in college and professional basketball. Women's basketball was even worse: as late as the 1960s, a player was allowed two dribbles, and then she had to shoot or pass the ball lest she "over-exert" herself.

With the exceptions of catcher/spy Moe Berg, running back/Supreme Court Justice Byron "Whizzer" White, and boxer/Shakespearian Gene Tunney, professional and amateur athletes are seldom esteemed for their intelligence. But when a better way of winning is found, jocks or their coaches are quick on the uptake. Except for some lip service paid to physical fitness, the intelligentsia historically has been careful to observe the "seam" of the ball that separates sports and education. The former President of Harvard Charles Eliot Norton typifies the ignorance and opposition of academe. Norton proposed eliminating the entire Harvard baseball program because pitchers had developed the curve ball, and such "a deliberate attempt to deceive," he said, should not be tolerated at Harvard. Coach Vince Lombardi, on the other hand, thought that a school without a football program was nothing more than "a medieval study hall." Too often, educators, to paraphrase a former Oklahoma State president, are trying to build a university the athletic department can be proud of. Such a bias led one Florida State professor to give test answers and final grades of "A" to forty-two athletes in his Russian history class. And in 1989 at the University of Nebraska, athletes who were declared "learning disabled" after admission became eligible for all the perquisites of a blind or deaf student. Texts were taped by tutors for their charges to listen to, the athletes went to class with their own note takers, exams were read to them, and they were given extra time to complete them.

Such a deplorable state is perhaps inevitable given the deterioration of the family in recent years. An examination of the miniature world of sports reveals a splitting of the "seams." Children, it appears, are increasingly likely to be taught a sport by a coach than a parent. And even among intact families, the typical American father can ruefully confess along with Joseph Epstein that "I've spent more time with Curt Gowdy than with my own father." When Pop Warner football and Little League baseball games become struggles of parental egos, how are children going to learn that one day they must mark their own score cards? Ideally, says Scott Russell Sanders, in an industrial/service economy:

> Instead of consulting the stars or the entrails of birds, father and son
> consult the smudged newspapers to see how their chosen spirits are
> faring. They fiddle with the dials of radios, hoping to catch the oracular
> murmur of a distant game. The father recounts heroic deeds, not from the
> field of battle but from the field of play. The seasons about which he
> speaks lead not to harvests but to championships. No longer intimate
> with the wilderness, no longer familiar even with the tame land of farms,
> we create artificial landscapes bounded by lines of paint or lime. Within
> those boundaries, as within the frame of a chessboard or painting, life achieves
> a memorable, seductive clarity.

Frequently, the reality of parental involvement is more sordid. In 1991 Mrs. Wanda Webb Holloway was sentenced to fifteen years in prison for paying $10,000 for an assassin to enhance her daughter's odds of making her high-school cheer-leading squad by murdering the mother of her daughter's chief rival. Heywood Hale Broun wrote, "Sports do not build character. They reveal it." Alan Page agreed but added, "They also build *characters.*" He was too polite.

Admittedly Mrs. Holloway is not representative of the vast majority of parents who interest themselves in their children's sporting lives. But the underside of the athletic "sphere" is not as taut as sport advocates would like for us to believe. Yankee pinstripes, for example, were adopted to make an over-weight Babe Ruth look svelte; John J. Audubon, progenitor of the modern conservation movement, painted only birds that he had shot, and Arnold Schwarzenegger, former President George Bush's sport czar, used steroids to help him win his four Mr. Olympia titles. When it comes to professional wrestling, everything that meets the eye is suspect. But candor is beginning to crawl out from under the thick mats and box springs of the wrestling ring. One promoter recently sued a wrestler in his stable because "he won too fast" and not as the promoter had choreographed it. A few diehards like Frank Deford think "pro wrestling is clean and everything else in the world is fixed." Even the courts have ruled that professional wrestling is an entertainment, not a sport. Of course, Deford was simply being as candid as Bill Vukovich who claims there was no secret to winning at Indy, "Just accelerate and steer left." If anyone thinks that any professional sport is that easy, just invite him to hit successfully against major-league pitching more than 26% of the time, the all-time batting percentage. If this foolish fellow is successful a mere 33% of the time, he will earn a place in the Hall of Fame! Even at Nebraska and Chico State, 33% is well short of honors.

The pressure to win and the commercial opportunities available today have made sportsmanship and fair play as welcome as a clean, dry ball on a muddy field. I have in mind such "stitches" on the ball as runner Emil Zatopek's gift of one of his four Olympic gold medals to Ron Clarke, who had none despite setting numerous world records. Former Ohio State coach Woody Hayes, who Jim Murray described as "graceless in victory as in defeat," would have been mystified by Zatopek's gesture. Bill Tilden, who advised his students of mixed-doubles strategy "to hit at the girl whenever possible," would likewise have been nonplused. And Knute Rockne, who wanted no one but "bad losers" on his team, would have despaired. Why is it that for years children are taught to shake hands with the opposition after a game, but as soon as they reach high school or college, the civil custom is dropped? Soccer is one exception as is boxing where opponents often embrace after a fight. After one welterweight fight in Miami, however, the boxer who had lost a TKO touched his gloves to the victor's and then knocked the referee, a sixty-year old man who had his back turned, unconscious.

That violence is an ugly gash in the cover of the "ball" should come as no surprise when often bodily harm is the very reason for a sport's existence. The purpose of boxing after all is to separate a man's *compos* from his *mentis* with punches that fly 135 mph and develop 1000 pounds of force on impact. Jack Dempsey, anticipating such violence in the ring, chewed pine tar to strengthen his jaw and marinated his face in pickle brine to toughen his skin. But even the fastest heavyweight boxer in history and one of the toughest, Muhammed Ali, could not avoid being hit in the head an estimated 1.5 million times. The result is a very rich man with Parkinson's disease. If according to George Will, football is "violence punctuated by committee meetings," then surely boxing is a few minutes of violence punctuated by handlers delivering long tantrums urging more violence. All this with no timeouts and no halftime. The only sport that is more violent is the Welsh game of "purring" in which two men in steel-toed boots hold on to each other's shoulders and then kick each other in the shins until one falls or lets go.

"War minus the shooting" is what Orwell called sport, but in the film *The Last Boy Scout* (1991), a running back high on drugs pulls out a pistol and shoots his way into the end zone. If that sounds bizarre, try reality: in 1969, the Nigerian-Biafran War was suspended for two days to allow both sides to watch Pelé and his Brazilian soccer team play exhibition games in the warring countries. In the same year in El Salvador, a fight on the soccer pitch boiled over the stadium walls into the cities and countryside resulting in the deaths of 2000 people in the Salvadoran-Honduran "soccer war." Whether war gives way to sport or sport gives way to war, there is no question that sport is a preparation for large-scale belligerence.

In Germany in the 1930s, for instance, a popular children's game was "I Declare War!" The strategy, strength, and endurance required of sports have obvious carryover values on the battlefield. That good athletes make good soldiers is the conventional wisdom. With this in mind, the Iroquois prior to battle would arrange two teams of about a thousand lacrosse players on a field several miles long. To keep the braves in motion over three days, squaws were stationed along the sidelines with birch switches that they freely used on any laggard.

The emphasis on winning, one of the loose threads in the sporting microcosm, is certainly understandable in a do-or-die situation, but realistically death is rare even in the boxing ring or the race track. In most amateur sports, you can always try again tomorrow. This is even true in some professional sport. Eddie Arcaro, for example, rode 250 losing mounts before winning his first race. What I worry about is the attitude summed up by famed billiard player Danny McGoorty, "Try to hate your opponent. Even if you're playing your grandmother, try to beat her fifty to nothing. If she already has three, try to beat her fifty to three." Professional football coaches like George Allen of the Redskins argue that "every time you win, you're reborn; when you lose, you die a little." Bill Veeck was perhaps closer to the truth when he observed, "A winning team can bring a city together, and even a losing team can provide a bond of common misery." One visit to Chicago during the baseball season in most years will confirm the truth of that observation.

The overemphasis on winning at the expense of everything else has inevitably led to a backlash—the anti-sport movement, which I personally have a hard time getting a "grip" on. This new trend has given us games like Infinity Volleyball in which two sides of six players chant the number of times the ball sails over the net without touching the ground. Everyone wins when the two sides break their previous record. Such games are fine when a parent is playing tennis or catch with a son or daughter because nothing sours a sport faster for a child than always losing to a crowing adult. But after adolescence, say, the game quickly grows cold without the risk of losing or the thrill of winning. The main stimulus that keeps me running and swimming during the week is the possibility of trouncing somebody on the softball diamond on the weekend.

But if I can't win fairly, I don't want my name on the trophy. The Emperor Nero won every event he entered in the 60 AD Olympics, but how he lived with his "victories" is not recorded. Some unfairness, on the other hand, like Harvey Haddix's loss of his no-hitter, lies only in the eyes of the beholder. In one semi-pro game, a reliever came in with two outs, a man on first, in the top of the ninth with his team trailing by one run. The reliever took his warm-ups; then, before ever throwing an official pitch, he whirled and picked off the runner on first. His team scored two runs in the bottom of the ninth, and the reliever was given credit for winning the game even though he never pitched. The victory wasn't gained by cheating, but neither does it seem just. Perhaps as Eddie Quinn said, "the only sport on the level is mountain climbing." Of course, blatant cheating like missing a shot in basketball to beat a point spread or striking out to lose the World Series is rare. But the temptation to cheat is always there because the thrill of winning is irresistible and addictive. In 1973, a father paid $20,000 for wind-tunnel tests and then built a "Soap Box Derby" racer for his son with a powerful electromagnet in the nose. The wiring and the battery were completely encased in fiberglass. At the top of the hill as the racers stood ready to start, the boy in the illegal racer pressed his head back against a switch buried in the seat cushion turning on the magnet in the nose of the car. The magnet was, in turn, drawn to a hinged steel plate that held the racers in line awaiting the fall of the starting gate. The illegal racer got a slight forward tug when the gate fell because of the attraction of the magnet to the gate. Observers said that the racer seemed to leap from its starting position. Not until the boy had won the national competition did someone demand an investigation which included an x-ray of the racer, and eventual disqualification.

On the other hand when the rules themselves are inadequate, there should be some way to redress the injustice. In 1985, for example, the 49ers were visiting the Broncos, and on one 49er's field-goal attempt, a snowball flew out of the stands and landed a short distance in front of the holder just as the snap arrived. The holder mishandled the ball, tried to throw a pass, and failed. There was a futile protest before the Broncos went on to win 17-16. The rules allowed officials to call for more security at the 49er's end of the field but, bizarrely, not to take the play over. On other occasions, officials have been more flexible and creative when they've been faced with impasses not covered by the rule book. In a football game between Kentucky and Tennessee, Kentucky fumbled in front of its own bench, and in the scramble for the ball, a box containing eight footballs was tipped over. This meant that a total of nine balls were loose on the field, and no one knew which of the nine was the game ball. The game officials coolly counted the balls and awarded Tennessee the advantage because they had five balls and Kentucky only four. Just as the referee makes boxing more of a sport than an animalistic brawl, so do football's "zebras" make a sustained, orderly existence possible on the Serengeti gridiron.

Speaking of foreign locations, the microcosmic ball may seem strangely tattered to sports fans who travel abroad. Ties, for example, are possible in Japanese "*besuboru*," but the British see nothing wrong with running up the score, a practice that appalls Japanese and Americans. German soccer players usually suffer a kick in the shins stoically, but the Italians and Brazilians writhe in agony both mock and real. The Japanese once thought that being hit by a famous pitcher's fast ball was an "honor exceeded only by being crushed under the wheels of the Imperial carriage," so in World War II the most derogatory insult Japanese soldiers could think of to taunt the Americans was "Babe Ruth go to hell!" Americans thought they were joking. And when the King of Sweden pronounced Jim Thorpe the greatest athlete in the first half of the twentieth century, Thorpe brightly replied, "Thanks, King!" Proper Europeans were horrified by this rift in decorum, but most Americans understood that in a democracy, this is how one addresses a peer of the realm.

Often what appears to be a chasm in international sports is really just some powdered lime on a field. Cricket, for instance, which is unknown to most Americans, is a brother to our national pastime. An anonymous Englander once tried to explain cricket to an American as follows:

> You have two sides: one out in the field and one in. Each man that's in the side that's in goes out, and when he's out, he comes in, and the next man goes in until he's out.

Except for the term *side*, the above could serve as a rough description of baseball, for cricket and baseball are twins who were separated at birth from "rounders," their mother, the ur-bat-and-ball game. Of course in the broadest sense, most athletic values such as teamwork, courage, and determination are universal. Everyone understands, as Wilt Chamberlain said, why "no one roots for Goliath" even when he scores 100 points in a game and averages 50 points a game over a season. And everyone can appreciate the astounding fact that Goliath or not, Chamberlain never fouled out of a basketball game in his pro career.

Jim Thorpe's candid reply to royalty quoted above is a sharp reminder that in the athletic microcosm sport operates as a pure meritocracy devoid of nepotism in which the last shall be first if he can hit the hard slider. Mickey Mantle's son could not and, therefore, despite his father's influence, never played major league baseball. Critics of the apparent "advantage" that blacks have in basketball charge that the sporting meritocracy has been violated by evolution Boston Celtic star Bill Russell answered these critics by saying that natural selection gave nothing to blacks that eight to ten hours a day of shooting basketball wouldn't give anyone. Indeed racial and class differences in most cases are blurred by sport, but a strict hierarchy still exists among sports with golf and tennis near the top, and bowling and boxing near the bottom. Tex Cobb summarized the difference between the ends of the scale, "If you screw up in tennis, it's 15-love; if you screw up in boxing, it's your ass." Geoffrey Bocca claimed, rather mistakenly I think, that "the personal charm of any sportsman is in inverse proportion to the social standing of his sport." Bocca cites John McEnroe (decidedly uncharming on the court) and Archie Moore (charming?) as examples of their sport but neglects to mention Arthur Ashe and Sonny Liston, a gentleman and a brute respectively from opposite ends of the sporting and social spectrum. Perhaps, as George Plimpton suggested, the differences can be explained by the size of the ball: the smaller the ball the higher the class. But while polo and squash are aristocratic games which use small balls, the handball is also small and in many urban areas it's played off tenement walls without the benefit of gloves. And basketball, which uses the largest ball of all, is a popular after-hours recreation for yuppies in "fitness Meccas" across America. Indeed, until social and economic justice prevail and everyone plays some middle-class sport yet to be devised, the rich, it's safe to predict, will continue to scorn their divots at their country clubs, and the poor will bowl in the alley. Until that time, we will continue to enjoy the spectacle of the arrogant being brought to earth as when Muhammed Ali told a flight attendant, "Superman don't need no seat belt," to which the attendant replied, "Superman don't need no airplane."

But high and low, rich and poor, finger the same rosary. Regardless of socio-economic class, many who find spiritual rewards in the sporting microcosm are unaware perhaps that a baseball has the same number of stitches as a rosary's loop has beads and spaces (108), and that the first baseball game was actually played on the Elysian Fields. Coincidences notwithstanding, there's no question that sports confer a spiritual dimension to people's lives, and as a result, sport and religion are often spoken of together. Red Smith called the 90' between the bases "the one absolute truth." Bartlett Giamatti said that speaking to Yogi Berra was like "talking to Homer about the gods." Many baseball fans think that you stretch in the bottom half of the seventh inning because God rested on the seventh day. And when the US beat the USSR in ice hockey in the 1980 Winter Olympics, good finally defeated evil, many claimed, because "the evil empire" had cheated to win basketball gold in 1972. Here was a nation's redemption; America was saved. But sport and religion in many ways are odd bedfellows. Christianity's ideal is one of poverty, meekness, and loving your neighbor, not just your teammate. Many athletes, however, are selfish, materialistic, and intemperate despite their use of words like *faith, sacrifice,* and *spirit.* The antics of some over-exposed ballplayers, however, who have kids everywhere spitting, chewing tobacco, and brawling, have only slightly diminished the meaning and cohesiveness that athletics can contribute to individuals, families, and, indeed, the nation and the world. Fans who stay long enough at the game eventually learn through a personal epiphany that it's not the goals scored but the assists that truly matter. And while the day of muscular Christianity is waning, the "doctrine of the strenuous life" is enjoying a renewed respectability "Sweat," as Heywood Hale Broun wrote, "is the cologne of accomplishment."

Before sweat stains the clean jersey, however, a new ball on the green turf is sweet and spotless as the interior of a new car. Indeed, though few men admit it, beauty is one of the sporting microcosm's strongest "stitches." Bill Russell said Kareem Abdul-Jabbar's sky hook was "the most beautiful thing in sports," but my preference (probably because Kareem was taller than Goliath) is the image of Jackie Robinson stealing home, Roger Bannister slipping by John Landy on the homestretch, or one of Bill Bradley's "hope passes." Bill Sharman admitted that the hardest thing about guarding Bob Cousy was the "temptation to stand back and admire him." Simply put, Sharman was in love with the beauty and grace of Cousy's play. The heart aches for the graceful achievement of a perfect pole vault, three-meter dive, or triple axel. Robert Frost, who admired individual accomplishment more than a team's success, thought a sprinter in full gallop was beauty personified. The ugly, Frost thought, was a three-legged race. But a perfectly executed 400-meter relay with three fluid baton exchanges at break-neck speed moves me profoundly every time that I see one. Sport is beautiful, and the aficionados of any sport are voyeurs.

Of course no ball lasts forever anymore than a ball player does. Some athletes know "death" before they die Reinhold Messner, for instance, climbed all fourteen mountains in the world over 8000 meters (26,250') without oxygen. Now, rather than climb anything under 8000 meters, he is, I imagine, weeping for new peaks to conquer. Other athletes even of Messner's caliber expect to be killed by their sport. Grand Prix driver Jim Clark said before he died in a fiery wreck, "Racing is one sport you get better and better at before it kills you." More than one athlete has suffered premonitions of their death. Coach Bear Bryant, for instance, told a reporter that he'd "probably croak in a week" after he stepped down as head coach at Alabama. He died a week after he retired.

Fans run a similar risk. One Pakistani cricket fan yelled, "Long live Pakistan!" as his country was receiving the World Cup and then suffered a fatal heart attack. Other fans let the team they support die for them. After Bill Buckner let Mookie Wilson's slow roller meander through his legs in the 1986 World Series, the Red Sox lost countless fans. The team effectively died for them. Buckner, however, did not take the loss as personally as Donnie Moore. Moore and his California Angels were one strike away from winning the American League pennant in 1986 when Moore served up a home-run pitch to the Red Sox's Dave Henderson. The Sox went on to win, and Moore, haunted by the pitch, committed suicide three years later. He apparently was not consoled by the argument that it was his pitching that led the Angels to the playoffs, or that a game, even a playoff or World Series game, is just a game.

Former Commissioner of Baseball Bartlett Giamatti said that baseball is "designed to break your heart. The game begins in the spring, when everything else begins again, and it blossoms in the summer, filling the afternoons and the evenings, and then as soon as the chill rain comes out, it stops and leaves you to face the fall alone." This is the sentimental view of a man near death. I prefer to think that the end of baseball is the start of football and just a point on the continuum of my own softball, biking, and swimming. Incidentally, I've got my eye set on Ted Mumby's record for the 100-meter freestyle for the 80-84 age group. I figure if I live long enough and stay fit, I can shave a few seconds off his record of 3:14, for I plan to go down swimming or swinging at that microcosmic ball.

The Older the Vintage the Better the Buzz: Reflections on and of a Retiring Teacher

Black and white and every shade of gray,
Skip gathered himself to give it away.

Knowing a damp sponge drinks more than one dry,
he urged his students to ask the world why.

Look hard, he said, *at the sand in the pearl.*
He taught them to see all of the world.

The sword's in the book, not buried in stone.
Until it is freed, none takes the throne.

Skip never sent any students to jail,
but he did think they had a right to fail.

When no one was watching, he seized the poor dears
and bit the shrink wrap that covered their ears,

saying: *We each have a rudder but lack a sail—*
we're shipping water, but we can bail.

Shoulder your small part with a fragrant grace—
every rose petal holds the world in place.

People, like water, are cleared by motion—
wind, waves, and current sweeten the ocean.

People, like arches, are strengthened by weight
and toppled by wind unless there's some freight.

Life without grit is a knob without knurls—
if oysters had claws, there'd be no pearls.

But—when each orifice dried up or leaked,
Skip knew that he was a drip-dry antique.

Though he hates growing old, it beats dying young—
better an old song than no longer sung.

When the leaves fall, ice hones every breeze,
but one can see deeper into the trees.

ON PLAY AND COMPETITION

You might say that I have a love-hate relationship with sport. In high school, I enjoyed taking long runs with the track team, running the steps of the gymnasium when it rained, and high jumping onto a mattress. But no sooner had our track bus brought us to the opposition's stadium than my seven-league boots turned to concrete, lunch congealed in the pit of my stomach, and I had an embarrassing urge to yawn.

I was never good at track by any standards other than my own, but my meet times and heights, those that counted, were always slightly worse than in training. Coach Ernsberger pleaded in vain, "Relax, son, you're trying too hard." I could not understand how I could run my fastest without trying my hardest, or why my most earnest efforts produced mediocre times. I soon hated competition for its pain, embarrassment, and anxiety.

Nevertheless, after three years in the Army and five years in college, I took up jogging to get rid of the "Milwaukee muscle" I'd euphemistically come to call the pillow of fat that preceded the bulk of me. I ran alone as a rule, entered no races, and progressed steadily from five miles a week to twenty, occasionally running with a stopwatch but mindful of self-induced stress and its enervating effects. Generally I was happy to get my aerobic points for the week and record them on the tiny, precise charts I'd become accustomed to keeping.

I soon found, however, that reducing my waist line and "running for life insurance," as a friend of mine called his exercise, were unduly practical motives. Running became, by accident I guess, sheer fun, and when it did, I was hooked as securely as any addict. Withdrawal symptoms usually began on the second rainy day. I found myself agreeing wholeheartedly with George Sheehan that "when we expose play to the function of promoting fitness and preventing heart attacks, we change its gold to dross."

Word of my new athletic endeavors spread across the campus where I taught, and I was invited to join a group that played volleyball on Tuesday nights. Some of the men had been playing together for twenty years, so I expected to meet some resentment, but my stamina and height helped me to gain the respect of the group, and in a few weeks I felt like a veteran. Typically the group would play two hours of three-, four-, five-, or six-man volleyball depending on how many showed up on a given night. If the first game ended in a lopsided score, one or more players would voluntarily switch sides to even matters up. Score was carefully kept and competition was keen, but I never saw a winner gloat, though there was much good-natured joking, and losers were seldom on a losing side for more than two or three games. If a serve or spike landed near a line, the majority ruled; if there was no majority, the ball was replayed.

Hitting a service ace, spiking, blocking, and even setting were more fun than jogging, though I loved the runner's high. On the other hand, running up the face of the dike on the cross-country course was not as bad as hitting a teammate's good set into the net. Nevertheless, competition, I decided after all, was great fun. When I was put in charge of a departmental lecture series, I deliberately scheduled all talks for Wednesday or Thursday to keep Tuesdays free for "v-ball."

Shortly after I began playing, I started hearing about the group's traditional dominance of the school's intramural volleyball tournament held each April. The Senile Setters, as the group called itself in the competition, had won just about every tournament ever held, and it had never finished worse than fourth. I promised myself I was not going to let a two-week tournament spoil my Tuesday-night volleyball fun. I had seen the finals of the softball and touch-football intramural tournaments the year before, and I knew from the bloody lips and torn shirts how intensely some of the fraternities played. A few days before the volleyball competition started, I caught myself daydreaming of an opposing team consisting of six students who could leap like Rudolf Nureyev and hit an overhand smash like Jimmy Connors. Furthermore most of these athletic paragons had failed my English composition course.

As the tournament turned out, the Senile Setters won with relative ease, and, for the greater part, the losers were sporting young gentlemen. I suspected that most teams we'd played resigned themselves to losing like the College All Stars, submissive before their almost certain defeat at the hands of the NFL champions. Perhaps the game of volleyball itself nullifies most hostile feeling. Since there is no body contact between the teams, most anger is channeled within or directed at the referees, but if the officials are knowledgeable, firm, and consistent, there is seldom an argument.

Knowing of my jogging and volleyball play, an acquaintance of mine asked me shortly after the tournament if I'd like to play tennis. Though I'd never enjoyed tennis very much, I accepted his invitation with some reluctance and apologies for my poor game. Blitzed, 6-2, 6-2, 6-0, and my dislike for a sport having turned to hate as I became a trophy, I turned again to the question of whether play and competition aren't a lethal mixture. A week before my tennis match, I'd watched my son's YMCA basketball team throw elbows and tantrums despite technical fouls in an obsessive concern for a "W" in some soon-forgotten record book. The boys, I thought, cared too much for the things of this world. I began to understand what sport critics like Jack Scott and George Leonard were talking about: grace, skill, and cooperation counted for much more than winning. As Leonard put it, "Out of a lifetime of sport's spectating, the moments that live for us are pure dance. We may forget league standings and final scores and even who won, but we can never forget certain dance-like movements." Who needs, I asked myself, what Olympic swimmer Don Schollander called "pushing through the pain barrier into real agony"? Who needs the sort of voluntary humiliation I'd subjected myself to in that tennis match? It wasn't that I wanted to win that match; I just did not want to lose, even if losing is a fine preparation for reality. I was not willing to die or kill to be a winner.

When I asked a friend in psychology about what I considered the problem of competition, he led me to a study on the value of play. Jerome Bruner had conducted an experiment in which five groups of children between the ages of three and five were tested to see which group could learn a task best. The problem confronting the children was the retrieval of a prize from a box out of their reach. The only tools available were two sticks and a clamp. The results of the experiment were interesting: forty-one percent of the children who observed adults clamping two sticks and retrieving prizes were successful. Forty percent who were allowed to play with the three tools, but who received no instruction or observation of adults, successfully retrieved a prize. The three other groups which had varying degrees of practice and observation had a twenty percent or less success rate.

After reading Bruner's account, I was more convinced of the value of play, but I wished he had introduced the element of competition. I had visions of four-year-olds splintering sticks over their tiny knees and flinging C-clamps in their frustrated attempts to whip their opposition and get their prizes. I remembered a story I'd heard as an undergraduate in a physics class of Albert Einstein as a sixteen-year old playfully imagining himself with a mirror in his hand traveling through space at the speed of light. At such a speed, he reasoned, he would not be visible in the mirror because the light reflected off his face could not catch up with the mirror. From Einstein's imaginative play came the Special Theory of Relativity.

With Einstein's mirror and Newton's apple in mind, I thought perhaps scientists would do well to keep a childlike attitude toward all their work. In fact, I learned that Erik Erikson had found in a thirty-year follow-up of people, who had been studied as children, those subjects who had the most interesting and fulfilling lives were those who had managed to keep a sense of playfulness at the center of things. As Karl Menninger put it, mentally healthy people play and take their play seriously. Those who fail at play, I thought, might turn out like the play-deprived monkeys at the University of Wisconsin Primate Research Center: incompetent in virtually every aspect of monkey social activity, sexually inept, aggressive to the extent that they will attack helpless infants or dominant males they have no chance of defeating, or self-aggressive to the point they will rend their own skin and muscle to the bone.

A philosophy teacher next suggested that I read a classic study of play: Johan Huizinga's *Homo Ludens*. Unfortunately for my purposes, however, Huizinga is more interested in man playing than man competing. Competition, he admits, does serve to give proof of superiority, but the passion to win sometimes threatens the levity proper to a game. A competitor, Huizinga believes, desires first "to excel others, to be first and honored for that." Only secondarily is his motive "a desire for power or a will to dominate." The faces I had observed at my son's YMCA basketball game seemed to contradict the philosopher: those faces had not been seeking any laurel crowns. Huizinga does grant that the systematization and regimentation of modern sport have damaged its pure play quality, its spontaneity and carelessness, but the all-out condemnation of competition I was looking for was absent.

Next, a Lutheran minister suggested Hugo Rahner, author of *Man at Play*. This Jesuit writer espouses the theology of play because earthly play is an anticipation of heavenly joy. Only at play can there be a harmony between body and soul; only one capable of play can find the crucial balance between buffoonery and boorishness. Rahner warns that one should never lose oneself in work or play, but like Huizinga, his concerns are much loftier than mine, and he does not distinguish between competition and play.

Unaided, I found a book in the library by M.J. Ellis that discusses why men play. In coming to his own answer, Ellis relates how others have answered the question: play is the mandatory release of surplus energy; it is a preparation for adulthood; it is the instinctive recapitulation of man's development; it is a way of compensating for our working lives; it is a cathartic response after unpleasantness; it demonstrates our competence and volition; or it is a way of avoiding boredom and seeking stimuli. The last explanation, man plays because he naturally seeks pleasure and interesting alternatives to his work, is most strongly supported by scientific research, Ellis asserts. Although the relationship between play and competition still was not clarified for me, I had gained a broader view of the subject.

I began then to compile my own argument against competition, and I turned to the writers who had influenced me to run regularly. Kenneth Cooper, author of *Aerobics* and my personal "guru," skirts the issue of competition in his first book despite his insistence on recording times and distances. As long as one gets thirty aerobic points weekly, Cooper doesn't care whether they are obtained jumping rope in the bedroom or swimming competitive time trials. Thaddeus Kostrubala, psychoanalyst and author of *The Joy of Running*, however, attacks Cooper's charts and point system as destructive because they orient the runner away from his inner self and focus his mind on an artificial target. Kostrubala complains of the "cultural net of competition, tension, false values, and despair." He recommends running to achieve a sort of mystical experience, to touch another level of one's consciousness, to "resonate with one's biological heritage." Fred Rohe, author of *The Zen of Running*, agrees: "You can be victimized by your imagination if you imagine yourself astonishing your world with your progress and prowess. This mechanism is called ego. . . ." Similarly, Joe Henderson, editor of *Runner's World*, realized after his college competitive days were finished that his "running had to be more like play and less like the work it had been before. . . . The biggest victory," Henderson believes, "is to want and to be able to run each new day."

The longer I looked, however, the less I was convinced by these amicable writers because competition is the lifeblood of nature, commerce, and politics, not to mention professional sports. Arguments for non-competitive games like Infinity Volleyball, in which the ball is volleyed indefinitely to the chanting of participants and in which both sides share the final score, sounded to me like "transcendent silliness, dime-store Marxism, and counterculture blather," as William Bennett observed. I imagined such a game as an endless theatrical rehearsal, or a game of poker without any stakes.

George Sheehan, who set a world record for the mile for men over fifty, was more convincing. He speaks of the agony and fear of athletic rivalry, yet argues that competition is essential. His strongest argument is taken from the poet Robinson Jeffers: "In pleasant ease and security how soon the soul of man begins to die." As a tenured teacher, I knew all about pleasant ease. But it was James Michener, more than Sheehan or Jeffers who helped me finally settle the question of whether competition was for me. In Michener's *Sports in America* he writes:

> I find competition to be the rule of nature, tension to be the structure of the universe. I believe that normal competition is good for a human being, and I am sure that flight from it hastens death. I am prepared to acknowledge every charge against fanatical competition, or senselessly prolonged tension, and I would not foist either upon young people. But I would not wish to avoid reasonable competition, for I like a world in which men and women test themselves against others or against abstract ideals....

Armed with Michener's reassuring credo, I signed up for an intramural five-mile race, reminding myself that no horse ever ran himself to death without a mad jockey aboard. I was determined to run, but my competition was myself: I wanted only to finish strongly in a time near my personal best and maybe learn something about myself along the way. I'd traveled a long distance from my high school coach's idea that any race you can walk away from is a lousy one. I promised myself that if I did improve my best previous time I would not regard this race as a criticism of every race run at a slower rate. I was prepared, in short, to accept what I was.

I started dead last in the field of twenty, but moved up to nineteenth when the fellow in front of me stopped to retie his shoes. He obviously had the same attitude as I had toward racing or at least I thought so until he passed me. I was content to run my own race, however, staying in plodding fashion about ten yards behind the next to the last man until we reached the 4.5 mile marker. At that point I realized from the dry, wheezing gasps I heard that the man in front of me was exhausted; he'd been running at his upper limit since he'd tied his shoes, and I'd let him pace me. I sensed I could pass him, but I worried about how he'd feel. Shouldn't we finish holding hands? No, I decided; how would I feel if I let him beat me and if I cheated myself of a good performance? Finishing last was a dreary prospect; I could run for substance and self-development another day. I charged through the last quarter mile finishing next to the last, and though my time was not a personal best, I was a happy man.

I shook hands with the man I'd beaten who said, "You should have passed me earlier." I replied, "I didn't know what I had." I was sorry he'd finished last, but he said he was happy to finish; he'd never run that far before. My guilt disappeared when I saw how satisfied he was. Running was more than a mere distraction for both of us, and I knew I'd done the right thing competing fiercely down the home stretch.

George Orwell called sports "war minus the shooting"; to others, it's a popular opiate. But finer distinctions need to be drawn. "Toughness without callousness," is the discriminating ideal William James set for sports. If the emphasis is a rational one, on processes more than outcome, then sport, or more specifically competition, deserves to be an integral part of human society. The Old Testament suggests such a rational integration, "The people sat down to eat and drink and rose up to play." But playing for nothing is as unrewarding as working for nothing. "Without danger," the wise man said, "the game grows cold."

A Love Poem
For Ingrid

The plural of grass is lea,
for rain it's sea,
and God is three,
but the plural of three is me.

A Racial Autobiography

I n Clyde Edgerton's novel *Raney*, Charles and Uncle Nate get into an argument at a family Christmas dinner about the propriety of interracial marriages.

   "'Do you see any difference between a rabbit and a coon?' says Uncle Nate....

   'Yes—but not between a black rabbit and a white rabbit,' says Charles, 'and that's the *real* issue.'"

As I stopped reading, my question to a class of college freshmen was, "Who has the better analogy, Charles or Nate?" After waiting the recommended fourteen seconds for a response, I asked a second question that I thought might evoke more than silence since several students in this class were from Aiken, SC where the breeding of racehorses is a cash crop. "If a black horse and a white horse are scheduled to race on a muddy track, is color something you consider before placing a bet?" Finally a middle-aged exchange student from Nigeria volunteered, "I don't believe color is relevant here, sir. I'd check the racing form to see which horse had the better record on a slow track." I had a feeling that the rest of the class thought I had planted this fellow's answer; it was precisely what I had been fishing for. In my experience, people are as reluctant to speak about race, even in the modern multicultural classroom, as they are sex and God. Frankly, race makes me uneasy as well, but I am determined to examine it here before my computer, my priest.

After class I wondered where I had obtained my own ideas about race, for I had no formal training in anthropology beyond reading Margaret Mead and a few of her colleagues. As our family's historian, I turned first to the letters that I had inherited from a genealogy-obsessed aunt. In a sense, the family ghosts were her children, for she never married or had children in the conventional sense. In her tenderly annotated files, I found a letter written by a distant relation who lived in western Pennsylvania and apparently dodged the draft during the Civil War. In a letter dated April 17, 1863, Barney Eisiminger wrote his brother John, who would soon see action at Vicksburg: "Dear brother, I was sorry to hear that you was in the army for I think that it is a hard place to live and I don't know what possessed you to go. You said that you felt it your duty to go and fight for your liberty but I think that you are fitting for the nigger and before I would fight for the nigger I would stay at home...." What my ancestor apparently did not know was that the black man also was fighting for his liberty. Some 32,000, or 18% of the black men who fought in the war, died in that noble effort.

Clearly our family has a racist skeleton in the closet, but it isn't the sort of thing that is passed along in one's genes, so I began to search closer to home—namely Columbus, Georgia. South Georgia isn't where I entered the world; it's where my mother was born, and it's where she and I spent several of the war years while my father was overseas. In the early and mid-40s, Columbus was part of the "parallel universe" that was nicknamed "Jim Crow." A black man there could buy a suit in a men's store but not try it on. If he wanted to buy shoes for his children, who were not permitted in the store, he had to bring a cardboard cutout of their feet to insert in the shoes. He could buy a meal in some white restaurants but not sit down inside to eat it—what Harry Golden called "the vertical integration plan." A six-foot fence between the black and white sections of the municipal cemetery was not torn down until the late 60s. It's what might be termed the "horizontal integration plan," for anyone standing up here was suspect. Columbus boasted separate but far from equal restrooms, drinking fountains, motels, schools, libraries, hospitals (in Atlanta the white hospital was called Grady Memorial; the black, Degrady's), theater sections, dance floors, churches, Pullman cars, taxis, bomb shelters, and Bibles. I didn't learn about the Bibles until much later, but the city courtroom had one Bible for black witnesses and another for whites. Since God was evidently white, He was assumed to take offense at blacks swearing on a white Bible and vice versa even though the texts of both had the imprimatur of King James. As far back as the seventeenth century, whites debated whether blacks would turn white at the Resurrection. It was agreed that they could go to heaven but not the white man's schools; it just wasn't clear what color they'd be when they arrived.

In a related but more personal vein, I recall that black delivery boys always brought their drugs and groceries to my grandparents' back door, but since there were no white delivery boys in the neighborhood, I never thought much of it until one made the mistake of coming to the front door where he received a tongue-lashing from my grandfather. Once when my mother and I were invited to eat at my grandparents' home, I sat down in the kitchen uninvited next to Sarah, my grandmother's black cook. Sarah had occasionally slipped me a moon pie fragment, so I thought for once I would eat with her rather than the rest of the family in the dining room just a few steps away. Sarah's response, however, startled me: "If I can't sit down out there, you can't sit down in here." I left the kitchen hurt by the rebuff and joined my mother who from the look on her face had heard the conversation. It took me quite a while to recognize the courage it required for Sarah to speak to a six-year-old the way she had; she could have lost her job. A decade earlier, she might have been lynched; some three thousand were. In Georgia after 1893, the penalty for lynchers was four years in jail. Presumably before that, one could lynch with impunity.

It's a small wonder Sarah wasn't reprimanded because my grandfather was an avowed segregationist who once told me, "Every white man should have his own nigger." Grandfather's "nigger" was named Jesse who with his wife lived in a "shotgun shack" on a red-clay farm owned by my grandfather. When the aging Jesse came to weed my grandmother's flower garden as he did every Wednesday, Sarah "helped him a plate" which he ate on his lap under a pecan tree in the back yard. Jesse grew most every thing my grandparents ate, and his wife put up the produce in Mason jars before freezers became common. Alas, Jesse was an alcoholic, and his wife was sporadically deranged. One Christmas my grandfather gave his hired man a bottle of Four Roses bourbon. As he drove off on his mule-drawn wagon, Jesse said, "I'm goin' home to let these roses bloom." Arriving drunk as he did many nights, his wife, her patience exhausted, split his skull with a meat cleaver. If Jesse had a last name, it was never used in my presence, and he probably could not have written it if he'd owned a pen or pencil. The poor fellow paid my grandfather a dime to dial a telephone number because he didn't know his numbers either.

On my paternal grandparents' side there wasn't much influence either way since they lived in East St. Louis, and we seldom visited due to the gasoline rationing occasioned by the war. My father, however, had a strong influence on my budding racial attitudes especially when he was made commander of an all-black engineer combat battalion. At Ft. Benning and then later at Camp Gordon (both in Georgia), I took great pride in my father and the men he commanded. Before going overseas, I saluted from the grandstand as my father's men passed proudly in review. Despite my best efforts, when a brass band plays a Sousa march today, the tears begin to roll. During the war, I recall gazing in disbelief at a picture in *Life* of some German POWs cavorting in a Mississippi swimming pool. In Columbus, they drained the whites-only pool every time a black kid crawled over the fence and went for a dip.

When my father returned home, he was most proud of the fact that he had not lost one of his 660 men in combat. When I pressed him on that statistic years later, he admitted that, in fact, four of his men had died: one drinking Sterno had poisoned himself, another cleaning his uniform with gasoline just prior to returning to the States had caught fire and died of the burns, and two of his men had been executed. It wasn't until 1995, however, that he told me of Cpl. Robert Pearson and Pvt. Parson Jones who had raped an eight-month pregnant British woman before going to the front. (Though I was the first person he'd told of the rape and hanging in fifty years, he recalled everything except the men's serial numbers.) Ultimately, the jury found the two guilty despite their protests that the sex was consensual. The woman's multiple bruises convinced the jury otherwise. Dad said that when he received news of the men's death he called the three companies of the 1698th together, climbed on the hood of a jeep, and lectured the men about what the dire consequences of rape would be whether the victim was friend or foe. Rape, he said, would never be a weapon in his battalion's arsenal as long as he was in charge. Some of the black warrant officers objected to the severity of the men's sentence, but that was in the hands of a foreign civilian court, and the majority of the men realized that.

Though one of Dad's warrant officers did write Eleanor Roosevelt complaining that the twenty-six bars in Chard, England were segregated, a colonel sent from Washington pronounced Dad blameless and the segregated bars a good thing because when they had been integrated, interracial fights were commonplace. Once the 1698th reached France and began to push east, the white officers and black enlisted men functioned and fought well together. After Germany surrendered and the 1698th was allotted some German POWs to help build "cigarette camps" in France, Dad often saw his own men step off the wooden sidewalks into the mud to allow approaching POWs to pass unimpeded. Even though back in Mississippi, some old slave chains had been donated to a wartime scrap-metal drive, the "mind-forged shackles" of the slaves' descendants were not so easy to shake loose. In the post-war era, American Jews sometimes advised blacks, "Don't wait for people to love you." Smart as that is, it's very difficult to accomplish without the self-confidence born of a first-rate education.

After the war, the Army sent my father to Ft. Hamilton in Brooklyn where he commuted to New York University in Manhattan where he worked on his masters. It was at "Ft. Ham" that I made my first black friend, the son of an engineer officer just like myself. Jerry Maxwell and I loved to roller skate, and most every afternoon we met on the one hill in the project where we lived, locked arms with several of our peers, and sped down hill like a Chinese dragon on New Years. In the winter, we sledded on the golf course hills of Prospect Park. Since Jerry was a trusted latchkey child, we were able to listen to any station on the radio after school that we wanted in his parents' apartment. Here I tasted the forbidden fruits of Ray Charles, Chuck Berry, and The Platters for the first time. Listening to baseball broadcasts with Jerry almost turned me from a St. Louis Cardinal fan to a Dodger fan because my black friend dearly loved Jackie Robinson. I did too except when the Bums played the Redbirds! When my bike was stolen from the basement of our apartment building, Jerry was mentioned as a suspect, but I knew my friend had a better bike than I had and didn't need another, especially one he couldn't ride in my presence.

Our bond, however, was sealed one summer day when my mother sent me to the park with my two younger sisters with strict orders to "watch out for the girls." Jerry had joined us on the swings when without warning a half dozen teenaged boys with stockings over their faces came screaming out of the bushes swinging nylons filled with colored chalk dust. It could have been an outtake from *Clockwork Orange*. Jerry and I placed ourselves in harm's way and got thoroughly pummeled in a multicolored and multicultural way. The boys were screaming something about the two of us on their "turf," but their voices were so muffled by the stockings, I never fully understood their anger. The girls were unharmed, and their screams probably saved the day when the building's super stuck his head out of the basement door, shook a coal shovel overhead, and swore at the masked gang. Off they went in a cloud of chalk dust as rapidly as they had appeared.

At PS 201, the public school I was attending ("Stalag 201" I called it because it was surrounded by a ten-foot, barbed-wire fence), Jerry and I heard rumors of our assailants' identities, but we were never able to confirm the stories mainly because we didn't have the courage to press the matter to a head. Just what would we do if we found them? Most of the older boys at this formidable institution carried a switchblade in a zippered pocket of their black-leather jackets à la *Blackboard Jungle*. The upshot was, the assault went unavenged, the motives undiscovered.

Paradoxically some of our best times together were spent at the Stalag. Jerry and I had an hour together every Wednesday afternoon because we were the only two Protestant kids in the seventh grade. While the Catholic kids went to confirmation classes at the church down the block, Jerry and I sat in a study hall together and did our homework while Mrs. Munnelly graded papers. He helped me with math; I helped him with English. When my father finished his work at NYU, however, I said goodbye to Jerry same as I bid farewell to dozens of friends over the years I haven't seen him since. The Army made sure that no friend I made between the ages of one and eighteen was known to me longer than three years.

In 1955, the family moved back to Columbus, Georgia where Dad began jump-school training at Ft. Benning prior to being sent to Korea. It was here that I came under the benign influence of the Reverend Robert McNeil, the minister at the First Presbyterian Church. Reverend Bob in the mid 50s stirred his congregation's passions into a maelstrom when he proposed that since the church was on the edge of a black neighborhood it should invite blacks to worship and open the Sunday School building during the week as a daycare center for the many working single mothers (both black and white) in the downtown area. This led to a conclave of the church deacons at which Reverend Bob was fired. The story made the pages of *Look* and the *Atlanta Constitution*, but the deacons' decision was final. Nevertheless, he left a lasting mark on me and many others who felt that the church's thunder had lost its lightning.

The Columbus school system was segregated while I was a pupil there, but after high school and a quarter at Georgia Tech, I impulsively joined the Army and promptly took a bus ride to Ft. Jackson, SC to start eight weeks of basic training. It was one of the most memorable trips I have ever taken. When a racially mixed group of thirty teenaged boys from the Atlanta area boarded a bus in the dark, every one of us was scared and solitary. But as conversation spread during the three-hour trip, white and black came together like the integrated keys of a piano despite the tone-deaf efforts of Jim Crow. Once we had our heads shaved and donned baggy fatigues, we were a unit as solid as the Confederate Memorial on Stone Mountain that we passed on the way to Columbia. After learning close-order drill, qualifying on the rifle range, surviving the tear-gas chamber, and crawling under barbed wire as live rounds whistled overhead, we were "brothers." Then in its wisdom, the Army broke us up. Unfortunately, the intelligence unit in West Germany, where I spent the great majority of my three and a half years in the Army, never achieved the *esprit de corps* our basic company had. The handful of blacks in our company, however, never had it so good because to German women, African-American men were an exotic, desirable species. Indeed, several of them married a *Fräulein* before returning to the States.

When I returned in 1963, I was married as well, and our first child was on the way. We decided to move to Columbus because Mother's youngest brother had generously lined up a bank job for my wife and a loan-company job for me. Like several family members, Uncle Jim was a paradoxical mixture of racial attitudes: on one hand he treated Stewart, the black foreman of his small construction company, like the heir he did not have. This kindness lasted for twenty years until my uncle caught Stewart embezzling. On the other hand, Jim was a segregationist like his father. He would occasionally invite my wife and me up to his lake cabin; then, after furtively glancing left and right, he'd tell us the latest racist jokes as he basted the ribs. About the time the Freedom Riders in Mississippi were making headlines, Jim told his assembled audience that, "A nigra had been dredged from a lake in Mississippi wrapped in chains. I reckon," Jim chuckled, "he stole more chain than he could escape with." He followed this gruesome tale with a laugh so hearty he never noticed that he was the only one laughing, and this included his wife.

While my wife was urging poor blacks to join her bank's Christmas Club (which paid no interest), I was working part-time in a rather sleazy loan office. In the late afternoon (that's why I was called a "sundowner"), I reported to the Broadway office, telephoned the mostly black clientele, and asked them if they wanted to take out another loan just before Christmas. Selling debt was the most dispiriting work I have ever performed. After a couple weeks, I noticed that my boss was hovering in my vicinity eavesdropping on the calls I was placing. He had already warned me that I needed a harder sell. Finally, he approached my desk, obviously exasperated, and said, "Is the glorification of the Negro now accepted? Listen, Skip, as long as I'm paying the phone bills, don't ever call a nigger 'mister.'" Without even thinking about it, I had asked to speak with "Mr. Johnson" unaware that I was violating company policy. In the 1940s, blacks had been lynched for not calling a white man "Mister," as he reminded me. "Have the Kennedys brought us to the point that every nigger now deserves the same title of respect enjoyed by white men?" he wondered aloud walking back to his desk. On November 22, 1963, a few hours after President Kennedy was assassinated, I walked into the office and found half a dozen re-po men and secretaries still rejoicing over the news. When I realized what was going on, I quit.

Shortly after Ingrid, my new German bride, and I arrived in Columbus, we decided that she needed to apply for her American driver's license. At the first opportunity, I drove her to the Department of Motor Vehicles, let her out, and went in search of a place to park. Meanwhile Ingrid entered the lobby and began reading her way through the thicket of crudely made signs. One sign beside some boxes of forms instructed those renewing licenses to fill out a white form and first-time applicants like my wife to fill out a pink form. When she was finished, she looked up and saw over one door leading into the office a sign reading "White" and over another door a sign reading "Colored." Having just filled out the "colored" form, Ingrid entered the door labeled "Colored." After standing in line a while, she noticed that the elderly black man in front of her was holding a white form, so in her best English she politely informed him that he was in the wrong line. The gentleman said in a thick Georgia drawl, "You ain't from these parts, now, is you, Missy?"

One hero I had in the racial "wars" of the 60s was my Aunt Clarice. Clarice was teaching first grade just north of Columbus in the tiny community of Waverly Hall. Civil Rights legislation had just recently been signed, and schools everywhere in the South were reluctantly integrating. At Columbus College (now Columbus State University) where I started back to school in 1963 after completing my military service, the first black student entered the following year. In the district where my aunt taught, school officials decided that they would test all the black applicants and admit only the two brightest in the first year. Both of these terrified children landed in Clarice's classroom. For a while the white and black kids got along fine, but soon the white parents found out who their children were sitting beside, and the class began to fragment as the kids brought their parents' racial philosophies to school. My aunt knew that she was in for a long school year, but she really had no ulterior racial motive when she praised one of the black children's homework papers as "a model of neatness that the rest of you might strive for." Word got around because the next day an infuriated parent, whose son was not even in Clarice's class, showed up after school and said, "How dare you use a nigger's work as a model for white children!" The parent then took his case to the school principal and the district superintendent. Though my aunt had served ten unblemished years as a teacher in Harris County, she was informed that she would not be re-hired even though at the time she was the only teacher in the school with a four-year degree. The principal of the local high school offered her a job teaching home economics, but on appeal to the state board of education, probably with a federal howitzer pointing at its head, Clarice won back her job as a first-grade teacher at Waverly Hall. Twenty years later Clarice told me that the young black man she'd taught was working as a private flight instructor and the woman whose work Clarice had praised was a medical technician at Emory Hospital in Atlanta. Clearly these two had not waited for anyone to love them.

After I finished my master's degree at Auburn in 1968, I was offered a job at Clemson University in South Carolina as an instructor in English. Looking at some maps of the campus on an orientation tour, I realized that Martin Hall, the building where I would be teaching, is located near the spot where John C. Calhoun's slave quarters had stood a century earlier. Calhoun was the man who said, "Show me a nigger who can do a problem in Euclid or parse a Greek verb, and I'll admit he's a human being." I don't suppose that it ever occurred to the former vice president of the United States that his mother and grandmothers probably could not parse a Greek verb either. In his defense, however, it's quite likely that Calhoun acquired his self-taught prejudice reading Hegel, Kant, Jefferson, and other luminaries of the Enlightenment. Just a few yards away from the old Calhoun family mansion stands Tillman Hall named after Benjamin "Pitchfork" Tillman, a former governor of South Carolina, who once said, "The black man must remain subordinate or be exterminated" presumably on the tines of a pitchfork. On at least one occasion while he was in office, Tillman aided and abetted a mob bent on lynching a black man even though the victim had declared the suspect was not the man who raped her. A few yards in another direction from the Calhoun home is the Strom Thurmond Institute building named for another former governor and a graduate of Clemson. Much like Gov. George Wallace in Alabama, however, Thurmond underwent a dramatic and apparently sincere transformation of racial attitudes. Early in his career as the leader of the Dixiecrat Party, Thurmond declared, "There's not enough troops in the Army to break down segregation and admit the Negro into our homes, our eating places, our swimming pools, and our theaters." Years later he said, "It seems to me that we ought to give this black man a chance. Years ago, minorities didn't have a chance." Of course, one reason opportunities were scarce for people of color, including his own mixed-race daughter, was obstructionist legislators like Thurmond.

Despite the bad karma created by the ghosts of Calhoun and Tillman, Clemson had admitted its first black student, Harvey Gantt, just five years before I arrived. After graduating from Clemson and MIT, Gantt became a successful architect, mayor of Charlotte, NC, and candidate for the US Senate. On a return visit to Clemson in the mid-90s, I heard Mr. Gantt tell an audience of over a thousand, "Thirty years ago, Clemson was a large salt shaker with a single fleck of pepper, and that was me. Tonight it is a pleasure to look out over this salt-and-pepper audience. There has been progress!" Well, racial progress in South Carolina is a relative term as I soon learned thanks to Dean Howard Hunter.

For some reason, Dean Hunter, Clemson's dean of Liberal Arts, took a personal interest in me, and shortly after we arrived, my wife and I were invited to dinner. But as soon as I entered the dean's lovely home, I felt like I was back in my grandparents' home in Columbus: a black cook in the kitchen was finishing preparations for our meal. After she served us, she closed the door and shutters between the kitchen and the dining room with a clatter, I thought, of protest. As we ate, I was uncomfortably aware that Mrs. Phillips, the cook, was eating on the other side of the louvered shutters, and I felt the same guilty urge to sit down beside her so that the clink of her silverware would not be quite so deafening.

The summer after our children's college graduation, I drove the family down to Columbus for a visit with, among others, my grandfather who was now nearly deaf and living in a retirement home. We stayed with one of my cousins who has two children herself. One afternoon the adults and the four children drove over to the retirement home to "set a spell," as my grandfather liked to say. At some point, one of my cousin's kids raised the topic of busing, and my grandfather snorted, "Niggers!" When all the kids laughed, he said it again, which evoked more laughter. It quickly became a game for the old man who could barely hear the laughter he evoked. What he failed to understand was that the kids were laughing, not at the offensive word, but at him, the dinosaur in the tar pit. All four of these kids were going or had gone to school with black children and had accepted the rainbow reality of a diverse culture. They had never known times like 1948 when, for example, the West Memphis, Arkansas school district spent $145 per year for each white student enrolled and $20 per year for each black.

The easiest part of desegregation for me was the friendships I developed in my life starting with Jerry Maxwell and continuing with several black colleagues from across the campus at Clemson. This socialization was epitomized, not by the department in which I worked for thirty years which continues to have problems retaining black faculty at the higher ranks, but by the interracial softball team that I played on for almost as long. There's something about tossing a ball back and forth that allows men of all races and ages to open up with each other. Often we would straggle sullenly on to the field, but as soon as the pepper game started, spirits rose and the banter began. Some of the closest friendships I have ever made with members of the human race have been made on a softball diamond. Occasionally on weekends, we would travel to tournaments across the state, and while nerves would occasionally frazzle in making travel or sleeping assignments, on the field it was sweetness and light.

Skin color is to me a biological irrelevance. If genetic engineering could make the next generation of Americans the same shade of brown, I'm convinced the change would be beneficial.

Along the way, we had better make all noses the same width and all hair uniformly curly, or people are likely to find something other than skin color to fight over. As my uncle in the Lions Club likes to point out to potential cornea donors, organs, bones, bone marrow, blood, and skin are all transplantable across racial lines. In the year 2006, about 70% of the world's population is non-white and non-Christian. By 2050, it is estimated that half of the American population will consist of "minorities." Like global warming, the handwriting is writ large on the wall.

Finally with regard to racial harmony, America today reminds me of the family of three who needed a new car. Problem was that while they had agreed on the model and make, the vehicle's color was unresolved: the wife wanted yellow, the husband blue, and their adolescent son wanted red. An ombudsman suggested white because when white light is passed through a prism, yellow, blue, and red are all visible. The family compromised and chose black.

Thy Will Be Done

Child of Auschwitz,
Mina was taught to pray
in the boxcar
that delivered her.

Nights, she beseeched the dark,
and days, the condensation trails
that diced the blue
beyond the smoke she breathed.

Some Baptists have concluded
Jehovah does not answer
the prayer of a Jew.
Of course He did.
He said, "No."
But while many were not listening,
Mina was.

She figured His cargo planes
and bombers were busy—
mercy temporarily snarled
by anger
and logistical nightmares.

She weeps for His inability
to set things right,
forgives Him for His failure,
and thanks Him
for the little strength
she has left—
He could have left her a void.

THE LANGUAGE OF RACE

I broached the subject of race one day in a class of college juniors and seniors by telling the story of Stephen Biko's confrontation with a South African judge. As recorded in Richard Attenborough's 1987 film *Cry Freedom*, the white judge asked the black African activist, "You people look brown to me. Why do you call yourselves black?" Answered Biko, "You people look pink to me. Why do you call yourselves white?"

After the laughter subsided, I explained that in the time of apartheid there were nine recognized racial categories in South Africa, and by law everyone was at birth placed in one of these pigeon holes. Since one's race determined where one could live and work, there were frequent applications to the government to change one's original designation. Indeed, in 1985, the state permitted 506 "coloreds" to become "white," but no "whites" became "black," and no "blacks" became "white."

I then told the class to forget what Biko had said about pink and to place a naked forearm, palm down, across a piece of white paper. "Now, scrutinize the color of your skin," I said passing around several sheets of black construction paper to remind them what black looked like. "Is your arm pink, white, black, or brown?" I inquired. The class of thirty, which had three African Americans and a young woman from Taiwan peppering the majority from the American Southeast, agreed that "brown" was the one word that best described their skin color. "Beige, tan, toast, snuff, sepia, chocolate, and buff," I unilaterally declared, were to be considered synonyms for "brown" in this exercise. No one objected. To be sure, some of the "browns" were darker than others, but no one was "black," and no one was even close to "white," but then it was late April in South Carolina. For 2005, it was a rare moment of agreement in a multicultural classroom.

At this point I unstabled one of my favorite classroom war horses. I said, "Imagine that all six billion of us are in a single file, in short-sleeved shirts, heads covered with paper bags, and arranged from the most nigrescent Nubian to the fairest Finn. Flying overhead in a helicopter, how confident do you think you would be saying where one 'race' began and another ended?" Judging from the show of hands, most of us agreed we would not be confident given the fact that the skin tones of the three African-Americans and the Asian student were identical to or lighter than some of the suntanned Caucasians seated beside them. Understandably, a few of the students, both light and dark, refused to raise a hand, for I was challenging something that lay very deep, and they weren't about to give it up after a ten-minute demonstration and lecture.

Suddenly a hand in the back row shot up, "Dr. E, why do some people call whites 'Caucasians'?" He had me. I knew the word had some connection to the mountain range in what is today Asian Georgia, but how it ever came to describe most Europeans and Americans, I confessed I did not know.

Back in the office, I found a superb essay on the net by the late Stephen Jay Gould that placed the blame squarely at the feet of Johann Blumenbach, a German social scientist who never traveled outside of Europe and rarely traveled within it. In the late eighteenth century in the generation following Linnaeus, Blumenbach was one of the finest taxonomic anthropologists in the world. In the collection of skulls gathered by field workers from the University of Göttingen, where Blumenbach taught, a handful of specimens collected near Mt. Caucasus years earlier and bleached white by the sun struck Blumenbach in his words as the "most beautiful" of all the skulls in the collection. Because of this

Christian European's subjective and surely biased appreciation of a few skulls and the fact that these bones originated closest to the area between the Tigris and Euphrates Rivers (think Eden), he made what Gould calls one of the most "fateful" decisions in the history of science: he ranked the races based on the "beauty," color, and "uniformity" of the skulls. Here for the first time, a recognized authority had given the imprimatur of science to racism. Blumenbach's thinking apparently went something like this: if the Caucasians are the most beautiful race, the Asian and African must be the least beautiful. Now he had an equilateral triangle. But Linnaeus had stipulated an American race, so Blumenbach situated the Native Americans between the Caucasians and the Asians. This, however, left the triangle unbalanced in an age when classical symmetry was a virtue. (If there's any doubt, see the work of Jacques Louis David and the compositions of Haydn, both contemporaries of Blumenbach.) Searching the Göttingen collection, Blumenbach found what he concluded were examples of the Malay race, and these he placed between the Caucasians and Africans to balance his triangle. Symmetry has always exerted a powerful force on the asymmetrical especially in the file-drawer minds of classifiers like Blumenbach.

Indeed forty years earlier, Linnaeus, while he did not rank the races he described in hierarchical fashion, he was not exactly objective either. He decided that if there are

four continents ("America, Europe, Asia, and Africa"),
four humors ("choleric, sanguine, melancholic, and phlegmatic"),
four body types or postures ("erect, brawny, rigid, and relaxed"),
four governing principles ("custom, law, opinion, and caprice"),
four body coverings ("fine red [painted] lines, cloth vestments, loose garments, and grease"),
and four temperaments ("obstinate, gentle, severe, and crafty"),

there must be four primary races, each with its own distinctive color ("copper-colored, fair, sooty, and black"). [Each parenthetical listing above, incidentally, follows the order of the continents and their respective races.] In other words, if a gentleman has four jackets, four trousers, four shirts, and four pairs of shoes, it's hard to resist buying that fourth tie. In time, the whole world begins to look like a multiple of four! Invariably, however, someone like Galileo comes along and finds five of something the whole world thought there were only four of.

In the next class, I summarized the origin of "Caucasian" and told the story of Blumenbach's unfortunate decision to rank the races. Even though most historians of science agree he was not a racist, I have my doubts just as I have reservations about the objectivity of Linnaeus. I then asked the class how many still used Blumenbach's word "Caucasian" to describe themselves, and no one raised a hand. Seeing this, I said, "Take a sheet of paper and imagine that your closest friend has asked you, 'What are the races of man?' Write down the words you would use to answer. I'm interested only in the terminology; don't give me any hierarchies, and don't include your name or race." The results interested me so much that I posed the question to my other two classes.

Out of eighty students aged nineteen to thirty, fifteen refused to take my bait and answered in elegant simplicity, "the human race." The great majority, however, forty-five to be precise, resorted to the familiar color terminology—twenty said, "white," twenty said, "black," two said, "yellow," two said, "red," and one said "brown." Clearly "black" and "white" are firmly entrenched at least in American Southern usage, but the political correctness movement apparently has all but killed off "red" and "yellow" as racial designations. These two colors appear to be drawing their last breaths in "the Redskins" and "Yellow Peril," but when they expire, few will mourn their passing. While "African-American" received four votes and "Negro" got one, "brown" only polled one vote. This strikes me as a mystery of perception, a curious blindness, when so many of us are a shade of that color as I thought I had so convincingly demonstrated just days before.

World geography has seldom been the forte of the American college student, and my classes were no exception. Many confused "race" with "continent" (the "African" and "European" races), or "country" (the "Mongoloid" and "Israeli" races), or "culture" ("Hispanic" and "Native-American" races), or "region" (the "Southern" and "New England" races), or "state" (the "Texan" and "Georgian" races). A few confused "race" and "religion" (the "Christian," "Muslim," and "Jewish" races); one answered dialectally ("white folks and black folks"); one Bob Jones University transfer, I suspect, responded "fundamentally" ("Semitic, Hamitic, and Japhetic" using the adjectival forms of Noah's sons' names), and one resorted to slang ("towel heads"). I'm pleased to report that no one used the term "nigger" proving once again that this remains one of the strongest taboo words in the language even when written work is unsigned. As proof that students did not feel compelled to take this exercise too seriously, one student answered, "The races of man—Darlington, Daytona, Talladega, and Bristol."

Lest the reader think these students unsophisticated in the matter of race, permit me to tell of one more classroom experience. In William Fleming's famed humanities text, *Arts and Ideas,* now in its tenth edition, there is a section on the rise of photography in the nineteenth century. The last of five early photographs is captioned, "John Lamprey, *Front View of a Malayan Male,* 1868-1869. Royal Anthropological Institute of Great Britain and Ireland." In the accompanying text, Fleming states, "Through photography, social scientists and the general public confirmed their belief in the inferiority of non-Western cultures." When I first read this gloss of Lamprey's photograph, I wondered how in one or more black and white images any cultural inferiority could be shown much less confirmed, so I asked some sixty plus juniors and seniors to respond to the sentence quoted above in a well-reasoned and well-supported paragraph of their own. I gave them a week to think about it.

I anticipated a series of observations about how the naked Malayan is dark-skinned, short (5'1"), uncircumcised, unkempt, and thus inferior to Western males. Although two men offered that the Malayan was inferior because his penis was "underdeveloped," I was gladly mistaken about the majority. Here's a paraphrased but representative sample of what most wrote:

"I fail to see any signs of Western superiority or Eastern inferiority in Lamprey's photo. If a European were stripped naked, handed half of a curtain rod, and placed beside this Malayan male, he would doubtless appear vulnerable."

"This poor man reminds me of a butterfly pinned in a shadow box for the delectation of voyeuristic Europeans. But since the butterfly is capable of flight and the viewer isn't, who's inferior to whom?"

"The author of our text should have explained that Lamprey's image is an ugly objectification of a complex human being and may lead the viewer to an unjustified sense of dominance."

"Lamprey's photo neither enhances nor down-plays this man's essential humanity; it merely records the truth of his appearance on a given day."

"Since Victorian-era Westerners were covered in clothing from head to toe, Lamprey's photograph may indeed have said to many that this man is subhuman. Fleming should have said that the model was paid to pose naked and was under the impression that the work was scientific."

"In all likelihood, this Malayan male was stripped, propped, posed, and photographed in a way to capture what European audiences, shaped by incipient notions of Social Darwinism, would have considered his 'simple barbarism.' Lamprey should be ashamed of himself."

Given the fact that the "experts" have at various times identified as many as sixty-three "races" and distinguished them based on a comparison of finger-whorl patterns, hair shapes in cross section, tooth shapes, and ear-wax compositions, it is not surprising that there is massive confusion when it comes to race. My position has long been, if all of us are 99.9999% genetically alike and have been for 3.93 of the 4.0 million years we've shared the planet, why bother to make racial distinctions, especially after the 5,000 years of racial strife we have a record of that got us nowhere?

To illustrate the futility of a hollow classification system, recall that in the seventh and eighth centuries, England was torn over the relative superiority of the Frisians, Jutes, Angles, and Saxons, all of whom incidentally spoke a dialect of Low German and could therefore understand each other. This internal conflict ended about the time the Normans invaded, and the country was torn all over again. As soon as speakers of Old English and those of Norman French began speaking the hybrid we call Middle English, the strife died down. Today few Englishmen know if their ancestors were Norman or Jute; however, they do know if they are Christian or Muslim, and herein lies the rub for the twenty-first century. The sooner we follow the lead of the American College of Physicians, which in 1995 voted to delete race labels in patient case studies, the better off we'll be.

The contributions of Blumenbach continued to haunt me, so I asked some German-American friends how they would answer the same question I posed to my classes. Three said "black, white, and yellow." A fourth, however, answered, "Asian, African, and Germanic." Though this came from a *Gymnasium*-educated woman who had lived in the States for thirty years, it's clear that racial and national pride dies hard. When I checked the *Brockhaus Encyclopedia* to see what terms German authorities recommend, I found, "European, Mongoloid, Indian, and Negroid." In the *Bertelsmann Lexicon*, another standard German reference work, I found, "Mongoloid, European, and Negroid." In the land that gave the world "Caucasian," the word appears to have been replaced by "European." But given the multicultural nature of the twenty-five-state European Union, it's hard to say how the Irish, Estonians, Portuguese, and Greeks at the EU's four "corners" share any classification other than political and "human." And one has to wonder what became of the Lapponoids, the Fenne-Nordics, the Alpines, and the Osteuropids last described by Ernst Häckel in 1879.

Besides "Caucasian," "Aryan" is another race word that even more speakers of English associate with the Germans especially the Nazis even though in English the word preceded that gang of thugs by about a century. In *Mein Kampf* (1933), Hitler wildly and irresponsibly uses "Aryan" as an antonym for "Jew." In English, "Aryan" (not "Arian") was first used as an adjective meaning "noble" in 1839 and as a noun meaning "gentile" in 1851.

By the turn of the twentieth century, however, writers like Madison Grant in 1916 and J. S. Huxley in 1939 were publicly discouraging the use of "Aryan" in English as a "term of racial significance." But Friedrich Schlegel and Max Muller in Germany, taking a heavy-handed cue from the anti-Semitic Frenchman Compte de Gobineau, had already waved their linguistic wands over the Sanskrit "*arya*" and declared that the German word "*ehre*" ("honor") was a cognate. And if the languages were related, the people must be related, or so Nazi scholars later emphatically opined, even though we now know that the Aryan people lived in northern India, not northern Europe. As the *American Heritage Dictionary* now succinctly states, "Aryan" is "no longer in technical use."

⁓

In North America over the last four hundred years, the unevenly punctuated evolution of "darky," "dinge," "nigra," "negro," "Negro," "colored people," "nigger," "black," "people of color," and "African American" has been slow and painful. Each of these terms (and of course there are more), may be understood to represent a point on a graph. Connect the points to make two lines, one drawn by whites the other by blacks, and you'll see two very different contours. Nevertheless, the progress of both lines is upward, and I for one interpret this trend as a sign of hope, which has led me to write the following verses:

> Between black and white
> are countless shades of gray.
> Where the lines should be drawn
> is hard to say.

> From Nubian
> to alabaster Swede
> are six billion dark,
> red mouths to feed.

> Their colors range
> from pepper to malt—
> however they're shaken,
> their tears are salt.

> Human skin shines
> in a rainbow of hues,
> but passed through a prism,
> they're all shades of blue.

> Black, white, or umber,
> all of us share
> the color we bleed,
> the conversion to air.

AN APOLOGY FOR EXPEDIENCY

Just prior to the bell, I was collecting the loose ends of Hawthorne's "My Kinsman, Major Molineux," as my students were gathering their book bags when I said that Robin, an adolescent minister's son who's telescoped a year's worth of growing up into one night, is shocked to discover his capacity for sin. Joining the mocking chorus of the mob, he denies any relation to the Major after having spent most of the night bruiting that kinship about town.

Rising to leave, Edwin, my brightest sophomore that semester, said, "I don't see the sin." I said that Jesus and Socrates would probably have handled the situation better, but then they were experienced speakers and men of the world; Robin was not. This "shrewd lad," as Hawthorne calls him, did remind me a little of Huck Finn cleverly lying to save his friend Jim, the runaway slave, from bounty hunters. Others might have handled the situation worse than Robin by prying up a cobblestone and hurling it at their defenseless victim. Though he has not behaved like a saint or felon, Robin feels terrible after his denial and rightly or wrongly senses he has betrayed an innocent man. His parents have firmly installed a Puritan conscience in the boy if not a sense of political history. As I told the class the next time we met, a priest might find Robin guilty of hypocrisy; a prosecutor might charge him with unlawful assembly; I would only say that Robin hasn't exhibited the heroic virtue of a Dietrich Bonhöffer. Nevertheless like Edwin, I didn't see the sin either. I cannot condemn Robin because I'm reasonably sure I would not have acted any more virtuously or heroically than he did, and I'm forty years older. Through his pretense, Robin took the expedient course and survived to tell about it. Though it is unlikely, he may have tailed the mob and rescued his kinsman when they tired of playing their ugly games. That's a plot twist Hollywood may one day consider. Unfortunately, Hawthorne concludes his tale of initiation without telling us the lad's decision or implying, except in the broadest way, how his protagonist will turn out. Another possibility is that he will return to his parents though he'll need a loan to cover his travel expenses. On the other hand, he may accept the mysterious Samaritan's invitation to go home with him where Robin might clip the story of the lynching from the morning paper for his journal and future reflection. Indeed, there's much to be gleaned from his expedient behavior even if he was flying on auto-pilot at the time.

As Socrates said, "In every sort of danger, there are various ways of winning through if one is ready to do and say anything whatever." The key word here is "danger," for that alone permits Robin and Huck to level the playing fields they did not survey or grade. It's the same reason one cannot condemn too strongly Peter's epic denial in the New Testament, an episode Hawthorne alludes to in "My Kinsman, Major Molineux." However, it is axiomatic in situations such as Peter, Robin, and Huck find themselves that humans have a right to defend themselves and their loved ones. Whether they exercise that right is another matter altogether. And Peter, knowing what the Pharisees and the Romans were capable of, was within his rights in denying his association with Jesus. Had he acknowledged his friendship, he might very well have been crucified. Yet dying on the cross in 33 AD instead of 64 AD might have jeopardized the church whose founding was crucial to the forwarding of Jesus' theology of doing for others. The failure to establish the church would have been a tragedy far greater than the death of the founder. It is interesting that

Peter alone, according to John, took up the sword to defend his mentor and was rebuked for it. Yet, after Peter denied his spiritual leader, Jesus did not rebuke him. Indeed, he charged the first pope with feeding the flock, not waging holy war, for Peter with all his human failings was still the rock to build the church of peace upon.

Expediency has a bad name in many circles, for many think it means only choosing the easiest, most self-serving option like the able-bodied father who mutilates his children so their appeal as beggars will be increased rather than go to work himself. (This is why *apology* in my title means both "a defense" and "an expression of regret.") But if the mutilation of one's children to avoid work is unacceptable, some self-serving choices are surely justified. In August of 1945 following the German surrender, my father volunteered to embark on a troop ship out of Marseilles headed for Okinawa to participate in the imminent invasion of Japan. Some military analysts have calculated that as many as a million people might have perished in this operation. When the Japanese surrendered, however, the ship's captain made a hard turn to starboard and steamed for Newport News, Virginia. With a forty-five-day leave in hand, Dad could have stayed around for the parades and the demobilization of his mostly-black combat engineer battalion now in New York, or he could have taken a well-deserved leave. Selfishly, he caught a train to Atlanta where my mother was waiting for him in the Ansley Hotel.

"What's the first thing you did when you saw Mother again?" I naively asked him.

"Well, son, that's a personal matter I'd rather not talk about."

"I understand. What, then, was the second thing you did?" I persisted.

"It's an old joke – I took off my boots."

Somerset Maugham observed, "If the circumstances are right, any principle can be sacrificed to expediency." Perhaps he should have spelled out what he meant by right or just circumstances, for too many ignore the first clause of that sentence, which might better have been stated, "If love is best served, any principle might be sacrificed to expediency." Ideally though, regardless of the modal auxiliary, love and justice should be the same. I would define love, incidentally, as doing for others as they would have us do, not as we think they deserve. This definition helps the would-be humanitarian to distinguish self-interest from love.

In the famous prosecution of Sir Thomas More, a devout Roman Catholic and former Lord Chancellor of England, principles were sacrificed, Maugham would agree, but altruism was not served. To insure that his royal employer won the case, Richard Riche, Henry VIII's solicitor general in 1535, gave perjured testimony, which led to More's conviction. Though the trial record is incomplete, Riche's testimony was based on a failed attempt to trick More into denying, what the English parliament had decreed in the Supremacy Act, namely that the British king outranked the Pope. Henry, More's nemesis, was so pleased with the court's decision that he appointed Riche attorney general of Wales. Before his execution, More turned to Riche and, according to James Humes, said that he could understand why a man might sell his soul to gain a great nation, but piddling, poverty-stricken Wales?

Now if Henry had taken Riche's wife or children hostage, one might understand the solicitor's perfidy, but there is no evidence of such external pressure. Riche no doubt rationalized his expediency by saying he was only doing what his divinely appointed sovereign wanted him to do, and what the king wanted was best for the country. Furthermore as solicitor general, every conviction was another jewel in the crown that was slipping over his eyes. These flimsy and self-serving explanations became fundamental truths to Riche, and they blinded him to the selfish reasons he perjured himself. Not surprisingly, the Marquis de Sade argued, "It's better to side with the wicked who prosper than the righteous who fail." The famed libertine could not have known anymore than Riche did that Pius XI would canonize Sir Thomas More, not Riche, and certainly not Henry, in 1935.

One of the earliest direct experiences I had with expediency occurred in 1961 when at eighteen I served with the U.S. Army in northern Germany. Sgt. Bill Perry and I were scouting some new sites along the East German border for our radar-intercept equipment when I noticed that the jeep I was driving was pulling sharply to the right. I stopped on the shoulder and discovered I had a flat and a spare held in place by one nut. As the two of us were wrestling the spare on, I accidentally kicked the rusty can holding the five lug nuts and watched helplessly as they rolled over an embankment into the Elbe River. "Not to worry," said my resourceful crew chief, an ex-farm boy from North Carolina. "Though Army training regulations discourage this, just take one nut off three wheels and the spare, and we'll limp back to the motor pool with four nuts apiece. It's only about twenty kilometers." Though I had to stop a couple of times on the cobblestone roads to tighten the nuts, Bill's solution worked beautifully. I don't know what I would have done without the jack and lug wrench Uncle Sam provided me, but Bill no doubt would have figured out something; he was a master of the expedient. As I learned from him and others I respected, many Army regulations, when they reached the "Eastern front," were not commandments writ in stone as I'd learned in basic training, but merely suggestions from Pentagon bureaucrats.

Driving on the German Autobahn taught me to drive aggressively, but the 1959 Volkswagen I came home with did not always provide me the means. After my discharge in New York City, my wife and I moved to Georgia where I resumed work on my college diploma. Heading to a family reunion in South Georgia once, I was driving our VW about 55 mph, which was the speed limit along that urban stretch of Interstate. It was also about all that car was capable of unless I was headed down hill. Suddenly I found myself in some very heavy traffic: an eighteen wheeler was hard on my rear bumper and another was on my left, but there was some breathing room ahead of me assuming the truck beside me didn't switch lanes as he appeared ready to do. As the three of us approached a cloverleaf intersection, I noticed a Lincoln racing down the on-ramp apparently headed for my right-front fender. I honked but the noise of the trucks drowned the warning. I flashed my "light-horn," but the Lincoln apparently didn't see it because of the angle of his approach. Moving left was out of the question. I could have reduced my speed, but there was that blinking truck on my tail, so I gritted my teeth, tossed the dice, and pushed the accelerator to the floor. Seconds later, the elderly driver braked hard and tucked himself in behind me with just inches to spare. When I looked back, the driver gestured sheepishly; apparently he had only seen the bigger trucks and overlooked my "bug." As my blood pressure returned to normal, I wondered what I would have told a highway patrolman if he'd caught me on radar when I surged past the speed limit: "Had I obeyed the law, sir, I might not be here for you to ticket." Law or no law, the last thing I want to be is dead right.

But I am not entirely self-taught in this delicate matter of expediency. One of my tutors was an old friend named Freddie Nemchek. Freddie had been a Hungarian border guard who was drafted when the ill-fated Revolution began in 1956. Stopping his countrymen from fleeing Russian tanks was wrenching enough, but when his unit was ordered to Budapest, where the revolt was centered, Freddie had to make a quick decision. His two younger brothers were students at the university there, and both were politically active in the uprising. Not wanting to be placed in a position where he might have to shoot at his brothers especially after promising his dying father that he would look after the boys, Freddie rolled three hand grenades onto the ten-meter-wide mined strip. He then rose from a drainage ditch and prayed that the detonations had cleared all the mines in his path; the barbed wire hardly slowed him down. He wasn't alone; nearly 200,000 refugees over several years fled the country with him. From a refugee camp near Vienna several weeks later, however, Freddie learned that his widowed mother had been arrested and charged as an accessory in her oldest son's defection and her younger sons' activism. It never occurred to any of the sons that their mother would be targeted. Furthermore after spending six months in jail, she was released to discover that the family's twelve-acre farm was scheduled to be collectivized. Freddie never saw his mother again, but she did write forgiving him for his expedient departure. The lives of her sons, she generously stated, were worth any time she might spend in jail, and the farm was more than she could handle by herself.

I met Freddie in 1985 a decade after he had earned a Masters degree and taken a job teaching high-school English in upstate New York. When he told me the story of his escape, he quoted his favorite American writer, Emerson: "We do what we must, and call it by the best name." When the Iron Curtain was drawn back in the late 80s, Freddie sent for his brothers, and today they all live within twenty miles of each other with a sprinkling of cousins and nieces. Most every summer, Freddie flies back to Budapest to lay two roses on his parents' graves. Understandably, none of the brothers has any interest in reclaiming the farm each is entitled to.

Another of my teachers was Ilse Barmwater, my wife's mother. In the tiny farming village of Wolsdorf, Germany she had managed to shepherd her two children and her aging parents through the Second World War while her husband was on the Eastern Front and later in a French war prison. Late in the conflict when her larder was seriously undersupplied, she begged Herr Otto Schulze, who employed her during the planting and harvest seasons, if she might buy or barter some potatoes. "You know the law, Ilse," said the farmer. "All I grow goes to our soldiers who are dying on two fronts. God forbid that they should starve as well. I can't sell you any," he said with a wink, "but you can steal some." So Ilse waited for a moonless night, dressed in black, and filled a gunnysack with Schulze's precious tubers. She knew at least one soldier at the front who would not begrudge her a few spuds though she did not conduct a public opinion poll to see how his comrades felt about her larceny.

In May of 1945 with rumors of the allies' advance on every tongue, Herr Hermann Bäsecke, the Nazi mayor of Wolsdorf, decided to rally Ilse and her neighbors in a last-ditch effort to stop the Allies. Afraid of doing nothing, his honor decided that a sandbag barricade placed at one intersection in the middle of this town of five hundred would blunt the Ninth Army's spearhead. A few residents including Ilse worried that any obstacle would say "stubborn Nazis" to the Allies, who if offended might flatten their homes, the one thing of material value they had left. It was bad enough to be hungry, but homelessness, assuming she survived the shelling, would crush what little remained of her spirit. One cloudy night, therefore, Ilse and some comrades sliced open the mayor's sandbags with kitchen knives so that only a modest speedbump remained for the tanks to cross. Once again Ilse defied the authorities, but in doing so, she helped to save her home and many of her neighbors. In June, the Nazi mayor was relieved of his duties and sent to a yearlong re-education camp.

Opponents of situational ethics like to remind people such as myself that Hitler's love of Germany is what led him to start the war in which some sixty million died. Indeed

Hitler did love the Fatherland and the blond, blue-eyed folk who populated it, but love which is defined so narrowly that it justifies killing millions of innocents is not a love or a god that I respect even in a world where, as Iris Murdoch opined, "love is the reality and God but a dream." Does the end sometimes justify the means for the situationist? Yes. Are love and justice the same to him? Generally. Is situational ethics relativistic? By and large. Is love the only moral absolute? Yes. Does situational ethics require judgment and maturity? Most certainly and lots of empathy as well.

Ethical maturity, however, may be found at any age, which is why the moral superiority of children so often embarrasses their elders. A case in point: our daughter Anja was asked on a sixth-grade ethics test if it was acceptable for a fictional hero to steal medicine to save the life of his wife since the poverty-stricken family could not afford to buy the wife's medication. Unfortunately, the question cast the hero's complex decision in black and white terms: the hero could either steal the drugs and save a life or obey the law and attend his wife's funeral. Anja quite properly left the ludicrous question blank. She knew that loans and handouts were available for desperate people; she had a few dollars herself she would have contributed. Though twelve, she already knew the good work that the Salvation Army and Red Cross did. I applauded her answer, but then I threw a monkey wrench in the moral machinery. What if the hero were a trusted Jew in Auschwitz with a job cleaning the infirmary. If his wife needed medicine in this slave-labor camp, the hero has an obligation to steal, for Nazi "welfare" did not extend to "undesirables."

Aware that reality trumps the hypothetical when it comes to morality tales, Gregory Jaynes tells a story about the unidentified small town in coastal Georgia where he once lived. As General William "Total War" Sherman and his men were approaching in December of 1864, the town elders decided on a boldly proactive response. They mounted their horses and, white flags flying, rode at great personal risk to greet the army that had burned Atlanta and promised to "scorch the earth" between Buckhead and Savannah. On the outskirts of town, the elders requested an audience with the commander of the flaming juggernaut. "General Sherman," the mayor said, "please, sir, we are peace-loving people; do not destroy our humble town. We wish you no harm and hereby surrender. Incidentally, sir, there are 4000 bales of cotton in the warehouse by the river, and every one of them has your name on it." Sherman at this point turned in his saddle and said, "Put out your torches, boys. We have some counting to do." Jaynes, who ungratefully complains that the town fathers "had no courage," lived safely and comfortably in an antebellum home that was saved by the expedient town elders he condemns. Surely there were many Georgians like Jaynes who thought the mayor's actions were treasonous, but I cannot imagine anything the defenseless town might have done that would have helped the Confederate cause in a substantive manner. I say that from hindsight, of course, but most Southerners knew the war was essentially over by the end of 1864. A warehouse full of cotton could probably be replaced in a year's time, but the town and its citizens could never be restocked as my German mother-in-law realized in Wolsdorf.

There's an African proverb which states, "If the snake's in the house, one need not discuss the matter at length." African elephants and nature in general seem to have gotten that message as well. In a poignant documentary on the Discovery Channel, my wife and I watched in tears as one herd's drought-crazed females butted a youngster away from the watering hole, which was little more than mud anyway. Survival of the family, it seems, meant more than a frail daughter's life. Expelling a defenseless youngster from the herd meant certain death, for the restlessly circling lions were just as thirsty as the elephants, and blood though salty, will slake a thirst in a pinch. Instinctively the elephant mothers realized that once the drought was over, the herd could be replenished assuming one bull and his harem survived long enough to reproduce.

If nature permits infanticide, is a human ever justified in killing or torturing another? Yes, when on those rare occasions that love is best served by extreme measures. If the police in New York City had observed someone padlocking a nuclear device to a lamppost beside the Empire State Building on the afternoon of September 11, 2001, would they have been justified in torturing their captive? Yes, indeed, if the bomb squad had reported that the device could not be safely defused or transported without a password for its timer. The terrorist in custody may not have possessed this information, but police authorities would have had every right to twist his arm until they were convinced of this even as they were piling dirt atop the bomb, and residents were evacuating Manhattan. Commenting on a similar situation, the journalist and physician Charles Krauthammer says that, "Only a moral idiot would say no [to torture under extreme circumstances]."

My convictions concerning expediency were sharply tested in the run-up to the war in Iraq. In January of 2003, my sister, a Methodist minister in New Jersey who had counseled some of the 9-11 survivors, e-mailed me that the looming war was depriving her of sleep. One of her two sons had just been called up to active duty at Ft. Drum, New York. For very personal reasons, she opposed the war, but with many hawks in her congregation, she was obliged to mince her words. I wrote back that the flimsy evidence for weapons of mass destruction, a weak link to the events of 9-11, and the existence of unexplored diplomatic avenues cast me in the unfamiliar role of dove. I copied my retired-military father in North Carolina and my neo-Calvinist sister in Arizona to see what they thought. Dad replied tersely, "Do we wait until a nuclear device is detonated in New York harbor before we take action?" My older sister said, "We have to assume the WMD still exist since their destruction was never documented. We have to wage war since the US in its role as the world's super power has the responsibility to preserve and protect freedom for all the world's citizens." She has not always been so generous in her concern for the rights of others, but she had a point. Stubbornly I replied that all great power has a seductive allure like the finely crafted sniper rifle, accurate to a mile that seems to whisper, "Use me." We have to guard against such enticing appeals.

My younger sister proposed a coin toss to put the whole matter in God's hands. However, I wasn't so dovish that I was willing to give Saddam Hussein a 50-50 chance of winning any war, and I told her, "I'm afraid my faith in the flipped coin is not as strong as yours. I believe God gave humans reason and free will to make complex moral decisions for themselves. I would not choose a spouse on the basis of a coin toss anymore than I would decide the fate of an accused felon if I'm serving on his jury."

A letter in the *Greenville News* provoked me to go public with my anti-war position. The letter writer had paraphrased Dietrich Bonhöffer, a culture hero of my own, as follows, "If you are on a bus, and you see that the driver is mad and clearly intends to ram a column of children at the intersection, you must stop the driver by the most immediate means possible. It is his life or the life of the children; thus, the moral imperative is to act."

I responded, "Analogies, as Lyndon Johnson learned the hard way, can often be treacherous in argument. The logic of the domino theory was so compelling, as Johnson himself eventually admitted, that he could not screw up his courage to withdraw from Vietnam.

Although he realized the US could not win, he feared that several more countries like Cambodia and Thailand would fall like tall thin blocks with a high center of gravity. Well, countries are not dominoes, and Saddam Hussein is not driving our bus; George W. Bush is. But for the sake of argument, let's say we are passengers on Saddam's bus. Before I would willy nilly shoot the driver and risk the lives of everyone on board, I'd want to know that he was mad and not just suffering a leg cramp. Bonhöffer's mad driver, on the other hand, had long ago jumped the curb, buried the accelerator, and run over millions of innocents before the Lutheran ethicist finally acted in concert with hundreds of high-minded Germans. If the moral imperative is to act, not kill, wouldn't it be prudent for someone to seize the wheel and emergency brake while another collars the driver? This isn't Hollywood after all, and the choke hold we have on Saddam has worked for a decade."

Fortunately for me, the *News* had so many letters before D-Day that it never published mine. In the back of my head, I kept hearing my older sister say we had a responsibility to the brutalized people of Iraq. Probably because her fundamentalist beliefs are so contrary to mine, I sometimes find it difficult to recognize the virtue of her position. Nevertheless one weekend, I found myself surfing the net for Human Watch and Amnesty International reports on Iraq. What I found was astonishing: an estimated 200,000 dead Marsh Arabs, an estimated 100,000 dead Kurds, torture by electric shock and acid baths, rape, and an estimated 10,000 still dying each year in Saddam's prisons. I imagined myself at Auschwitz in 1944 thinking, "Where are those Americans?" When the Rev. Brian Herir, former dean of Harvard's School of Divinity and philosopher of peace, spoke on campus, I asked him about the Kurds and the Shi'as after he'd made an impassioned speech about maintaining the status quo in Iraq. His answer was, "As was seen in Bosnia, the human rights argument is the strongest for war." His reference to the Balkans reminded me that I had supported our bombing of the Serbs; was Hussein any different from Milosevic'? Shouldn't Americans aggressively oppose any state that uses rape, torture, and "ethnic cleansing" as various means to an end, no matter how gloriously it dresses it up? I thought so, and soon said as much in an e-mail that I sent to the family and a few friends: "The upshot is that I have come to accept the inevitability of war, and, indeed, its desirability."

My Methodist sister was suddenly silent, but my Dad and older sister welcomed me back in their good graces, happy that I'd "finally seen the light." My friend and former colleague John Idol was the only one seriously to challenge my flipflop just days before the war began. Though I had warned the *Greenville News* letter writer about arguing with analogies, I devised one of my own to explain my position to John. Imagine one day you hear screaming coming from your neighbor's house, and good Samaritan that you are, you go to investigate, but in the rush you forget your cell phone. Through the living room window, you see a clearly berserk father chasing his small son with a baseball bat. The boy's mother lies near the door unconscious and possibly dead. The father swings his bat wildly a few times, but the agile youth wards off the worst of the blows and scampers out of reach. He tries the door, but it's locked as you have already determined. It is clear to you that the boy, who is tiring, cannot avoid the blows much longer. You continue to yell and beat on the door, but the hysterical and possibly drunken father ignores you.

Some neighbors who have heard the screams join you. Breathlessly, you suggest breaking down the door and gang tackling the father as those courageous airline passengers may have done on 9-11 before crashing in Pennsylvania. The neighbors know this man; he has a history of irrational and violent behavior. The majority, however, say that it's none of their business; it's a domestic dispute, an internal matter; leave them alone. Another volunteers to run and call 911, which you agree to, but in your estimation, the boy inside does not have five minutes to live as you wait for the police. Frustrated by the lack of support from the people you thought were your friends, you break in the door, and at considerable risk, you wrestle the father into a neck lock. However, now the father is striking you with the bat over his shoulder. As the two of you fight for control, you accidentally snap the madman's neck. You only meant to subdue him and save the boy from further harm, but you have killed him in front of several witnesses clucking, "We warned you this might happen."

Now if this case came before me as a juror, I told John, I don't think I could in good conscience vote to convict this defendant of murder or even manslaughter. I might fine him or vote for a short jail term, but no more. John suggested breaking the glass and helping the boy escape. I said this boy had no precedent for defying his father after his older brother had run away. If that didn't work, said John, how about passive resistance, but the mother still tucked in the fetal position had already tried that, I said. Jewish passive resistance in the 1940s, had there been any, would only have made Hitler's job easier. Great democracies don't engage in preemptive strikes, said John. He's right of course, but when Israeli intelligence showed Arab tanks had crossed into Sinai in 1967 prior to the famously brief Six-Day War, it was wise to strike before Arab tank gunners had time to load their chambers and the pilots had an opportunity to launch their jets. Indeed, over four hundred were destroyed sitting on the tarmac.

In most cases, expediency is shortsighted, costly, and immoral. The Society of Jesus' motto, "Any means are justified if the end can be achieved," permitted the Jesuits to convert any non-Catholic at the point of a sword. And Leo Durocher's slogan, "Win any way you can as long as you can get away with it," presumably allowed his Giants to cheat with impunity. (The other side of the "anything goes" coin is John Henry, Cardinal, Newman's callous observation, "The Church holds that it were better for all the many millions [on the earth] to die of starvation in extremest agony...than that one soul...should commit one single venial sin." To this I would only say that no credo, whether "nothing goes" or "anything goes," should be a suicide pact.) But as I trust I have shown, there are times when love is best served by the expedient, whatever that might consist of. My mother-in-law understood this when she stole potatoes. The Rev. Dietrich Bonhöffer understood this when he entered a plot to kill Hitler. Mohandas Gandhi understood this when he made salt in violation of British colonial law. Henry David Thoreau understood this when he refused to pay a poll tax because some of the money went to support an imperialistic war against Mexico. Moreover, Mrs. Rosa Parks understood this when she refused to surrender her seat to a white man on a municipal bus. What I hope is that no one would ever be prevented from doing the right thing because it is technically or generally considered wrong. For those worried about the slippery slope, there are effective crampons to fit all boot sizes. E.D. Martin argues that, "Knowledge of means without knowledge of ends is animal training." The education of humans requires infinitely more than hunting dogs and show horses. And if like Benjamin Franklin, Thomas Jefferson, and George Washington, people hedge their bets by maintaining their church memberships when they are more deist than Episcopalian, I cannot blame them.

Doing the Best He Can

"If God is good, then he is not all powerful. If God is all powerful, then he is not all good. I am a disbeliever in the omnipotence of God because of the Holocaust. But for thirty-five years or so, I have been believing that he is doing the best he can."
Norman Mailer, *The Gospel According to the Son*

In the literature classroom discussing American Puritan writers such as Edward Taylor, Jonathan Edwards, or Michael Wigglesworth, I have often found myself trying to make the same point as Mailer. Knowing the popularity of gambling in the Clemson dormitories, I usually resort to a stud-poker metaphor to explain myself. In the imaginations of John Calvin and many of his Puritan followers, God calls the game, antes, stacks the deck, and deals. A few rounds of betting may follow, but no one is surprised by the outcome. A humanist's view of the poker-playing God (let's call Him Zeus to sharpen the distinction) still has the Almighty calling the game, but then He shuffles, and passes the deck to be cut. He does not arrange the cards to His liking, and His odds of winning are just slightly better than the others at the table because presumably, He has called His favorite game, plus He comes last in the betting order, often a decided advantage.

In one Olympian game of seven-card stud that I had the privilege to sit in on recently, I received a pair of nines showing, but nothing in the hole. Several face cards were then dealt to my opponents, but my heavy betting drove them to concede; indeed, Zeus Himself folded with the ace of spades up. Three rounds of betting later, I drove off the last contender who was showing a pair of queens. My poker-faced bluff saved the day, and a large pot was my reward. I found it interesting that after Zeus folded His cards, He walked around the table but gave no indication that I did not have that third nine, another pair, or anything else of value. In other words, Zeus was the most powerful player at the table and the most knowledgeable, but He still lost as did my other opponents, some of whom spend a lot more time in church than I do. In Calvin's game, God or His "elected" (because God casts the only vote) always wins. Bluffing is not only unfair but impossible; consequently, those Puritan games are short, dull, and monotonously predictable.

However as Norman Mailer says, one wants to think that Zeus, cheering like a t-ball dad in the bleachers, is doing His best. Indeed, the game is always held at Zeus's comfortable home, and He generously supplies the chips and dip. But if you want to drink something other than water, you'll have to supply that yourself. He doesn't make you stay to clean up, but I feel sure He appreciates the help. What I enjoy most about the competition is watching the old guy in His green visor shuffle several billion cards at once: He throws the cards in the air, and a cyclone whirls them about until they fall neatly back into His outstretched hands. What a guy!

His shuffling reminds me of a super slo-mo film of the wind blowing across a field of coreopsis. Most of the pollen falls on the ground to be sure, but some of it falls in the ovaries of blossoms hundreds of miles away. I suppose if I wanted to give *all* the glory to God and none to man or nature, I might (as Calvin believed) say that God knew where every grain of pollen would fall because His aim is unfailing. But is the grain of pollen lodged between two rocks or the acephalic fetus evidence of perfect marksmanship or a divine miss? I know that many things that appear wrong turn out to have value down the line: think of the South's view of the Union in 1865; then think of it in 1945. But a child born without a brain, as reluctant as I am to admit it, has little or no redeeming value and never will as far as I can see. The everlasting sorrow inherent in such a birth far outweighs the pleasure of its conception. And still with all the practice God has had, He continues to supply mothers with one acephalic fetus per 10,000 normal ones. Were there no such specialization as prenatal research, I expect this number would remain roughly the same. However, the day may come thanks to human efforts when brain stem cells could be implanted in an empty skull before the fetus ever sees the light of day. Intrauterine surgery is already being performed, so why not imagine a day when a fetus without a brain can be supplied with one. No one will be happier on this occasion than the Creator who has given man the brains and body to accomplish what once was thought to be miraculous and today is routine. Indeed if it were not for the efforts of man, aspirin and thousands of other drugs would still be dormant in the plants where man first found them.

Ben Herlong an old friend and a veteran of World War II once told me a story that helped me to understand God's limitations. One day in the terrible French winter of 1944, Ben and his infantry platoon had come under mortar and rifle fire. Several of Ben's buddies lay dead about him as he furiously tried to dig himself a foxhole in the frozen earth while the company medics cleared the field of the wounded. Hunkered down at a depth of about two feet, Ben heard a mortar round land ten yards or so in front of him. The explosion generated a wave of adrenalin in Ben followed by some wild digging, so that when the second round fell ten yards behind him, he was crouching about four feet down. Suddenly Ben realized that he was being bracketed, and the next shell should fall right on top of him. He was digging his own grave. Ben cast about for some other shelter, but the trees were too far away even if he had been fleet of foot, which he was not; in fact, his burlap-bound feet were near frozen. Suddenly in the dying light, he saw a fresh mound of dirt about two hundred yards away, and he realized that even though he could not see them, his mortar-firing enemies had to be crouched behind the mound doing the fatal math. "Though I trusted God," Ben said, "it was time for this ostrich, metaphors be damned, to seize the charging bull by the horns!" He threw his shovel aside, grabbed his rifle, and emptied a clip into the only earth visible that was not covered with snow. Perspiring profusely, he waited for the third shell to fall, but it never came. Later in the darkness, he cautiously made his way to the suspicious mound and discovered two German soldiers slumped over their mortar. After he'd pulled the bodies off a few yards and slammed a fieldstone against the mortar's barrel, he bedded down in the spacious German foxhole he'd just liberated and fell asleep.

The next morning before word came to move out, Ben wondered what the outcome would have been if the shelling of the previous day had occurred in the summer. With the ground thawed, any mortar or artillery shell landing within a few yards of a properly dug foxhole might well have buried him alive. In basic training at Fort Benning, Ben had been taught that it was not enough to dig *down* in the Georgia clay; a good infantryman also had to dig *forward* a couple of feet to protect himself from a round exploding overhead. But as many had learned too late, a shell exploding beside a foxhole occasionally caused a landslide that buried the occupants. He knew that the hole he had dug the day before was not deep enough for that to occur, but the memory gave him pause. He wondered what God's role in all of this was. Both of the adolescent Germans that he'd killed had

Catholic crucifixes about their necks. And while Ben was a Baptist, he fairly assumed that all three worshipped the same God. Was God then cheering for one Christian side and not the other? Nonsense, he decided; God just made the ground rules, one of which is: water freezes at thirty-two degrees Fahrenheit. In four months, the very foxhole he was resting in might collapse around him if a mortar round exploded a few feet away especially if it burrowed a few feet into the soft loam before detonating. God does not wage war, Ben concluded, nor does He aim the mortars, guide the shrapnel, or decide what time during the year the two sides will meet. The rules are the same for all combatants, and man is free to fight or flee, dig or shoot.

But if God makes all the rules and knows everything in advance, isn't He responsible even if He doesn't pull all the strings? When this question comes up in class, I find myself resorting to the hypothetical again. As in the Olympian poker game, Zeus knew more about the deal than anyone else at the table, but unless He's holding a divine flush, He often doesn't know the final outcome. This ignorance relieves Him of absolute responsibility though the Calvinists believe He has and never will relinquish full control. Now, imagine me Zeus-like in my eighth-floor office musing out the window eating a sandwich. Suddenly amid the lunch-hour traffic, a van pulls into the library parking lot and stops in front of a good friend's car. I know it's Ray's car because he arrives every morning at six to get that coveted space. I assume Ray has called a mechanic because emerging from the van is a man in dirty overalls carrying some tools. He disappears under the car for less than a minute, crawls out, gets back in the van, and drives off. Suddenly I see some fluid gleaming in the sun running out from under Ray's car. I take my field glasses from my desk to be sure, and who do I see but Ray entering his car from the side opposite of where the leak is. Is it gasoline, I wonder, anti-freeze, *brake fluid*? I open the window and yell, but he doesn't hear me. I then grab the telephone and call Ray on his cell phone—fortunately, I have him on speed dial. Before he can leave the parking lot, I am relieved to hear his voice and tell him to stop his car immediately. His foot goes all the way to the floorboard, he tells me in a panic, before the vehicle stops against a curb scattering students in several directions. I wave to him from the window as he slumps against the steering wheel. Taking the elevator down stairs to investigate, I think back over my role-playing: was I playing God or just acting like a responsible human? I tell myself that God may have given me the raw materials, but I derived the conclusion and made the call. Silently, I thank God for His gifts; then, I strike up the little Dixieland band in my heart to celebrate a life saved. As for my "omniscience," I have no idea why anyone would have cut Ray's brake line much less who it was. So, when my neo-Calvinist sister tells me that God has all the knowledge *and* all the power, I politely ignore her. If God had the knowledge, why didn't He call Ray while I was yelling out the window? If God had the power, why didn't He derail the Holocaust? The God that Norman Mailer and I worship waves a lot from the sidelines, but sometimes we just don't see Him or pay Him any attention.

Whether we worship Zeus, who could not or would not save His own son from dying in battle though He saw the Greek spear before it was thrown, or Jehovah, who either could not or would not save His son from the Roman spikes before they were driven, we are left with a God whose powers are circumscribed. The sooner we recognize that, the sooner we humans can get down to the business of feeding the hungry, housing the homeless, curing cancer, and slowing global warming. Surely even the terrorists among us would welcome those goals. Squabbling over whose God or prophet is superior is a tragic distraction that prevents us from improving the lives of billions.

I've long loved the story that Jews and Muslims alike tell about the wise old farmer who is planting a tree in his orchard when he is interrupted by a neighbor excitedly yelling, "The messenger of God has come!" Says the rabbi or mullah to his listener, "When you find yourself like the farmer in such a conflicted position, first finish planting your tree; then, go and meet the messenger who claims to be from God." Stories like these lie about the fringes of every religion in the apocryphal writings that didn't make the final cut, but it's here that we often locate the nuggets in the mud.

Speaking of the fringes, I can't imagine many places more remote than the Sinai Desert. In the shadow of Mt. Sinai in the midst of that vast desert stands the monastery of St. Catherine built in the fifth century A.D. to wall in what was considered the Burning Bush of Moses' day. As the Egyptian crow flies, the monastery lies about a hundred and fifty miles from Jerusalem, nine hundred miles from Athens, and sixteen hundred miles from Rome. For some fifteen hundred years, the famed Old Testament shrub had grown in the desert before Greek Orthodox monks built massive stonewalls to protect it. How they located the right plant is not recorded. Orthodox Christians, Roman Catholics, and Jews alike admit that the bush has not burst into flame in three thousand years; nevertheless, in case some cheeky Muslim youth douses it with gasoline and strikes a match, a fire extinguisher stands at the ready. The silent admission of this modern precaution speaks volumes about the reality-based faith of the brothers who maintain the monastery. I doubt that there are any lightning rods at St. Catherine's, but plenty of them and lots of sprinkler systems as well have been installed on and in churches where lightning is commonplace.

If I were a guide at St. Catherine's and a tourist asked me about that extinguisher, I'd say, "The monks here trust in God to be sure, but they recognize that with a universe of immense size to watch over, divine oversights may occur. The next time your back goes out, remember that for some two million years the hominid spine traveled parallel to the earth, not perpendicular. The responsibility for the once-divine shrub is now man's, so it is he who waters, prunes, and fertilizes it. Long ago when the monks observed that the pruned branches of this *rubus sanctus* do burn, the installation of a fire extinguisher in proximity to the shrub was considered prudent."

❧

After discussing free will in a class once and announcing the first examination, one student asked if I thought he'd pass: "Is it in the cards, professor?" he wondered aloud alluding to my fondness for poker. I said that like God before testing Abraham and Job, I had no clue what his or anyone else's score would be. To the best of my ability, I said the test would be a fair measure of their comprehension of the material we'd covered. Moreover, while I might predict some failures and notable successes, all my predictions are non-binding and subject to error.

Murmurs of discontent from the back rows led me to assume that some didn't believe me, so holding up an empty grade book, I said that like God, I could only pray for their best efforts, but that all of them, prepared or not, have the option to pass or fail. With tuition as high as it currently is in 2006, students often don't consider the value of failure, but after running up a grade-point average of 1.5 on a scale of 4.0 as a civil engineering major at Georgia Tech in my first and only semester there, it was comforting to know I would never design a bridge that would collapse in heavier-than-I'd-anticipated traffic. Indeed, the D's and F's I'd accumulated were not just a good thing for me, but for drivers everywhere.

I prayed that I'd never have to take another calculus class, and my prayers were answered when I dropped out of Tech and enlisted in the army. When I returned to school four years later, calculus was not required for English majors. Who among us, I wonder, has not prayed and discovered what he prayed for within his grasp? Regardless of one's faith, it is often tempting to think that the answer to one's prayers is merely a coincidence, but it would be a bizarre world indeed, if coincidences never occurred. The law of averages states that occasionally red, black, or green is going to show up on the roulette wheel three, four, and even five times in a row. No mathematician who's ever lived, however, could predict without technological assistance when a given color will show up at any given time. Indeed, the odds of red appearing on one turn of the wheel are 38:18 unless you're in Europe where they are 37:18. Too often, however, people pray for rain; the rain falls, and those happy wet souls attribute the rain to their heartfelt prayers. If, however, they'd checked the weather forecast, they would have seen that cold front sweeping down out of Canada toward another front pushing up from the Gulf of Mexico.

One afternoon, I took my poetry workshop outside to enjoy the spring weather, and the first young woman to present her free-verse poem (a reworking of the Adam and Eve story) announced that she regretted the poem's "blasphemy." The class's most outspoken critic suggested that she apologize forthwith, but I said that if God seriously objected, He'd throw down a lightning bolt that instant. Actually, the sky was darkening and a very light rain was starting to fall, so lightning was not out of the question. Instead, the poet's cell phone rang just as I said "lightning." We all laughed at the synchrony while the poet had a muffled, red-faced conversation. As she hung up, we all wanted to know if God had called.

"No," she said, "it was my Indian friend Krishna." Thirteen jaws dropped simultaneously before we all broke into laughter again. After class, I asked if she'd been kidding about Krishna calling.

"No," she said, "Sri Krishna is his name."

"Sure am glad it wasn't Shiva!" I said and wished her a good day. Walking back to the office, I thought such is the coincidental stuff that most if not all mystical experiences are comprised of. The radical deist Thomas Paine in *The Age of Reason* (1793) called these experiences "hearsay" and argued that they shouldn't be admissible in the court of public discourse. My personal beliefs, however, are much closer to the twentieth-century American poet James Dickey's than Paine's. Dickey, a mentor of mine in graduate school, was puzzled by people who deny the existence of God with no more evidence than those who vouch for His intimate involvement in human lives. "The thought of a Creator makes the world sweeter," said Dickey in class one day, "and helps all of us feel more secure as when we see a uniformed pilot boarding the plane before we do. Who is so callously self-confident, I wonder, that he could deny a lonesome child an imaginary friend? I see a lot of bumper stickers saying, 'My boss is a carpenter.' Well, my boss is the primal electrician who let there be light before creating the stars! Whoever or whatever made this universe, even if it's nothing more than the mystery of life or the blind force that refused to leave a vast void unfilled, deserves to be worshipped." And whatever the Creator is, I would add, It deserves our knee-bending respect if for no other reason than the obligatory worship which rescues us from pride.

I'll never forget a Clemson physicist at a faculty forum who mocked a reference of mine to "God the prime mover." Said the smiling astrophysicist, "Creation just happened like spontaneous combustion." I replied, "But *someone* had to douse those rags in linseed oil and pile them in the corner, didn't He, She, or They?" As Edgar Poe says in "Sonnet—To Science," science is a vulture that alters everything by its ceaseless questioning and scrutiny, and though the bird's appetite is insatiable, its food is never completely consumed. The situation is every student's nightmare—answer one question, and two more appear beckoning the test taker to some black hole of absolute reason where God has no purchase.

The American poet Wallace Stevens referred to the spiritual reality that humans universally have a need to believe in as a "necessary" or "supreme fiction." In 2006 incidentally, 92% of Americans agree with Stevens. Call it a lie or call it faith, but few of us are willing to make a long trek through a pitch-black tunnel without a light to walk toward. Without the "fiction," Stevens suggested, humans are emotional cripples with dangerously inflated notions of themselves. I recently asked my five-year-old grandson Spencer who he thought God was, and without hesitation, he said, "He's the great spirit who started everything with a BIG explosion. Now He takes dead people and turns them into spirits like Himself." Not a bad definition for a kindergartner or an astrophysicist especially if no one *really* knows either way. If one cannot know, why not opt for the utilitarian view that brings the most people the most happiness? No harm is caused by such innocent belief because I'm not speaking about organized religion, just faith. And as Nietzsche observed, "With a 'why,' any 'how' is bearable."

Though I regularly attended church services for over twenty years and I appreciate the fact that the church rescues alcoholics and addicts long after families and state agencies have given up on them, much of organized religion is "the poison in the blood" as Salman Rushdie has argued. I saw first hand how religion drove a wedge between my maternal grandparents when my grandmother decided that full immersion was the only acceptable form of baptism. She left the Methodist church that she and her husband had attended for close to forty years, and in doing so, left my grandfather a very lonely man on Sunday mornings. Similarly, a friend of mine's Northern Irish Catholic family refuses to lay a wreath at a World War I memorial in Belfast because the shadow of an Anglican church occasionally falls across the memorial. Another friend's mother became a Jehovah's Witness after the baptism of her seven children in a Baptist church which meant that she refused to be a witness to any of her children's weddings in the church where her husband retained his membership. I've seen enough instances of such divisiveness that I've decided there's no reason to pay for another layer of bureaucracy between me and the Creator. In about 10,000 years of recorded history, man has established some 100,000 religions; which one would I choose?

On the other hand, I've watched enough goose-stepping state funerals and eight-minute Soviet weddings to convince me that a God-less culture has little appeal either. But the "fill-in-the-blank" Episcopal services that hardly mention the deceased don't assuage my grief either. Give me a convivial wake with family and friends in my living room or a local tavern, and my spiritual needs are usually met.

My own innate faith might be called "the faith of the unsqueezed rat." In the 1950s, some psychologists at Johns Hopkins had the bizarre notion that if a rat was squeezed in human hands to within a whisker of its life, the poor beast might become more passive than a Native American infant wrapped in a papoose. The rats were each held until all struggle ceased. As if nearly pressing the life out of them wasn't enough, these sadists in white lab coats then placed the despondent rats into a bucket of water whose sides were so high and steep that no escape was possible. Thousands of rats were squeezed or not squeezed and then placed in the water. Some rats were tame; others were wild. Sometimes the water was warm; other times it was cold. All of those rats who'd been squeezed, however, quickly drowned. A few swam for up to an hour, but many sank like stones without any effort to save themselves. The rats who'd not had their "faith" crushed, on the other hand, swam for as long as eighty-one hours!

Like Albert Einstein, the unsqueezed rats, my grandson, and myself, many of us want to believe in a benevolent God, not a cosmic crap shooter, but a charitable uncle in the garment business who has wrapped us in the biosphere's cloak (but not too tightly) even as He has left us to our own devices. We can sink or swim. "With the right attitude," Robert Pirsig observed, "anything is possible."

When Einstein's beloved sister Maja was near death, however, he did not advise her to place her faith in God, but to "look deep into nature, and all will be well." However, the vast majority of us, Einstein charged, are like "fish who know nothing of the water." Yet if the fastest human swimmer moves at four m.p.h. and the fastest fish at sixty-eight m.p.h., and if man has inhabited the planet for four million years and fish for 450 million years, I'd be willing to bet that fish know a lot more about their environment than Einstein gave them credit for. On the other hand, what *do* humans know of their "water"? We know, for example, that the life span of the atoms which comprise the human body is ten to the thirty-fifth power or 1,000,000,000, 000,000,000,000,000, 000,000,000 years. That may not be an eternity, but it's a lot longer than the Bible's "three score and ten," ample time for scores of incarnations both animate and inanimate. We know too that the pineapple, the chambered nautilus, the spiral nebula, and many other seemingly unrelated things share the mathematical organizing principle known as the Fibonacci Sequence. It may be just a coincidence, but it's a staggering one.

The German philosopher Georg Hegel famously argued that the Fibonacci Sequence, which he compared to one orderly room in a mansion, doesn't prove the existence of a master architect. In 1779, sure as Hegel was of the pre-eminence of chaos, he could not have known that even the mansion's formal living room lies in disarray. Our subatomic closets are a rat's nest according to quantum physics, a quaint notion that Einstein never took seriously. Indeed, given the uncertain behavior of neutrinos and muons, he was ridiculed for his belief in an order-maintaining God. But even if the quantum theorists are right and Einstein is wrong, what's wrong with a messy sub-basement as long as the landlord does his best to run a tight condo? Don't we all have some place where chaos reigns?

There's a great adventure ahead, I believe, and it has nothing to do with pickling oneself for eternity or strumming a harp. We have nothing more to fear from death than what we felt at birth—death's equivalents of the forceps and surgical shears. I won't pretend that meeting my Maker doesn't make me apprehensive especially when I dodge a "bullet" on the Interstate or wrestle in the dark with a flu bug, but when I stand on Table Rock Mountain, where I wish some of my ashes spread, with a clump of bluets at my feet and look out over the Blue Ridge Mountains into that "blue yonder," what's to fear? It'll be like coming home.

THE COMMONWEALTH OF BELLS

Like a medieval apprentice residing snugly in the shadow of his church, I spent my fifth, sixth, and seventh years living within a similar circle of well being. My family and our German governess, of course, had a lot to do with the structured serenity I enjoyed, but I realize now that I also owed much to the bells of Heidelberg's churches. Most had escaped damage during the war though some had contributed their bells to the Nazi war effort; those not volunteered were confiscated. By the end of the forties, however, many in the German campanological armory that had not been sent to the furnace were returned to their rightful ecclesiastical and civic owners. Annelore, a self-confessed "bells and smells Catholic" and our family's nanny, filled my head with much of the bell lore that still chimes there. Walking, biking, or taking the trolley through Heidelberg on one of our many excursions, she would point out bells that had lost their voices following some perfidy or regained them pursuant to the proper reparations. I'm sure she was the one who tried to convince me that the chocolate I'd received one Easter had come from a bell recently returned from the Vatican, not the Easter Bunny as I'd been led to believe. This may have been the birth of my rational faith as I challenged eighteen-year-old Annelore's notion of a wingless brass bell flying back across the Alps with enough chocolate for every Christian child on earth. It wasn't long before I began to question, among other things, the possibility of an extravagantly generous rabbit as well.

When I misbehaved, Annelore would remind me of the great *Glockenspiel* in Strasbourg and its skeleton bell-jack that struck the hour with a human femur! From time to time, the bone splintered, she said, and the bell-jack would go in search of bad boys with plump thighs just like mine. On another occasion when I was caught escorting the family cat into the living room to see if it could get a rise out of my sister's aging canary, Annelore told me of a similar malicious lad. This jokester cut the bell from a cat's collar to give his lord's feline a decided edge on some recently hatched chickens. The lord's cook caught the boy and strung him up feet first inside a bell where he served as the clapper until his skull burst! That was the last time I exposed any defenseless creature to our unbelled cat.

John Idol, a close friend who grew up in tiny Deep Gap, North Carolina in the 1930s, came to respect bells in a decidedly different way than I did. As a callow youth after mowing the church's lawn and cemetery, John would sneak into the belfry of his clapboard church, briefly ring the bell, and light out for the safety of the woods much the way urban children screw up their courage to ring the doorbell of someone they fear. After John was confirmed, however, the deacons often would ask him to ring the bell calling the faithful to church services. Proud of his new role and responsibility, he became a defender of the church bell against any upstarts who might sneak a tug at the bell rope. Like my friend, I too became a defender of the bells.

The Nazis, however, were not so protective. It has been estimated that the Nazis seized over 100,000 of Europe's bells mostly for the tin, not the copper. (To achieve maximum resonance, incidentally, most bells are between one quarter and one fifth tin; the rest is copper.) Germany has no tin mines to speak of, and late in the war, cut off from her peacetime sources, her war lords desperately needed this soft, silvery metal for soldering electrical connections. Yet in some ways, it's surprising that the Nazis commandeered any continental bells at all because many like Annelore still believed that ringing them provided a roof certified against everything from the plague to falling bombs. After Oxford had been targeted for a Luftwaffe bombing raid and the town escaped virtually unscathed, the Nazi "Occult Unit" attributed the lack of success to the university's secret weapon: the seven-and-a-half-ton "Great Tom" bell which had complained furiously during the attack. Believers say that Gerard Manley Hopkins' "bell-swarmed" village was saved by its bell. After all, it was St. Thomas Aquinas who said, "The tones of the consecrated metal repel the demon and avert storm and lightning." Realists argue that if the Germans had flown a little lower and opened their cockpits they might have heard the audible "bull's eye" Great Tom painted on Oxford. And skeptics claim that poor visibility had more to do with the campus's salvation than the bell's "umbrella."

Annelore probably knew nothing of Oxford's good fortune since she spent much of the war with her head between her knees in dimly-lit bomb shelters. Nevertheless, she still believed in the protective aura afforded by ringing bells, especially those that had been baptized. Roman Catholics had consecrated new bells for centuries—bestowing blessings complete with holy water, hymns, a sermon, a starched baptismal gown, and the assignment of a godparent. Afterwards, indulgences were granted to those who needed them. If an unbaptized bell was rung in a farmer's field during a hail storm, for example, and this bell ringer's crop happened to miss the brunt of the storm, the bell was considered blessed. Sensing the erosion of the church's power, Charlemagne issued a proclamation in 789 banning the private use of bells whether they were blessed or baptized, but many of the folk defiantly rang them right through the plague years. Belief in bell efficacy was so strong in many communities that some victims, who had died at the ends of their bell ropes, were replaced by volunteers without missing a beat.

Luther and Calvin were the next to tackle the bell issue. The Northern European Protestants banned the baptism of bells and did their best to banish their "magic" even as their cohorts were smashing stained glass windows and "pillar people" in the old Catholic structures they came to occupy. In many instances, the belfry bells were just too difficult to pull down without damaging the church's infrastructure, so many Protestants continued to worship under bells covered with Catholic iconography. Since few ever saw the bells high in their towers, it seldom became an issue. If there were several bells in a Roman belfry, often only one was used as a concession to Protestant austerity. In the early Congregational churches of America, it was rare to find any bell at all, but that may have had more to do with the absence of a foundry and the expense of importing something that weighed tons.

When a new bell was required, the time-honored method of acquiring one was to pass a bucket through a community asking for contributions in the form of money or metal scraps. At the foundry, the scraps were sorted before the furnace was lit, but not before greedy churchmen and mayors pocketed the gold and silver. Contrary to public opinion, these precious metals lowered bell resonance, but the unscrupulous didn't want that information to circulate since fewer widows would contribute their husband's wedding bands to the pot. Riding the trolley to Heidelberg's university museum once, Annelore told me what became of Judas's thirty pieces of silver. I imagine that she'd heard the medieval legend from some anti-Semite in the Nuremberg school she attended. It seems that after Judas's suicide, the silver coins in his purse were contributed to some church trying to gather enough metal for a bell, but the result was a "mongrel pitch." Of course, the Nazis attributed the tenor's failures to Judas's Jewishness, not the brittle alloy achieved when copper, tin, and silver are combined. Over the centuries, many a misbegotten bell became another reason to persecute the Jews.

Though bells have occasionally been used as an excuse to harm, more often than not they've been regarded as benevolent creations. Doubtless, tales of bell generosity, such as the Catholic Easter bells mentioned earlier, can be traced to the music which is undamped, freely given, and once broadcast, independent of its maker. Imagine a sexton striking the wrong bell and trying to retrieve the sound! Such is the independence of the bell. And a bell's ability to fly can surely be traced to the way its tones "wing" their way to every quadrant of a town. The instrument's most common form has given rise to the belief among some Asians that the bell's body represents the womb and the clapper a phallus. The fact that bells call the faithful to worship but do not enter the sanctuary has made the bell a symbol of hypocrisy for a few Englishmen and Americans. In Africa, a widespread belief exists that if stuttering children drink from an inverted hand bell their speech will become clear as a crystal bell. And in the American South, the bell is sometimes given the attributes of eloquence and piety because it speaks from the church without ambiguity. One exception might have been the result of an earthquake in New Madrid, Missouri which shook that frontier town to its foundations in 1811 and 1812. The quake was so powerful that bells in Charleston, South Carolina, a thousand miles away spontaneously began to toll.

While our family was living in Europe in the 1960s, my parents took several opportunities to stretch my intellectual horizons. I recall visiting the Uffizi once and overhearing a tour guide's lecture on Michelangelo's *David*. It seems that as a young man the precocious sculptor was ordered by one of the Medicis to sculpt a statue in snow. The result was the *Madonna of the Centaurs*, a glittering success that inevitably melted in a Tuscan courtyard when the weather turned warm. Art's loss, however, was nature's gain when a bubbling spring was discovered where the Madonna once stood. Several years later, the guide said, Michelangelo was commissioned by some French lord to make a bronze *David*, similar but smaller than his marble colossus. Michelangelo did as he was instructed and shipped the bronze off to France. Unfortunately, war broke out, and *David* was melted down for the lord's ordnance. Not even a sketch remains.

In a poem, "Molecular Memory," I speculate optimistically on the possibility of the snow and the brass spontaneously reconstituting the form the master once gave them. At the resurrection of Michelangelo's bones, the snows of yesteryear, I imagine, will take the form of his *Madonna*. And shrapnel from all over Europe will rise up from ancient battlefields to be rejoined in the lost *David*. This scenario reflects not so much my rational faith as my reasonable hope.

Some have speculated that most of the bells of Europe have been melted more than once to make ordnance, which was then recast following the war into bells, reduced to artillery in the next war, and so on in a monotonous and deadly cycle of war and peace. In an epigram titled "In a Monastery Belfry," I begin by quoting a gunnery sergeant I met once who joined the Dominican order when the war ended:

> "Most bells were bells
> before they were cannon,"
> said the ex-Nazi
> who now is canon.

For the poet, the irony of the same substance and in this case the same person, being used to protect on one hand and destroy on the other is irresistible. Bell metal is a little like the fugu, a fish whose preparation the Japanese have raised to an art as well as a science. Cleaned and cooked properly, the meat is reported to be delicious, but carelessly prepared, it contains a potent poison. For centuries, I imagine, monarchs have mused the calling bells of their fiefdoms as the brass reverberated between heaven and earth. And as their bones have vibrated in unison with the carillon, some apparently wondered, "Shall I permit these bells to continue, or should

I have them melted down and declare war?" It seems there are two kinds of ruler: one who looks at a bell and hears a cannon explode, and another who looks at a cannon and hears a bell chime. Perhaps the church should do for bells what the Scots once did for the bagpipe: issue a license to operate only after the owner and user understood the instrument's potential.

Though Pope Pius III in 1503 abolished a society doing meteorological research because, "It is well known that God and witches alone cause the weather," the Catholic church for nearly three hundred years continued to sanction the ringing of bells to avert storm damage. If St. Anthony could banish demons by jingling his bells, surely a baptized bell could disperse a few dark clouds. But if lightning struck despite the pealing, the usual response was, "Imagine how much worse it would have been without the bells' interference." The Campanile of San Marco was struck at least nine times between 1388 and 1762. In 1766, the new Franklin rods were installed, and ever since, the famed bell tower has not been damaged by lightning (though it did collapse when its foundation crumbled in 1902, but then Franklin never claimed his invention was effective against dry rot). When the Parlement of Paris discovered that over a thirty-three year period 103 sextons had been electrocuted by lightning, the French passed the first law forbidding the ringing of church bells in thunder storms. Yet just a few years earlier, the Roman church had tried to ban lightning rods because they interfered with God's vengeance. Despite the progress of the Enlightenment, for many years into the more theistic nineteenth century, a church steeple protected by Franklin's rods and insulators was said to show a lack of faith. Most churches today are discreetly grounded in recognition of the fact that there's just so much the Creator can do to control lightning and arson after setting the universe in motion and issuing humans free will.

Incidentally, the ex-Nazi priest referred to above is a man I met touring The Church of Our Lady in Munich. Following his retirement forced by arthritis, he generously agreed to lead tourists around the church and up the double belfry. "Belfries," he said, "originally had nothing to do with bells. In old German, the word literally means 'peace tower.' Despite the ironic name, these war machines were actually siege towers which, when gunpowder rendered them obsolete around 1400, were rolled into walled cities, equipped with warning bells, turned around, and used as watch towers." I asked him if anyone had ever measured how far the pealing of Our Lady's bells carried, and he said approximately four miles though some bells in the Alps were reputed to have a range of thirty miles. Because the church was situated on a low promontory, it was visible on some days though not audible from a distance of twenty miles. He then volunteered that while on retreat in Belgium recently he'd learned some interesting local history: three times Antwerp had torn down its walls, circummurred new ones further out, and then cast larger bells to insure that each new house was protected by the invisible umbrella of its bell tones. Stone walls and oak gates were a physical barrier between the inhabitants and anyone who wished them harm; the bells, however, offered defenses less concrete but more vital to the spirit.

As proof of this contention, I would add that in the six years I have spent within the commonwealth of bells (I returned to Germany for three more years in the 1960s), I have never heard anyone so jaded as to express anything more than a passing annoyance with the laughter emanating from the belfries. No one ever seems to grow weary of this minimalist music any more than they tire of the lark's song. Indeed, how could anyone, whether atheist or pantheist, object to an instrument whose pure sound is free and useful. "I sing for joy," "I cry for the dead," "I console the living," "I dispel the storm," "I torment demons," "I repel the enemy," "I call to worship," "I mark the hours," and, "I celebrate the festival." These are just a handful of benevolent claims engraved or embossed on bells around the world; not one seeks to harm those living within the commonwealth of their appeal. Indeed in Northern Ireland, the Catholic and Protestant bells harmonize beautifully setting an ecumenical example for their human audience.

The music, of course, is the important thing, not the instrument which produces it. On several military bases where my father was stationed while I was growing up, a bugle that was played into a microphone and broadcast from speakers on the post-chapel steeple often substituted for big brass bells. For years I rose with reveille and was tucked into bed with taps along with hundreds of others within the gates of the garrison. There was something pleasantly reassuring and grown up about knowing others much older than I were doing the same thing at the same time. As John Huizinga says in *The Waning of the Middle Ages*, a town's bells "lifted all things into a sphere of order and serenity. . . ." The post bugle did likewise for me.

Alma Bennett, a widely traveled colleague who now lives a short distance from the Southern Railroad's "grand funk line," as she calls it, and who misses Europe's bells as much as I do, feels like the trains passing her home have an "engaging effect" on her emotions. "Trains make a charming clattering rhythm which draws you out of your cocoon. The tattered but homey racket is a very different sound than the bells I've known, but I've lived with the trains long enough now that I would mourn their passing if they stopped." As her bed starts to vibrate even before the whistle is heard, she feels connected to the world beyond her bedroom. She rejoices when the trains run on time and is worried when they run late as they did for weeks following September 9, 2001. I don't live quite as close to the tracks as my colleague does, but I have often felt like Thomas Wolfe in *Look Homeward, Angel* that the haunting rhythm of a train's "music" is as evocative and poignant as anything composed by Beethoven or Big Ben. Just as the curfew bell once was a warning to "cover the fire" and go to bed, so is the 9:55 departure of the Southern Crescent a communal reminder to put out the cat and turn down the covers, for it's time to catch that Pullman to dream land.

As a rational human who is unabashedly moved by the intangibles of life, I am proud to say that my spirit is often lifted by pealing brass, train whistles, and the wind in the willows. Lest I forget the transformational power of bells, I bought a recording of Cologne's famed church bells joyfully tolling the advent of Christmas. A dozen or more bells, high and low, near and far, fat and thin, ring the changes across the Rhineland for all to enjoy gratis. In America, a young land that is largely and sadly without bells, Christmas would be seriously diminished for me without our recording playing near the *Weihnachtsbaum*.

I should add that Clemson, South Carolina, where I have lived and taught for over thirty years, has never been entirely without bells. When I arrived in 1968, I discovered the E-flat bell, nicknamed "Pitchfork Ben," in the bell tower of Tillman Hall marking the hours, but its range was only a few hundred yards; it did not extend to the suburbs where we lived just two miles away. But even this small bell had what I called a "dominion of appeal," a phrase I used to title a poem about the school bell that once hung in the landmark named for the state's former governor, Benjamin "Pitchfork" Tillman.

> This place is not Oxford,
> nor is Tillman's tenor "Great Tom"—
> that brazen dome a shield
> against the German bombs.

"Pitchfork Ben" does not grieve
or shout at peace—
he chimes forth the hour
beneath the tower eaves.

Of gentle blood,
its rim sows crystal "E's"
over cool, trim lawns
and streets lined with trees.

Beyond its appeal,
oak turns to beetled pine,
red clay manges the rye,
and mill whistles whine.

In 1987, "Pitchfork Ben" was replaced by a carillon courtesy of the Clemson Alumni Association and hundreds of generous contributors. But before the carillon's installation, it certainly seemed as if the area within "Pitchfork Ben's" circle, the university and the close-by, more-established neighborhoods, drew sustenance from the bell while the area beyond looked forlorn and impoverished.

As much as I miss my German bells, I was amply consoled a few years ago when a member of Clemson's class of 1943 telephoned to ask a favor. Would I write a few verses to be embossed on a bell his class was donating to the university as a part of the new carillon? Of course, I agreed and eventually produced the following ditty:

I sing for those
        who now soar with the bird.
I speak for those
        who have given me words.
I sound for those
        who have yet to be heard.

The bell committee voted to accept what I'd submitted, and about a year later I was called to see the completed work before it was raised into Tillman's bell tower. My wife grabbed our daughter and a camera, and the three of us rushed to catch a glimpse of "my bell." There it stood, $55,000 worth of copper and tin, the largest bell of all forty-four, the "C" bell that would strike the hour, when it wasn't carrying the bass in the carillon, for tens of thousands of students and faculty for years to come. Though I had signed my verses, "Class of 1943," the committee had kindly placed my name under the poem. A reporter who was covering the carillon's installation spoke with me briefly about the unique way I'd been honored, and the next day, her article had the following headline: "Local Poet and Clemson Professor Achieves Immortality in Tillman's Bell Tower." It was all I ever wanted.

HELLO AND GOODBYE: THRESHOLD RITUALS AND THEIR IMPORTANCE

Perhaps the most cordial greeting ever extended to me by a stranger came from Bishop Desmond Tutu in December of 1991. My wife and I were attending the graduation ceremonies of our son and daughter at the University of South Carolina, and to our great surprise and pleasure, Bishop Tutu from South Africa was the keynote speaker. After the school president introduced him, the bishop stepped to the lectern and said to the hushed crowd of perhaps ten thousand, "The God in me greets the God in you." Whatever tension caused by a black man addressing a mostly white audience in a red state was instantly dispelled. Bishop Tutu, I believe, would agree that polite greetings and farewells are a lot like sacraments: outward and audible signs of an inner and spiritual grace. In Robert Frost's words, they're "temporary stays against confusion."

After the ceremonies, I added a line of my own to Bishop Tutu's greeting:

"Whether you are Christian, Muslim, or Jew,
The God in me greets the God in you."

Occasionally I use these verses when meeting a literature or humanities class for the first time. After one such occasion, an Indian exchange student informed me that Tutu was simply but elegantly translating the Sanskrit *Namaste,* which means, "I bow to the divine in you," or, "I honor the spirit in you, which is also in me." After a trip to India, my sister, a Methodist minister by trade but an ecumenical at heart, started saying *Namaste* when she would meet members of her congregation in town or after Sunday services. Before some people started complaining about it, she would bring her hands together prayerfully at her chest, bow her head, and pronounce the foreign compliment. Then like the Dalai Lama, she would take the extended hand of the person she was greeting in both of hers like a mother warming the hands of a child who has just come in from sledding. Most Methodists, however, preferred a firm handshake, and she eventually abandoned the practice.

Children, however, aren't as tied to society's rituals as their parents are. I once was asked to speak to a fourth grade class about the origins of personal names including the students' own. The class was already in a playful mood, and I didn't help matters when I went up to several of them and said, "Give me some hungry chicken." A college student had recently taught me this greeting as a variation on the old "Give me five" routine, and suddenly it occurred to me that something new and comical would help me gain the class's attention. Of course, I had to explain that when I said, "Gimme some hungry chicken," the person being greeted should extend an open hand. It was from this that the greeter would hungrily "peck" the proffered "grain." Unfortunately for the class's teacher who'd invited me, the kids continued pecking long after I'd left.

An adult hand tickling the excited hands of children is an unmistakably friendly gesture in any culture. The same must be said for the topless greeting given by British wives to their husbands and boy friends who were steaming into Southampton harbor on a troop ship following the Falkland Island War in 1982. No mistaking the sincerity of that greeting. However, what is one to make of a welcome mat I once saw that read, "You're not unwelcome"? To be effective, a greeting should be more than an abrupt "Don't get up" extended by a standing visitor to a seated co-worker. My response to this opener once was, "Well, don't sit down." Neither one of us quite understood what I meant nor where we should go from that point. Thoreau complained about the "ruts of tradition," but I regard most properly observed social rituals as long, steel rails that enable people to travel smoothly and efficiently together. The ritual observance, however, must be clear and precise.

Clarity is precisely what was missing when a twenty-something black stranger greeted an African-American acquaintance of mine in 2003. Dressed conservatively, freshly barbered, and bling-free, my thirty-something acquaintance had driven himself to a self-serve gas station in Greenville, SC where he filled up his aging Datsun. After paying inside and as he was leaving the station, he was greeted by the stranger with, "What's up, player?" My acquaintance was offended because to him *player* is synonymous with *pimp*, or what he refers to as the "BET-Blaxsploitation-Superfly meaning of the word." *Cassell's Dictionary of Slang* (1998), however, says that since the 1950s *player* is anyone who uses "wit, charm, or intelligence to gain his objectives." ("I sure do miss Cary Grant and Sidney Poitier; now they were players.") When I polled my students about what they thought *player* meant in the gas-station context, one said it was an acknowledgment of common culture, six had no idea, fourteen thought it was an insult as my acquaintance did, but forty-seven thought it was just an innocent variation of *hello*. I sided with the majority and suggested to my acquaintance that he assume the best until he knew otherwise. When he wrote a newspaper column about the incident, his mail ran thirty to one in his favor; the majority thought that "Hello, brother" or something similar would have been more appropriate. Perhaps it would have, but not even Hitler had the power to change a language try as mightily as he and his henchmen did. The young will be served, and there is no way to stop them from using words as they please even if it doesn't promote collegiality. At least he wasn't greeted with a *nigga, killer, gangster,* or *dawg.*

Embarrassment, of course, is not what a greeting should accomplish, unless the two involved are intimate and have a history of playfulness. In Aristophanes' famous 4th century B.C. comedy *Lysistrata*, an Athenian magistrate greets a visiting Spartan herald, knowing the man has not had sex in months because of a sex strike the women of Greece have called, "Say there, are you a man or Priapus?" Says the visitor, "I'm a herald, you lout! I've come from Sparta about the truce." Unwilling to stop his teasing, the magistrate says, "Is that a spear you've got under your cloak [or are you just glad to see me]?" Thus was born the joke that survives to this day. I'm not sure who first added the tag line, but what's interesting are the variations on *spear* that show up over the next two millennia: everything from a cigar during the Bill Clinton presidency, to an iPod, a joystick, a phaser, a nightstick if the visitor is a policeman, an Oscar if he's an actor, a putter if he's a golfer, an inflated ego, a bankroll if he's rich, a vibrating phone or pager, some mojo, or a banana to mention but a few. Nevertheless, few husbands would object to their wives privately "roasting this chestnut" even if it is as old as the Parthenon.

Perhaps seeking some relief from the Depression or the war, playful rimed greetings were popular in the 1930s and 40s. "Hello, Joe, what do you know?" "What's cookin', good lookin'?" and, "What's knittin', kitten?" were, according to my parents now in their eighties, commonplace. Punning greetings like, "Hi gossip, what's news?" "Hi, sprout, what's growin'?" and, "Hi Sugar, are you rationed?" likewise were all the rage in the Big Band era, and apparently few took offense.

A punning greeting, however, is seldom appropriate especially when there has been a long and painful absence. One of the most heart-felt greetings in the history of literature is that given to the prodigal son when the father of the born-again wastrel commands his servants to "kill the fatted calf." For nothing in the ancient world quite said, "You are welcome in my home" as meat on the table, and the more fat there was, the more welcome one felt. Two thousand years later when Old Lodge Skins in the film *Little Big Man* says to his adopted son, Jack Crabbe, after a long absence, "Greetings, my son, you wanna eat?" the viewer knows the much-traveled Jack is truly welcome. But perhaps no greeting has been as soulful as that which Lodge Skins speaks a few scenes earlier, "My son, to see you again causes my heart to soar like a hawk—sit here beside me. We must smoke to your return." I suppose the contemporary equivalent would be, "Daddy's home—release the doves!"

This brief discussion of welcoming ceremonies may remind us that in recent years *welcome* has become decidedly unwelcome. How often have we heard an NPR or CNN interviewer's "Thank you" met by an interviewee's "Thank you"? Not, "Thank YOU [for inviting me]," or "No, thank YOU [for your gracious invitation to speak on national media]," just, "Thank you" with *you* unstressed? Another annoying habit is the British use of "not at all" in replying to an American's "Thank you." It appears to be shorthand for, "My services have *not* been any trouble *at all* for me to supply," but I find the phrase dismissive and bordering on the rude. It's like the American habit of replying to a "Thank you" with, "Hey, no problem." I suppose the speaker is saying that the service he's provided was not a problem to deliver; he was just doing his job, but then the speaker probably knew that. The worst substitute for "You're welcome" is the "Don't mention it" response to an expression of gratitude that may have been clipped from, "My services were so insignificant that they do not deserve any mention at all." But if that were taken literally, where would discourse and the web of sociability woven by grateful recognition be? My feeling is that every kindness should be thanked, and that gratitude should be respectfully acknowledged.

∾

An Austrian proverb states that "Parting is a lot like grief," but for gentle souls like my mother-in-law, some arrivals are like grief because they anticipate the imminent and inevitable farewell that will soon bump the heart out of plumb. Goodbyes have by definition always been harder than greetings especially for those whom "party in peace" is just not adequate or appropriate. One of Camus' best stories, "The Guest," illustrates the obligations of the host and the difficulties of a guest's departure. As Arab anti-colonial fervor builds, the French police charge a colonial employee in a remote section of Algeria with the responsibility of turning an Arab suspected of murder over to government authorities in a distant town. After the Frenchman has informed the Arab of his travel options, he hands his guest, a man he has known for less than a day but for whom he feels a primal obligation, a two-day supply of food and a thousand francs. When the Arab attempts to thank his host, he cuts him off saying, "No, be quiet. Now I'm leaving you." And off he walks. To be sure, there are cultural obstacles and language difficulties between these two, but that doesn't entirely explain the awkward irresponsibility of their separation and the host's generosity. Does the Arab feel potlatched? Two women probably would have handled it a lot better.

In the offices adjacent to the building where seventy of us in the Clemson English Department teach, it is common to hear a colleague announce his or her departure especially as a class hour nears. A professor setting out to discuss Frost might ruefully say, "And I have miles to go before I sleep." Another professor who loves T.S. Eliot often leaves his office with, "Let's go raid the inarticulate and beat our wings for the truth" unless he's leaving with someone when he'll often say, "Let us go then you and I." If the someone he's leaving with is a stickler for grammar, he might hear, "Do you mean, 'Let us go then you and me'?" No matter who or what I'm teaching at any given hour on any given day, one colleague who loves vintage aircraft will often say as I pass his office, "Keep 'em flying." My usual response is, "Once more into the breach." The closest either one of us has ever come to combat was a desk job in the Cold War, but war and sport imagery is what many males resort to in difficult moments when nothing else springs to the lips.

At critical and not-so-critical junctures, men more than women, says Deborah Tannen, are likely to sound a note of levity to dispel the tension of the moment. Not once has a woman told me, "Au Reservoir," or, "Abyssinia," or, "Later, tater," or, "Let's make like an atom and split," or, "Don't let the screen door hit you where the good Lord split you," or, "Keep your nose between the ditches and the bears out of your britches." During the First World War, Southern country boys often would depart with "Well, butter my butt, and call me biscuit, but I have to be goin'." In the Second World War, many men who left with a "Bye, bye bonds," had sons who grew up to say in the 1960s, "Plant you now, dig you later." The sons of these men may have signed off with "Live long and prosper" if they were Star Trek fans, or "Escalator" if they were gay. However, in each case, humor substituted for heartfelt emotion as men continued to struggle with their "inner children" and "feminine sides" that psychologists assured us we all had. Rare is the male like the orphanage director in John Irvine's *Cider House Rules* who can announce each night, "Good night, my Princes of Maine, my Kings of New England" and convince his boys that he's not mocking them, that, indeed, he loves them.

When anonymous joking farewells fail us, many of us turn to the celebrity *du jour*— Alan King's "May the wattle fairy never darken your door," Groucho Marx's "Go and never darken my towels again," Cosmo Kramer's "Giddy-up," Elvis Presley's "Elvis has left the building," or Kinky Friedman's "May the god of your choice bless you." When Joseph Epstein retired from writing his quarterly essay for *The American Scholar*, he summoned the spirits of Jimmy Durante, Jackie Gleason, George Burns, Fibber McGee, Walter Winchell, Red Skelton, Jack Benny and perhaps some others unknown to me to conclude his poignant farewell piece. Wrote Epstein, "Good night, Mrs. Calabash, wherever you are. How sweet it is! Say goodnight, Gracie. Good night, Molly. Good night all. With lotions of love. God bless. We're a little late, so good night folks. And thanks."

Many years ago, an African student told me that in Swahili the equivalent of "Good night" is "Wake up living." This frank recognition of the dangers of sleeping in lion and elephant country led me to wonder what foreigners really are saying when they say goodbye because we sponges who speak English have absorbed so many foreign exit lines. Many of these farewells like our *goodbye* (a contraction of "God be with thee") express a wish that God accompany the departing guest as in the Spanish *adios, vaya con Dios,* and the French *adieu*. Often speakers of English leave with "I hope we see each other again soon" or simply "Later," as in the Russian *do sivdanya* and the German *auf Wiedersehen*. Another standard approach is to wish one's departing guest a safe journey as in our own *farewell,* the German *gute Reise* (though speakers of English may prefer the cross-language pun *gute Fahrt*), and the French *bon voyage*. Wishes for peace include the Hebrew *shalom*, the Arabic *ma'a salama*, and the Latin *Pax vobiscum*. But perhaps the most touching and melodious farewell is the Japanese *sayonara* which might be translated, "Thus if it be." I cannot imagine any phrasing more wistfully indirect yet satisfyingly incomplete. The full idea when the implied subject and predicate are added seems to be that Fate or Time has conspired against two people who must part. Anne Morrow Lindberg in *North to the Orient* thought *sayonara* was the most beautiful of all the goodbyes because "it does not cheat itself by any bravado" or provide "any sedative to postpone the pain of separation." Like me, she appreciates its indirect direction. By its very opacity, "Thus if it be" adds no pain to the separation, nor does it give any false hope of a god's protection, world peace, or a quick reunion.

In 1996, the *New Yorker* ran a cartoon drawn by Michael Crawford showing two yuppies going separate ways at a street corner. Said the man to the woman, "Plutardo, babe." "*Plutardo*" appears to be some idiosyncratic Esperantesque coinage meaning, "Later," but it also appears to have died the instant it was published, for I cannot find another trace of it in English except as a proper name. Apparently inspired by the Italian *a più tardi* ("till later"), the English word (if one can call it that) was created from the Latin roots "*plu-*" meaning "more" and "*tard-*" meaning "late." Most people I've shown the cartoon to just scratch their heads in bemused wonder.

As long as I'm parsing foreign farewells, let me deconstruct a few in English. The British *ta-ta* appears to be a child's simplification of *bye-bye*; *toodleoo* and *toodlepip* are comic variations of the French *tout à l'heure* (roughly translated, "[I'll be] back presently"); *cheerio* seems to have devolved from *cheers*, and *olive oil* is a late-nineteenth-century mispronunciation of *au revoir*. The English *so long* has inspired glosses from the Hebrew *shalom*, the Arabic *salaam*, and the German *so lange*, but Occam's Razor leads me to believe it's just a clipped form of, "Let us not be apart *so long* again," or, "I hope it's not *so long* before I see you again." Finally "eighty eights" and "thirty for now" are remnants of telegraph slang. "Eighty eights" was an arbitrarily chosen numerical sign-off meaning "love and kisses" like XOXO which is widely used today by senders of email to represent "hugs and kisses" with the X standing for an embrace and the O an open mouth. "Thirty for now" or, "That's thirty" comes from the telegraph convention of ending a sentence with an X to represent a period, XX to represent the end of a paragraph, and XXX to stand for "End of message," or, "Goodbye; I'm signing off."

But from high to low, from James Joyce's, "I go…to forge in the smithy of my soul the uncreated conscience of my race" to the anonymous, "May your genitalia never fail ya," exit lines are often personalized as a way of telling the other, "I'm bored with *goodbye*, but not you." A few years ago, my son and I started imitating those NFL players who after an interception, run toward each other, jump straight up, and bump their padded pectorals. We dispense with the running and jumping parts and just turn a farewell hug into three "pectoral thrusts" each followed by a manly, "Uh!" My daughter, on the other hand, gets a peck on the cheek and a conventional hug. Devoid of jumping but not kissing, my German wife and I have also evolved a rather elaborate bilingual departure ceremony: after I kiss her goodbye every weekday morning, I say, "Juice" (an anglicized variation on *tschüs* or "bye"), and she says, "*Luba du* or *Lova du* (anglicized forms of "*Ich liebe dich*," or, "I love you"). I then say "See-ox" (because the German *Sioux* is pronounced "see-ox" which sounds a bit like "see you"), and she goes to the window to wave as I back out of the drive way flashing my "light horn." Elements of this routine come and go, but in one form or another, it has served a worthy purpose for over forty years. At day's end, my reception is not quite as elaborate as my leaving but every bit as ceremonious. I suppose we just don't have the energy. The important thing is that I greet her and she me before I tell her of the stack of papers I have to grade, and she tells me she has jury duty.

And speaking of personalized farewells, my friend Dr. Jim Skinner of Presbyterian College fondly relates his mother's habit of asking her children whenever they left thhouse, "Do you have a handkerchief?" Initially, this ritual was a helpful reminder, but it soon became annoying before eventually turning into an endearing trademark. Jim and his three brothers finally reached the point that when they heard the question, they would simply pull their hankies from their back pockets and wave them without so much as a backward glance as if to say, "Yes, Mother, I *have* my handkerchief." When she died a few years ago, the four men concluded the funeral service by pulling out their handkerchiefs and waving them in silence over the casket. Mrs. Skinner, of course, had known all along those handkerchiefs would come in handy one day, and they did.

Briefly in closing, William James thought habitual ceremonies, both public and private, were the "flywheel of society…its precious conservative agent." Others have regarded them as the ballast in a ship's hold, which in a storm are worth their weight in platinum. I could not agree more, for whatever the metaphor, the brevity of these rituals belies their steely-stony weight.

LIKE NAIL CLIPPINGS IN THE FIRE

For Ingrid

"Then the dust shall return to the earth as it was,
and the spirit shall return unto God who gave it."

Ecclesiastes 12:7

The sudden abridgement of heart and brain
should let my soul make its sighing exit
like light passing unobstructed through glass.

Then, assuming proper ventilation,
the gases will vanish up the flue
and be shuffled back in the mix.
Methane and phosphorus should flash blue-green
and head to some black hole starved for light.
Blood and tears will gradually boil off
and join Aeolus stuffing the stomata
of Pickens County and Jupiter's moons.
Soon, only the solids will remain—
enough iron for a ten-penny nail—
some of the same stuff, I imagine,
that stiffened the spines of Adam and Eve.
Though the skull may require a pestle,
please scatter the carbon and calcium
with their emptinesses now dismantled
into that bed of perennials
we weeded and fed for thirty years.

Watch for me in the spring.
Should you choose to wear me on your breast,
draw me into your lungs, dear, one last time
or as long as the fragrance shall last.

SINGING FROM THE SAME HYMNAL: SEARCHING FOR A COMMON BOND

Item: For centuries, historians of religion have quietly noted that Islam and Christianity are derivatives of Judaism. Item: In 1991, the Christian and Muslim armies of thirty-eight countries gathered under the flag of the United Nations to free Kuwait from Saddam Hussein. Item: A few years later a DNA study conducted among Syrians, Palestinians, Lebanese, and Jews concluded that they share a common set of ancestors. Judging from these three random observations and facts, many of us are lighting our candles from a common torch, yet prospects for an enduring peace in the Middle East range from dim to dark. In such a climate, man's common humanity seems a hopeless subject, barely a dream at the start of the twenty-first century. Searching for a compatible human denominator brings those of us who would later major in English the despair we felt in the fifth grade when, grasping at numbers like floating straw, the only denominator we could find for two incongruous fractions was a fifty-seven. "Could it be? Please, dear Lord, let it be!"

Despite the complexities, mathematicians and scientists surely have enjoyed more success in the search than most. Harlow Shapley, former Director of the Harvard College Observatory, found the common denominator in the inert gas argon. Each human breath, Shapley calculated, is filled with 3×10^{19} argon atoms which have never combined with anything since the Big Bang. Consequently every breath that any of us takes contains roughly 300,000 of the argon atoms Saddam Hussein or George W. Bush or anyone else has breathed at some time in the past. Without argon, which makes up about one percent of the atmosphere, our lives would be largely unchanged (the gas is used primarily in welding and in insulating windows), but nitrogen, which makes up eighty percent of the atmosphere, is absolutely essential to all life. Shapley calculates "that every breath...contains, on average, three of the nitrogen atoms from any given human breath...." Is there anyone who would not feel more connected to the past, the cosmos, and his fellow humans reading these calculations?

Our mutual dependence on science was further illustrated in the 1960s by Raymond Fosdick of the Rockefeller Foundation when he noted the contributions of the global health community. While the world is guarded from polio by what an American did, Fosdick observed, humans are guarded from smallpox, rabies, pellagra, and diphtheria by what an Englishman, a Frenchman, an Austrian, and a Japanese respectively did. A similar service has been provided to domestic animals by the world's veterinary researchers. As the German Arab Hafid Habid once wondered playing off a notion expressed by Terence and Montaigne, "If your car is Japanese, your pizza Italian, your coffee Brazilian, your numbers Arabic or Indian, your alphabet Latin, your carpet Persian, and your democracy Greek, how can your neighbor be an alien?"

More importantly, how can ancient allies become adversaries as when France fell from favor in America for refusing to invade Iraq in 2003? Some American enophiles emptied their wine cellars of all French vintages. One wonders what these nationalists would have done had they known that French vines once had been saved by rootstocks from Missouri just as California vines were saved by rootstocks from France.

Today the discoveries of medical science often come to us after years of research and great expense, but one wonders sometimes if the time and money were well spent reinventing the truth. In the 1980s, scientists announced that three alcoholic drinks a day are permissible and may even be salubrious. Ironically, over two thousand years ago the

Greek philosopher Eubulus wrote, "Three bowls only do I mix for the temperate; one to health…, the second to love and pleasure, the third to sleep. When this bowl is drunk up, wise guests go home." A transcendentalist might have argued that the truth of the three-drink limit resided from the beginning in the Oversoul and that anyone has access to this universal truth if their perceptions are refined enough to extract it. A Jungian psychologist, on the other hand, might argue that this specific truth has resided in the collective or racial unconscious since about 8000 BC when humans began drinking alcoholic beverages and experiencing the consequences of overindulgence.

Regardless of the source of any medical or scientific discovery, one can only hope that the truths of biological mutuality make themselves known as soon as possible, for people of different races have far more in common than not. The difference in genetic material between any two humans on the globe is only one-ten-thousandth of a percent. Bone, organ, and blood transplants among the races have all been successfully performed. More than one white man sees the world today through the corneas of a black man and vice versa. In Brazil, about one quarter of all marriages are interracial. Furthermore in Europe and the Americas, Negro women have long suckled white children. And the melanin that makes a Mongolian's skin brown is chemically identical, though the concentration is different, to the substance that makes a Negro's hair and a Caucasian's freckles dark brown or black. Other biological differences among the three major races, such as the shape of hair cross sections and the width of noses, are absurdly superficial. The similarities should come as no surprise since all humans trace their lineage to a tribe of East African ape mutants who lived about four million years ago. Further differences of behavior and intellect, for example, are cultural and of doubtful validity. Despite differences, there are few Mongolians, Caucasians, and Negroes who are incapable of enjoying a cup of coffee while watching a re-run of "The Muppets" and chatting about the virtues of Fuji's film or Volkswagen's automobiles. Now if these representatives of the races are literate, the possibilities of discussion are almost endless.

Take the commonwealth of folk tales for instance. How many of us could not appreciate a tale from India in which words are employed as love charms, or a Jewish tale in which an angel is conceived in each of God's words, or a tale from Finland in which a hero searches for the magical words which will save his people, or a West Indian tale in which a literal reading of a text leads to a misinterpretation of some religious words? Stith Thompson who has recorded these folk motifs (are they dream motifs too?) also makes a reference to an English folk tale in which negligent priests are buried beneath bags filled with words never spoken in their church services. Stated without the trappings of culture, the folk motifs are scarcely foreign to us, but how are their similarities and common appeal to be accounted for? Jan Harold Brunvand has observed that there are two basic possibilities: the materials originated in one place and were diffused, or the materials came into existence independently in many places about the same time. Whatever the source of this folk wisdom, we have more reasons to form associations for our common benefit than not.

Like students of folklore, students of cultural anthropology in search of the common bond (though some would call it the Holy Grail) have recorded similar proverbs in several languages. Mario Pei has observed, "whether we use our own 'Too many cooks spoil the broth,' or the Italian 'With so many roosters crowing, the sun never comes up,' or the Japanese 'Too many boatmen run the boat up to the top of the mountain,' or the Persian 'Two captains sink the ship,' or the Russian 'With seven nurses, the child goes blind,' the basic idea is the same." Writers of proverbs, it seems, have drawn extensively from Emerson's Oversoul and Jung's racial memory even if the metaphors chosen are widely divergent. The figurative language in which most proverbs are couched is just a smoke screen; blow the smoke away, and the similarities in the following examples should be apparent. In a letter to a friend, Lord Byron once called hope a "hollow-cheeked harlot." An anonymous Turk, who in all likelihood had never read Byron, observed, "He who lives on hope dies of hunger." A Pole, equally ignorant of the British writer, stated, "He whose coach is drawn by hope has poverty for a coachman." And a Dane once wrote, "Hope is a fool's income." Whether the metaphor is drawn from the realm of sex, food, transportation, or finance, the message concerning the fleeting sustenance of hope is the same. After a deep disappointment, I imagine that all four of these writers had grown cynical, and searching for a means to express themselves, they stumbled on their metaphors. What they felt was very nearly identical; how they expressed it naturally varied. One does not have to read very far in Sophocles and Moses before realizing that human emotional responses like grief and joy have not changed in three thousand years of human history.

Like proverbial literature, all cultures have their myths and legends which are remarkably similar. Hardly a society exists, as students of cross-cultural mythology have learned, that does not have its flood, birth-of-the-sun, or racial-differences myth. Likewise, basic artistic themes like man's quest for freedom, and subjects like birth and death are universal. Observe also the wide appeal of French film, African sculpture, Italian painting, American jazz, and Japanese poetry. Were aesthetic tastes formed before our ancestors migrated out of East Africa about 50,000 years ago? How is it that children around the world have their own version of *our* Pig Latin, *our* jump-rope rhymes, and *our* superstitions? I have no better answer than the Transcendentalists' Oversoul, but here are several more illustrations of our fascinating mutuality.

Iona and Peter Opie, who initially studied the lore and language of schoolchildren in England, Wales, and Scotland, noticed a great similarity of custom when children say the same word at the same time. The custom usually entails linking fingers and making a wish. The similarity was so striking that the Opies informally broadened their study of these ceremonies to include Ireland, Italy, Austria, Germany, the Netherlands, Sweden, Norway, Spain, Bolivia, and Egypt. Concluding, the Opies stated:

> It appears, indeed, that the rite would bear detailed investigation in the U.S., and possibly throughout the world, for the coincidence of two people accidentally saying the same thing at once is marked by some little ceremony in every country in which we have made inquiry, and almost invariably it aims at influencing or finding out about the future.

Why the Opies omitted the United States is indeed odd, but I can assure them that American children have been linking fingers and making wishes for generations.

Like the children of the world in the Opie's study, those who write on walls, sidewalks, and other public surfaces also have much in common. Robert Reisner and Lorraine Wechsler, who compiled the *Encyclopedia of Graffiti*, have noted how similar men and women's motives for writing are, especially in the privacy of a public toilet. The wall, as these editors argue, becomes a therapist for the graffitist, for the deepest and darkest impulses are expressed there. Not uncommonly, there are many similarities in the fundamental and usually vulgar expressions of hostility, scatology, fantasy, and propaganda. To take one mild set of examples, the editors observe that an Englishman once wrote, "How shall the Man e'er turn to dust who daily wets his clay with ale." Echoing this sentiment, an American wrote, "Old Grand-dad is dead but his [alcoholic] spirits live on." The graffitist universally writes to say, "I exist, and this wall is my outlet." That alcohol and other intoxicants may be responsible for some of what Wallace Stevens called mankind's "necessary fictions" is a denominator that goes a long way toward helping humanists discover what we have in common.

As proponents of Esperanto have been saying for a century, a common language, as Latin used to be in Christendom, would be very useful in the world peace process. Of course, English is already functioning as a *lingua franca* and has been since the end of World War II. Words and phrases like *Internet, computer, airport, passport, hotel, telephone, bar, soda, Coke, Marlboro, McDonalds, sport, gold, tennis, stop, OK, weekend, jeans, know-how, sex appeal,* and *no problem* are virtually universally understood. One is no longer sur-prised to hear of the Filipino second grader living in Frankfurt, who when asked to bring some authentic cuisine representative of the child's homeland, brought the class a ham-burger. What is surprising is that many Germans don't know that the hamburger minus the bun originated in Germany. "Run a 'burger through the garden," and it's thoroughly American, but one may buy one in most countries of the world.

If this reciprocity is beginning to sound vaguely inevitable or deterministic, a brief examination of color terminology should be reassuring. While blue, for example, in English connotes Puritanism, melancholy, and the aristocracy among other things, the same color in Italian means soft (as in *a blue voice*). In French it refers to a political conservative, and in German it suggests mild intoxication. The connotations of red, furthermore, show a similar confusion: in English *to see red* is to be angry; *a red tale* in Spanish is an indelicate one; in Ital-ian the yolk of the egg is the red, and in Russia a *red speaker* is not surprisingly an eloquent one. In fact, anything red in Russian is beautiful or valuable though that has been changing since the demise of the Soviet Union. Perhaps the Tower of Babel is responsible for these dis-parities, but it is interesting that pink is everywhere in the world more positive than negative, and yellow is everywhere the reverse at least in phrases in which these colors are found. Such similarities can probably be explained by the universal high regard for blood and health, and the fear that all cultures have for disease, which is often manifested by a yellowing leaf or limb. More difficult to explain is the unanimity Brent Berlin and Paul Kay found among the world's languages: no language, it appears, has more than eleven basic color terms. If a lan-guage has only two basic terms, these are always black and white. A language with three basic terms will have acquired black, white, and red; one with four terms will have black, white, red, and either green or yellow; one with five will have black, white, red, green, and yellow; one with six will add blue to the preceding five; and one with seven will include brown. If a language has eight, nine, ten, or eleven basic terms, it will have acquired purple, pink, orange or gray, but not in any predictable sequence.

Berlin and Kay make a very strong case for cultural unanimity, but a survey of ges-tures leaves one awash again in the flux. Sticking one's tongue out can mean anything from defiance and disdain in the U.S., to a welcome in Polynesia, respect in Tibet, teasing in Jordan, and copulation in Colombia. Dropping one's pants and flaunting one's naked buttocks, on the other hand, is regarded as insulting most everywhere in the world. During the 1967 stalemate between China and Russia, for instance, an entire platoon of Chinese soldiers marched to the front lines, dropped their trousers, and bowed in a southerly direction. But in Lapland, the "moon" is believed to blunt enemy swords, and in Pomerania, if the buttocks are female, "mooning" prevents the flight of bees. It has been estimated that body language may be responsible for over 70% of what humans communicate face to face. Gestures like rubbing one's belly ("That was a good meal.") or cupping one's ear ("Speak louder."), therefore, come as close to a *lingua franca* as the Hawaiian *aloha* and the Spanish *adios*.

Turning to religion, seriousness must prevail though humor is a major cultural denominator that has only been hinted at in these pages. Every culture, it seems, has a variation on, "Is that a banana/spear/pistol in your pocket, or are you just glad to see me?" Religion, however, like humor, is an element shared by all. Observe the importance and the similarities of incest taboos and of birth, marriage, and death ceremonies worldwide. Helpfully, Jeffery Moses, in his book *Oneness*, has collected many of the moral tenets which adherents of the world's great religions share. These include: "Honor thy father and mother," "Heaven is within us," "Conquer with love, not revenge," "You are known less by your words than your actions," "Judge not lest you be judged," "Follow the spirit rather than the letter of the law," and "God is love." But the foundation of the ecumenical movement may very well be the universality of the altruistic ideal. It is comforting that the golden rule of Confucianism is, "What you don't want done to yourself, don't do to others." For the Buddhists the rule is, "Hurt not others with that which pains yourself," and for at least nine other major religions across the globe, Christianity included, the same idea is not just an ethical proposition, but the *Golden* Rule. Perhaps that is cause for hope, perhaps not because these "rules" have been in place for close to three millennia. Good news, it seems, travels exceedingly slow. At any rate you will have something to talk about the next time you take a Muslim to lunch where a sign in the window may well read, "Come in, or we'll both starve."

No where have people "come in" in the last thirty years quite the way they have entered sports arenas and stadiums the world over. In 2002, for example, when Yao Ming first played for the Houston Rockets, an estimated 300 million people tuned in the game in China and presumably rooted for the Rockets. So much for the value of rooting; that season the Rockets finished fifth in the Midwest division. In the same year, 201 nations sent at least one representative to the Olympic Games; that's ten more member nations than the United Nations claimed at the same time. Back home some two billion fans watched the home team on television. Of course, the 10,500 athletes competing in Athens needed 45,000 security personnel, but that's a story for another day. As Isaac Newton discovered, the falling apple is attracted to the earth just as the earth is drawn to the apple. The same might be said of most any ball used in sport—the entire globe, it appears, is drawn to the ball especially at massive tournaments like the World Series, the Stanley Cup finals, and the most global of all, the World Cup of Soccer.

Art shall be my final venue even if its numbers are not as dramatic as sports. Because of the billions of fans drawn to sport, there is a natural divide between athletics and art that continues to widen, for few who are drawn to sport are drawn to art with the same intensity. Nevertheless, conductor Seiji Ozawa bridged the sport-art gulf effectively in the opening ceremonies of the Winter Olympics held at Nagano, Japan in 1998. He positioned choruses on each of the five continents and led them all simultaneously via a television satellite connection even as he conducted an orchestra in Nagano in a performance of

Beethoven's "Ode to Joy." And a joyful, uplifting performance it was, for man's arbitrary boundaries are no obstacle to electronic transmissions and nature.

Another Japanese artist, Yukinori Yanagi, has brilliantly underscored nature's indifference to human boundaries in an installation entitled *World Flag Ant Farm* (1990). Mounted on two connected museum walls, the work consists of 182 Plexiglas boxes each containing a flag made of colored sand representing a sovereign nation. (At the time of the installation, there were 182 member states in the U.N.) Once the sand had been painstakingly poured into the boxes and the flags had taken shape, Yanagi connected each box to its neighbors by a network of plastic tubes. Into the boxes and tubes, he then released a colony of ants, who, of course, know nothing of the sacred nature of flags. Over the course of several months, the ants slowly deconstructed each flag, some more than others, as they transported parts of one "country" to another. One day we may all carry the "passport" that ants and birds have always enjoyed.

As Peter Farb has observed, "one society's sin may be another society's virtue." Certainly there is almost as much evidence in this essay for cultural relativity as there is against it; in fact, there may be no absolute truths among the world's cultures. But while two people may comprise a multitude, in divisive times, little is gained by dwelling on differences and belaboring the problems which divide us. Defining cultural distinctions can, of course, lead to greater understanding, but with the Four Horsemen of famine, poverty, war, and disease galloping across the Middle East and much of the rest of the world, it is well to recall the Hebrew psalmist's words, "Behold, how good and how pleasant it is for brethren to dwell together in unity." Neither should one forget these words from the Koran, "Allah loves not those who create disorder."

FATHER-SON TALK
For Shane

Their talk in the parlor
is dry and small—
thoughtful speech blossoms
when tossing a ball.

The End Is Nearish

I come from a long line of crystal-ball gazers most of whom eventually lost their faith in crystal. Take my uncle Ted, for instance who in the early 1940s was projected by his high school peers to be the "Least Likely to Succeed." True to form, Ted was expelled from Gordon Military College in his freshman year and took up welding. A perforated eardrum kept him out of the military when the army was accepting anyone standing more than 5', weighing at least 105 pounds, and having twelve teeth. Ted says that initially he believed his peers' predictions, but that all those veterans who needed houses after the war made success in the building business so easy even a "failure" like himself could succeed. As an independent building contractor today, Ted is worth a vast fortune, owns three homes, uncounted automobiles, an airplane, and recently set up an educational foundation with an endowment of ten million dollars. I realize that success is measured in different ways, so I should add that Ted is also married, has three children (all successful themselves), and six grandchildren. So much for the accuracy of yearbook predictions. Some would say that the very gloom of the forecast launched Ted's career, but that would make crystal balls ironic. Forecasters cannot have it both ways—if the weatherman announces that it's going to rain, and the sun shines, consumer confidence is not bolstered knowing he may have been teasing.

Another uncle, an exception who never lost the faith, once phoned a psychic hotline and learned that he had a "better than average chance of winning the Publishers' Clearing House grand prize." Uncle Bill, who was close to senile in his eighty-fourth year, calculated that he could guarantee a victory if he purchased every subscription Publishers' Clearing House offered—at the time 120! When he lost, he was despondent, of course, but he had plenty of magazines to console him. I told him that phone psychics, who gross about a billion a year in this country alone, are just in it for the money. He said that wasn't the case because if they were, they wouldn't stay on the line for as long as you needed them. Aunt Laurie, Ted and Bill's sister, also shared a faith in clairvoyance but lost it about five years before her death. In her mid-80s, she voluntarily surrendered her driver's license after a near accident. On a five-lane highway, she had approached a green light in rush-hour traffic wanting to make a left turn. The turn arrow was not lit, but since she was first in line in the turn lane, she thought she could sneak a left when the light turned red. We've all been there. But when the light changed, the cars to her left and right started across the intersection so quickly (or maybe she was just too slow), she thought she'd better wait, so she backed up a few feet to wait for the green arrow. While she was sitting there, a complete stranger drove up on her right, rolled down her window, and asked, "Are you in 'Drive,' dear?" Laurie looked at her automatic-transmission indicator, and seeing that she was still in "Reverse," went suddenly cold. She realized that if the light had turned green a few seconds earlier, she would have accelerated directly into the car behind her. For days she told this story thinking her anonymous benefactor was a mind reader until she realized that the woman had merely seen her backing up at the light and then noticed that her back-up lights remained on when she forgot to shift into "Drive." Laurie's Samaritan has the eyes of a lynx, but she's not a seer. The only 20/20 forecasters I know of are the meteorologists stationed at McMurdo Sound, Antactica. Their daily forecast is "cold."

They've never been wrong.

Edellyn, another aunt but on my father's side, was surprised to be told by her college roommate, an accounting major, that she might be diabetic. Publicly my aunt ridiculed the prediction, but privately she worried. After a fretful week, she went for a blood test because she had been feeling somewhat feeble and feverish. The blood work revealed she had, indeed, developed a case of diabetes. For a couple of years Edellyn told people of her roommate's uncanny diagnostic ability, until a doctor asked her if she recalled ants around the toilet.

"As a matter of fact," Edellyn replied, "we did have ants in that dorm room. We sprayed; the school sprayed, but nothing seemed to help. The ants always came back."

"Well, there you have it," her physician opined. "The ants were attracted by the sugar in your urine. Your roommate wasn't Nostradamus, but by any chance, was she related to a health-care worker?"

"Yes," Edellyn said, "her mother was a public-health nurse."

Very often, what appears to be a product of pure intuition turns out to be a subconscious reading of subtle but empirical clues. (The Greeks called ants "piss prophets," by the way, largely because of their "uncanny" ability to diagnose disease.) Though an infestation of ants is not very subtle, few people associate them with human disease. Why the roommate never revealed how she knew what the prognosis would be remains a mystery. I suspect she enjoyed the sibyl's throne and didn't want to relinquish it. The Italian astrologer Girolamo Cardano was so disappointed when he awoke in good health seventy-two hours before the day he had predicted he would die, he committed suicide.

Predictions become more dangerous when clues are open to arbitrary or subjective interpretation. My wife, Ingrid, was a victim of such a prediction as a child. In the fourth grade, she came to school in Wolsdorf, Germany and was confronted by a friend in the schoolyard. The friend had made a small paper device that in America used to be called a "cootie catcher." It's folded from a single piece of paper in such a way that it fits over the fingertips of one hand, and depending on how the fingers beneath are moved, it's capable of opening in one of two ways. American kids who have these innocuous devices usually run amok collecting invisible "cooties" from their victims in their origami-style "catcher." In Germany, though, in the hands of budding psychics, the gizmo once had an eschatological function. Standing by the swing set, my future wife was casually asked her birthday, the numbers of which were then totaled to indicate how many times this device was to be opened and closed. When the schoolmate concluded, she poked the device in Ingrid's face and said, "See the red? You're going to hell!" The prognosticator then showed how her birthday sum insured that because she was "blue," she was heaven bound. As often as the device was fed Ingrid's odd sum of five (she was born on the 23rd), "Hell" was her ultimate destination. Needless to say this prediction caused my wife-to-be a great deal of worry until she confided in her mother what had been bothering her. A simple demonstration of odd and even numbers sufficed to lift the sinking heart that the forecast had caused her.

One of Steven Wright's stand-up routines goes something like, "I'm a peripheral visionary. From time to time, I get sidelong glimpses of the future. Sometimes I'm right; sometimes I'm wrong. It's a lot like guessing." Actually guessing is more accurate than some soothsaying: Punxsutawney Phil's Groundhog Day predictions, for example, have only a 39% accuracy rate over 114 years. But guessing whether spring will be early or late is profoundly different from stating unequivocally the fate of someone's immortal soul, and for this reason my wife and I were careful never to tell the above story to our own children before they could handle it. In fact, I was careful to avoid any mention of such hocus pocus, but you can't inoculate your kids against every germ. Once I went up to the tree house where I knew our son was playing with the neighbors' kids to call him for lunch, and I walked in on an impromptu séance. A child had drowned in Lake Hartwell a few days earlier, and this innocent threesome was trying to make contact with their school chum's soul to find out how he liked heaven. I excused myself for interrupting the session, but after lunch, I asked our son where he'd learned how to conduct a séance. "Oh," he said, "all the kids do it."

Children are often the focus of prognostications made or caused by their elders, and these speculations, which soon become unpaid debts, can be heavy burdens to bear. Think of Oedipus hearing for the first time the famed prophecy that he would kill his father and marry his mother. These words came as such a shock they recklessly led the young man to abandon home and family, climb a mountain, kill the first man he met old enough to be his father, descend the mountain, and marry the first nubile woman he met. Yet impulsiveness was only part of this young man's problems. Unknown, of course, to Oedipus was the information that the man slain and the woman wed were his natural parents, but what the son may never have realized is that he'd already fulfilled the oracle's prophecy. Figuratively fulfilled it that is. Indeed, he satisfied the god's command as every child fulfills it because every one of us labors under the same curse. All of us one day will "kill" our mother and father with disappointment in some form, yet even as their hopes lie dashed, we are "married" to our parents for as long as we live, for in many ways the umbilical cord is never completely severed.

Unlike hindsight, however, prescience is not 20/20, and timing has much to do with the success of the rain dance. Aeschylus knew that as well as Sophocles did, but he still went outside on the day the oracle said a falling house would kill the writer. Logically enough, he assumed that the house was his own and an earthquake would rattle his foundations as they frequently do in Greece, so he spent the day taking a walk so blithely unaware of any danger that he didn't even wear a hat, much less a helmet. Legend has it that an osprey flew over and, mistaking Aeschylus' bald crown for a smooth rock, dropped the turtle he was carrying. The blow, of course, killed the careless playwright who was slain by the turtle's falling "house." If a tree had fallen on him, the "house" surely would have been a bird's or a squirrel's. If a landslide had buried him, some pantheist would have claimed that the hill was a god's house. Indeed, is there anything that cannot be construed as a "house"? I've read of meteors arriving on Earth after striking Mars a glancing blow "housing" evidence of some extraterrestrial organism or another.

Of course, the oracle was always right; her life and livelihood depended on it. We know that Heinrich Himmler's astrologer died in a Nazi concentration camp, but I know of no other prognosticator who perished as a revealed fraud. The longevity of prophets is largely a factor of their language: it's hard to build a case against anyone whose diction and syntax are a Rorschach. One ancient Greek prophecy urged an army general to lead his men immediately across the river that ran beside his camp because, the oracle reported, "The army that crosses the river first will destroy an empire." Win or lose, the oracle was correct unless someone called a truce. But if hostilities ensued, as they did, one empire or the other was lost, and the oracle was left smelling like a rainbow. Cash offerings were left at the door unless one wanted to risk angering the oracle, who may have been a bit testy sitting on a tripod all day inhaling sulfurous fumes. Others say the aging virgin smelled a rotting python carcass or chewed hallucinogenic laurel leaves. Whatever it was that caused her trance, few dared to challenge her.

A good though circumstantial case can be made that at least some of the oracles were outright frauds. It's likely that at least one of the Delphic sibyls used carrier pigeons and some trusted associates (oracles in training) to bring word of what King Croesus was doing on a given day—making a turtle and lamb stew—in the monarch's very risky attempt to prove the seer wrong. Moreover, the *Encyclopedia Britannica* states that the Temple of Dionysus at Corinth was turning water into wine long before Jesus attended the wedding at Cana. Apparently, there is some archeological evidence consisting of pipes and vats which once allowed priests to "make wine" from outside a sealed temple by operating some concealed controls. The water was drained from one vat, and the wine flowed in from another.

My own experience with oracles began when I was fourteen. On the grounds of the Muscogee County Exposition and Fair, a gypsy palmist told me that what I'd taken as an extraordinary "love line" was really quite short. This interpretation proved false when I met the lovely Ingrid; to date we've been married for over forty-three years, and my teeth have been set against prophets for even longer. Nevertheless, I've slowly come to the conclusion that I may be prescient myself; it's just that I'm so far sighted that nothing has come true yet. H. G. Wells is the first futurist I know of who used the trick of dating one's predictions so far in the future that no one in all likelihood will remember Wells or his projections when the time comes. At the present, 3000 to 4000 years appears to be the limit of our cultural memory, so Wells' predictions for the year 800,000 AD in *The Time Traveler* appear safe.

Seriously, though, I do have premonitions. Once as I approached a red light, an interior voice said, "Put the car in neutral." I hardly ever follow my father's advice to save some wear on the clutch by placing the transmission in neutral while stopped in traffic, but for once, I heeded the advice. So there I sat musing cloud formations when I suddenly noticed the light was green. Embarrassed (there were cars behind me now though no one was honking), I pressed down hard on the accelerator, and though there was a mighty roar of my Tercel's sixty-five horses, I went nowhere. Just as the racket subsided, a white pickup sped brazenly through the red light from my left. I stared after its dust in disbelief. If I had not put the car in neutral as the voice told me, I very likely would have pulled into the path of the scofflaw, who may have sensed that I was going nowhere. Technically, I was in the right, but I was nearly dead right, so the incident gave me considerable pause. Indeed, I have seen the future, and in it I am dead. The wild card is knowing how far in the future that sad event lies, and I have no desire to know that date anymore than I want to see the video of my prostate being reamed out which is also in the near future, one of my favorite oxymorons.

Guard as I may against the nonsense of the modern entrails reader, I find myself subconsciously reading the "signs" in the chaos of daily life. I recall that just before going in for my doctoral orals, I stopped by the canteen and bought a Coke from the machine that once had taken my money and given me nothing in return. As I stood before this unreliable vendor, I thought, "If this sucker works today, I'm in like Flynn." (I often forecast in clichés.) Whatever convinced me that this refrigerated roulette wheel knew my ineluctable fate, I do not know, but just then the paper cup dropped with a reassuring rattle, a few hollow ice cubes followed on cue, and the cup then filled to the brim with my soda. Not a drop was wasted. I walked off to meet my inquisitors with a renewed confidence born of a newfound proficiency in the strange language God uses to communicate with mortals. There is no doubt that a psychic like a trusted priest or teacher can lift one's spirits even if all they do is listen and dispense caffeine.

Yet if I am a medium, I am not a happy medium. I still firmly believe that there is no way to examine the railroad tracks and determine which way the last train passed unless it is within earshot. If tea leaves, playing cards, dice, fire, excrement, mole and freckle patterns, stomach-gas rumblings, dreams, stars, and tabloids have our fates recorded, I should have died seven years ago. In late 1993, the *National Enquirer* published a list of predictions, one of which said, "In 1994, a South Carolina teen will detonate a nuclear device in his basement killing thousands." If there was such an explosion, I must be living upwind from ground zero. However, there never has been a Hiroshima-style disaster in South Carolina though the Air Force accidentally dropped an "unarmed atom bomb" on tiny Mars Bluff in 1958. "Only" the non-nuclear portion of the device exploded injuring a family of six and leaving their home in ruins on the brink of a 60' wide and 30' deep crater that once was their garden.

My wife's Magic-8-Ball is not much better than mine, but she's a believer nonetheless. One evening after supper, she went for a walk in our neighborhood. As she passed by a vacant, over-grown lot and its two beetle-infested pines, she felt a distinct shiver and consciously quickened her step to put some distance between her and the looming trees. Less than six hours later, a windstorm blew the larger of the pines down across the street that my wife had recently traveled with sudden trepidation. In the safety of our bedroom, we heard the explosive sound of the trunk snapping. It is sometimes said that the present is pregnant with the future, and indeed, on closer inspection the present was about eight months along that night. My wife had heard the weather reports of an impending thunderstorm, we'd agreed that the lot's out-of-state owner should cut his trees, the pines had been without bark or needles for at least three years, and the wind was beginning to gust as she made her way around the neighborhood. Subconsciously, she assembled the data, read the clues, and realized that nature might soon be making its will known. But to her, dodging the falling tree was a miracle, and I could not convince her otherwise. Frankly, I didn't try very hard because I dearly wanted to believe someone other than myself was looking out for her, just as a "clairvoyant" drink machine had once comforted me.

When my rational nature manifests itself in a classroom full of young fundamentalists, however, the class often stirs uneasily. I recall telling twenty freshmen after Elvis Presley died that contrary to received opinion some adoring fans were convinced their idol was alive based on (among other things) the fact that "Elvis" can be scrambled into "lives." I said that "Elvis" is also an anagram for "Levi's," but that coincidence meant neither that he was alive nor that he'd morphed into a pair of relaxed-fit denim trousers. (Remember that this was the "Fat Elvis.") Indeed if anagrams were perfect predictors, "moon starers" would be an anagram for "astrologers," not "astronomers." A few days later, one of my freshmen told me he expected to be raptured away with the rest of his small-town congregation over the weekend and not to expect him at the next class. I assured him that the Rapture was an excused cut and wished him Godspeed. I never saw the young man again, so I cannot say with certainty if he was assumed into heaven or not. It did not make the papers.

Living in the Bible Belt, I've grown accustomed to ministers preying on the fears of their flock, but occasionally there are incidents that no amount of rational analysis can entirely explain. Dr. Wolfgang Fernow, a music graduate of the University of Freiberg and a reasonable man, believes in humanity's intuitive power because it once saved his life. Off and on, he has spent the better part of his life trying to understand how it worked for him. Wolfgang was arrested after the Second World War simply because he was a German male. He was sixteen and had successfully dodged the draft for about a year living with his parents in a forest retreat near Wurzberg, but he could not escape the post-war Allied search for Nazis. Despite his protests of innocence, he spent about a year in a dismal French war prison outside Lyon. He had been anemic before his arrest, and the prison diet only worsened his condition. In April of 1946, however, word came that repatriation was at hand for a select few. Buoyed with hope, he fell into a ragged formation, marched to the Lyon train station as the French hurled rocks and insults, and strained to hear his last name called by a French official who apparently had no German. When the last name was read and "Fernow" had not been called, Wolfgang, near panic, pressed his way to the front and said in broken French, "'Sernow,' please check under 'Sernow!'" The bureaucrat, apparently moved by the boy's pallor, did as requested, found the name, checked the serial number on his roster against one that Wolfgang handed him, and allowed Mr. Fernow-Sernow to board the train with his last ounce of strength. To this day, Wolfgang credits an intuitive flash of supernatural origin with saving his life.

I've never had the heart to tell my friend that a capital "F" written in the Sutterlin cursive style of pre-war Germany looks strikingly like the Latin capital "S" that most French were using in the 1940s. That possibly explains how the mistake was made on the roster in the first place; it may also explain how Wolfgang knew where to look if he'd seen any cursive French in prison. Wolfgang, however, says that he had nothing to read for the duration of his incarceration. He had picked up a few words of French from the guards that enabled him to make his desperate and apparently inspired plea.

ॐ

Consider a newborn babe; call him Ralph. If he is normal, all of his senses are intact from the start. Put some salt on his tongue, and he'll spit it out. Place some milk there, and he'll suck. Blow some cigar smoke into his bassinet, and he'll turn his head away. Shine a light into his eyes, and he'll shut them. Drop a heavy book on the kitchen floor or draw some blood from his heel, and he'll cry. Now consider an infant born deaf, blind, and unable to taste, smell, or feel; call him Steve. Most of his reflexes are fine, so he's breathing and his heart is pumping, but that's about all. Does either one of these infants have a "sixth sense"? In either case, we simply cannot know. If Steve has a premonition, how would he know it, much less communicate it? If Ralph has an intuition, he should eventually develop the means to make it known, but it's always going to be subject to scrutiny and doubt by people like me.

Nevertheless, when the bullet with my name inscribed on it is fired, I can only hope I have the faith and foresight to duck. Perhaps the voice that told me to put the car in neutral at the stop light years ago will speak again.

A BOUQUET OF REINCARNATIONS
For John Idol

One winter afternoon, my grandmother told me as she put a kettle on a cold stove that "a watched pot never boils." Shivering from a rare Georgia snow I'd just left, I studied her pot on what slowly became a flame-orange burner in about five minutes or an eternity, whichever came first. Sure enough, she was right: no sooner had I lost interest in that kettle than it started to whistle. This got me to thinking in Sunday school that if I never took my eye off the clock above the crucifix, I'd never get any older, and I wouldn't have to go to another school that I didn't like. (My father was a career military man, and we moved every two or three years.) The troubling hierarchy of clock and crucifix, however, went unnoticed.

When a great aunt died not long after my pot study, I said that she'd "gone to the dogs" by which I meant that she'd gone to be with my pet Labradors who had gone, I'd been assured, to a better place. The dog comment, however, must have conveyed incipient cynicism to my grandmother because she marched me over to a light switch.

"You see this switch, Skipper?"

"Yessum," I said.

"Now if I turn off these lights, are they out forever?"

"No mam," I responded.

"That's right. Just because the light goes out when I mash the switch doesn't mean the electricity that made the light is gone, does it?"

"No, mam, it's right there hangin' fire in the wall just waiting to be turned loose again."

"Yes, and that's where Aunt Lucille is—not in the wall, of course, but just waiting somewhere to be lit."

That was a powerfully convincing analogy for a youth, and for years I felt guilty every time I threw away a burned-out bulb. "Cheaper to buy new bulbs than fix the old ones," Granddad said, confusing the issue even further.

A year later, my father provided still another reason for a callow youth to believe in reincarnation. Only four months after he arrived in Germany, the war ended. I guess that wasn't enough time for him because he volunteered to go to Japan to fight those people too. But it wasn't too long before that war ended as well. I figured the Japs heard that my father was on the way and decided to save themselves a lot of trouble. When Dad got home, he told me the ship that had been transporting him and his men to the Pacific was one of twenty-or-so ships which our Navy salvaged after Pearl Harbor. Only three ships were so badly damaged that they were left on the harbor bottom; the rest were raised and repaired to fight those who had sunk them. God had to be on our side, I concluded, and the rumors of immortality I was hearing had to amount to something.

Any doubts that I might have had were dispelled when my cousin Diane and I launched her dog. Diane's terrier Roscoe had moved in with us when her sister was born. Mostly the animal stayed outside, which meant we forgot to feed him sometimes, which meant that sometimes he made a meal of our grandfather's prize pullets. After Roscoe raided the hen house for the third time, Granddad issued an ultimatum—"get shut of that dog!" When we asked how we might do that, he said, "Just lose him in the woods." Well, that was an exhausting enterprise for an August afternoon in South Georgia, but what options were left to us? Granddad would never let us use his shotgun, there was no animal pound, stoning was too slow and unreliable, and a knife was out of the question. So we got some rope and went down to the banks of a neighbor's fish pond. Here were several supple sweet gum and sourwood saplings which I sometimes used as giant sling shots to chuck stones on days that I tired of counting to a thousand. I picked out one tree that still had some snap, climbed it, and then swung to the ground. As I held it down, Diane tied one end of the rope around Roscoe's neck and the other end to the sapling's crown. At her signal, I released my hold and off flew Roscoe. At the apex of his flight, however, he slipped his noose and plummeted into the bulrushes ringing the shallow pond. When we saw no signs of life down there, we returned disconsolate to the house where we told Granddad what we'd done. About that time, up ran Roscoe covered in mud and ready to play despite the raw wounds on his ears. Since neither of us had the heart to do him any further harm, we implored Granddad to dog-proof the hen house. "Seeing that Roscoe is tough enough to bounce back from an autopsy," he said, "I reckon I have no choice. In the future," he continued, "if you bury someone, bury him face down. That way if he starts digging his way back, he'll have a lot farther to go." For myself, I was sure we'd snapped Roscoe's neck when we launched him, but here he was licking my hand like Lazarus raised from Abraham's bosom. I wasn't about to bury my oldest friend face up or down.

A couple of months later when Roscoe was killed by a car, my sisters and I were, nevertheless, obliged to bury him in the peach orchard beside the house. After a few days, I got to missing him so that I dug him up. When Granddad saw what I'd done, he wrung the neck of an old rooster that had always given Roscoe fits, and we buried them together with Roscoe's head resting on the rooster's side. "Even the son of God had to die to get to heaven," Granddad said. "No one gets a bye. The Good Book says 'a live dog is better than a dead lion,' and though I've never met the king of beasts, I reckon the prophet had it right. Anyway, Roscoe can chase his chickens forever now or die tryin'." We muttered a few more words over his grave while my sisters wept as they tied two sticks in a cross. Then we all sang "Amazing Grace." A few days later, Granddad came back from town with a pecan tree sapling and planted it beside the grave, which had already begun to sink.

My sisters regarded me with awe after I rescued our pet from the grave, so when Miss Goldie was discovered floating upside down in her algae-choked bowl, they brought her directly to my attention. I reasoned that if a fish swims upstream to die, swimming down-stream must be good for its health. I took the fish into the bathroom and turned on the cold-water spigot. Then while holding the lifeless creature by its tail under the tap with one hand, I gently squeezed her sides with the other. After a few seconds as Goldie began to wriggle, I dropped her and an Alka-Seltzer into a bowl of fresh water. With the help of a new aerator, recycled Goldie lived several more months to our utter amazement and joy.

Shortly before Christmas one year while I was still basking in my family's glow, my mother bought a Christmas cactus which she explained was one that bloomed every year to honor Jesus' birthday and "to remind us," she said, "that the only thing standing be-tween immorality and immortality is the sign of the cross." As we waited in vain for that plant to flower, Mother, her faith shaken, threatened to take it back to the nursery. About March of the next year, however, we began to notice buds developing at the ends of each long pendulous branch. On Easter morning, Mother came downstairs to hide some pastel eggs and declared, "Glory be! The Christmas cactus has bloomed at Easter!" She took those blossoms to heart the way Mary rejoiced at the stone rolled away from Joseph of Arimathea's tomb. The connection may have been specious, but it sure made us happy, for when Mother was happy, her kids were ecstatic, and thoughts of a better life never crossed my mind, for my plate was full.

Throughout my childhood and well into my adolescence, the sun followed me wherever I went. I could not conceive of the earth without me, and I seldom tried. My faith was rocked, however, as a freshman in high school when our often profane and iconoclastic general science teacher said, "The only way to reach Paradise is through Intercourse [long pause] Pennsylvania! No, seriously, after death all of us return to the same state we'd enjoyed before birth. How bad is that?" To illustrate, he suggested that the soul might be compared to a drop of water. "Let's call it Drop A," he said. "Now if you reduce that drop to two parts hydrogen and one part oxygen, where is your drop of water or your soul? If you examine the same hydrogen and oxygen atoms after the distillation, where is the evidence that they have ever been water, much less Drop A?" Even though Drop A's oxygen and hydrogen are virtually indestructible, that analogy bothered me for a long time until I took a sophomore earth-science class. Here I learned of aquifers, great bodies of water that may lie untapped in the earth's bosom for millions of years. I was wise enough to see that the aquifer-as-heaven analogy, which I'd hastily constructed, was not perfect because clearly the body undergoes a chemical decomposition after death, and all the vital fluids eventually dry up, including Drop A. Alas, the soul is not a drop of water that slips blissfully unchanged and discrete into a heavenly reservoir at death, but all was not lost.

In junior chemistry, our study of the inert gases, which make up about one percent of the earth's atmosphere, was for me metaphorically fertile. Inert argon, for example, tasteless, colorless, and odorless, never combines with any element; it never changes in any fundamental way as it courses and mingles with other gases about the earth. Remarkably, argon is part of every breath we take, yet it is unmarked by any apparatus, animal, mineral, or vegetable, that it passes through. There is a very good chance that in every human breath at least one argon atom exists that percolated through the mortal lungs of Socrates, Attila, Mary, Jesus, and anyone else who has ever drawn a breath on this planet. It occurred to me, then, that the soul might consist of a single atom of an inert gas, inviolate for eternity. Hidden in its subatomic rain forest, I was confident, is the memory of its original body, life, and personality. About the time that I was concocting this theory, however, I read of a Swedish mortician who observed that the human body on average loses twenty-one grams at the instant of death. Could an argon atom weigh twenty-one grams, I wondered? Senior physics disabused me of this quaint notion.

I'm old enough now to recognize the soul-as-argon theory as a comfortable fiction (though it's never been disproved), but I find no harm in such myth-making, for like crutches, myths make forward motion possible when just standing is painful. Who wants to wake on a beautiful spring day and think, "In X years, I'll be food for worms and nothing more"? With the right crutch beside the bed, be it a multi-vitamin or a pair of running shoes, one can at least get up, fix breakfast, water the garden, and succor the spouse. "With the right attitude," Robert Pirsig wrote, "nothing is difficult." I've long admired the plucky Incan flutist who left his femurs to musical science. When he made out his will, he had to know that everyone who would ever play or hear the instruments carved from his thigh bones would be moved by his musical soul and his defiance of death's finality.

My own myth-making ability was tested when my grandfather died. Granddad had asked to be cremated, and though his wife disapproved, she was faithful to her husband's last wish. One night as we sat staring at his funeral urn wondering what to do with five pounds of ashes, I remembered my old Watched Clock Theory of Immortality. I suggested that we place a few ounces of Granddad's ashes in an hour glass and let him mock the stasis of death every time we used it. Finally, however, we sprinkled a generous scoop of his remains in the garden that he had spent fifty years of his life making fertile. Grandmother then took the remainder to the Crystal Palace, her potting shed, where she mixed them and a dollop of tears into some potting soil, which, in late October, she worked around the roots of her forget-me-nots. The long unfurling clusters of petals were never as blue, their eyes never as gold as they were the subsequent spring.

Grandmother herself died not long afterwards. I like to think of her in the Crystal Palace cultivating the "reincarnations," as she nicknamed her favorite hothouse perennials. When the doughty French woman Jeanne Calment publicly jubilated on her 121st birthday, Grandmother was cheered by news that the Bible's limit of 120 years was not absolute. Though Grandmother fell short of the "limit" by forty years, she didn't think Jehovah had ever intentionally placed such an arbitrary restriction on human longevity. When Mrs. Calment celebrated her 122nd birthday, Grandmother's intuition was proven correct though she could not be present for the festivities. She was in the cemetery which she liked to remind anyone who would listen was Greek for "sleeping place."

She was equally encouraged when she read in the local paper that her oldest grandson, yours truly, had achieved immortality. It seems that when the Class of 1943 decided to donate a bell to the new Clemson University carillon, their president called the English Department where I am employed and asked if anyone could supply them with a poem for the four-thousand pound "C" bell. The secretary gave them my phone number; I sent them six verses suitable for a bell, and a year later the newspaper headlined, "Local Poet Achieves Immortality." I submitted this headline with my annual evaluation the following year with the marginal annotation, "and a two-percent raise?" In fact, I received no raise. Immortality like virtue, it seems, is its own reward. The ironic thing is that every time I begin to feel immortal, my back goes out or I get a cold.

∾

Since immortality has been so generously bestowed on me, I have made a short study of the subject like the blind man inspecting a white elephant.

First I wondered what is the evidence that any living thing is immortal or even close to it? Lotus seeds have germinated after 1288 years which is a long time but not a bronze bell. Cancer cells, on the other hand, will reproduce forever if nutrients are supplied. Pollen appears to be immortal; ten-thousand year old pollen grains have caused allergic reactions in archeologists exploring long-sealed tombs. Bacteria locked in a rock crystal for 250,000 years have recently been resuscitated. Emily Dickinson thought a letter was immortal because its envelope enclosed a mind without a body. I suppose the same could be said for any poem, symphony, or water color on good paper. Art has long been haled by its creators and sympathetic critics as immortal despite the dust swept from museums and libraries every day. James Joyce thought that if he made *Ulysses* arcane enough scholars would be kept busy forever. No sign of any let up yet! If Steven Spielberg and Michael Crichton have it right, genes are immortal, but a clone is a poor substitute for immortality. I can't imagine anyone rescued from despair because a scraping from their meatless bones will some day regenerate their body. The flesh of mother and clone may be identical, but their intimate selves are altogether different. Finally, the past and future are immortal; we measure the present in nanoseconds.

Another question that occurred to me is, though immortality is widely touted, who are those opposed to it? Pindar exhorted his soul to enjoy and exhaust the limits of this life before it began preparing for another. Odysseus was offered immortality by Calypso, but he surprised many by turning her down. Medieval French kings had a seneschal among their courtiers one of whose duties was to whisper, "Remember, Sire, you are mortal," even as the worshipful masses shouted, "Long live the king!" The Greek Tithonus and Swift's Struldbruggs both made the mistake of achieving immortality without acquiring youth, so theirs are cautionary tales. The centaur Chiron renounced his immortality when he realized that eternal life meant eternal suffering. Many since Chiron have felt that neither centaur nor man is capable of immortality like the single mother of eight living in a Mississippi trailer who wanted nothing of her preacher's "eternal life." The contemporary novelist Tom Robbins has little apparent use for the immortal soul, something that he variously refers to as, "a billow of sacred flatulence..., a shimmer of personal swamp gas..., or a cross between a wolf howl, a photon, and a dribble of dark molasses." Finally, it has been suggested that the gods themselves, bored with their own perfection, might envy man's mortality. But to rephrase Susan Ertz, whereas the gods, who don't know what to do with themselves on a rainy Sunday, long for surcease, man desires an infinitude of football. That strikes me as a long-term goal to reconsider.

What does science have to say about immortality? Until the evolution of the death gene about three billion years ago, biologists think that many simple organisms enjoyed a form of immortality—splitting endlessly unless the food supply disappeared or they were struck by lightning. Such was Eden for the protozoa. Some scientists see cryonics as a legitimate attempt to regain that deathless state, but to date only some small mammals have been frozen alive and thawed unharmed. No humans have been reanimated following their descent into a stainless-steel cylinder of sub-zero dimethyl sulfoxide. At last count, about forty people had paid their $80,000 and been placed in cryonic suspension, but three-quarters of these have been thawed and buried when their bank accounts dried up. Indeed, many are cold, but few are frozen.

Computer scientists have suggested that immortality might be attained in cyber-space. This would involve placing everything one knows, family albums, financial records, home movies, diaries, and so forth on the Internet. The drawbacks to such an afterlife are summarized by Lily Tomlin's observation, "There is sex after death; we just don't feel it." Nevertheless, an eternal presence on the Worldwide Web might accomplish what William James thought was the principal virtue of believing in transcendence: "a genuine difference in our moral life."

Like science, pseudo-science has long offered a variety of schemes tailored to every wallet. The Chinese philosopher Ko Hung thought that a steady diet of cinnabar (mercuric sulfide) and white honey would render the diner incorruptible, but no one since Ko vanished like milk in the mattress has been able to duplicate his results. A more cynical but unnamed pseudo-scientist facetiously suggested that since copulation produces life, necrophilia ought to yield an afterlife. Today there are plastic, Tupperware-like coffins that are burped regularly for freshness, $125,000 hyperbaric oxygen chambers which enclose a sleeper in pure oxygen (non-smokers only), and $7,000 injections prepared in Swiss clinics from a potpourri of cells drawn from aborted sheep. Finally, there's the $399 Fountain of Youth Reincarnation Kit. "If you can conceive it and believe it," the literature promises, "you can achieve it." The kit consists of a pamphlet and map informing the temporarily dead "how not to get hopelessly lost in heaven or hell." Candidly, the Fountain of Youth home page does not say that their kit will make the purchaser immortal; it will only show the way to a second life because, as super spy James Bond presciently noted, "You only live twice." (Curiously, Bond is quoted several times in Fountain of Youth literature as if he were a real authority.) How can a purchaser be sure that humans have a second life coming? "Well, everyone has had at least one *deja-vu* experience, haven't they," Fountain of Youth asks, "and surely everyone by now knows the benefits of Past-Lives Therapy." The kit, which is only offered for sale on the Internet, lists a post-office-box return address in Evergreen Park, Illinois. My guess is that it's a cemetery.

$$\text{\large ۵۵}$$

Despite the two-ton bronze bell ringing in Tillman Tower with my name and verses embossed on it, I long for something more. I sympathize with the youthful Roman emperor Elagabalus who sent for the "breast of a phoenix" to insure his immortality. Unable to locate the mythic bird that rises from its ashes, the emperor's soldiers killed and salted a flamingo, which they called an African bird of paradise, and sent it to Rome. Predictably, this substitute failed, for the emperor was murdered at eighteen, an age when many of us, not just emperors, are feeling like permanent fixtures on the planet.

So I shall ask to be buried in the fetal curl with a goblet of nectar and a bowl of ambrosia beside me. Should cremation be mandatory by that time as it is in India, I'd like my ashes scattered in a costly fireworks display. Should all these charms fail, may I live again like George Eliot "in a few minds made better by my presence." In case I do return, I've willed everything to myself. Just kidding. Either way:

> To know the punch line
> is to spoil the joke,
> so heaven's gate
> is shrouded in smoke.

> It's best not to know
> if the wind will rise—
> then if it does,
> it's a fine surprise.

Index

www.ingramcontent.com/pod-product-compliance
Lightning Source LLC
Chambersburg PA
CBHW031119020726
47495CB00007B/2266